2013

3

REGIMES OF MEMORY

In recent years memory has attracted increasing attention. From analyses of electronic communication and the Internet to discussions of heritage culture and debates about victimhood and sexual abuse, memory is currently generating much cultural interest. This interdisciplinary collection takes a journey through memory in order to contextualise this current 'memory boom'.

Regimes of Memory focuses on memory's 'outside' – on the many fields within which understandings of memory have been produced. This book is divided into parts – Believing the body; Propping the subject; What memory forgets; What history forgets; Memory beyond the modern – which trace the genealogies of our contemporary Western under-standings of memory. Through studies of the early modern arts of memory, nineteenth-century evolutionary museums, and the modernist explorations of artists and writers, it explores the differences between Western and non-Western concepts of the lived past and compares understandings of memory in history, psychoanalysis and anthropology.

Individual essays by many of the foremost international scholars in memory studies trace memory's intimate association with identity and recognition, with cities, with lived time, with the science of the mind, with fantasy and with the media. The collection demonstrates the importance of contemporary Western preoccupations with memory to Western ideas of history, identity, and the relation between the personal and public.

Regimes of Memory will be of essential interest to those working in the fields of cultural studies, history and anthropology.

Susannah Radstone teaches in the School of Cultural and Innovation Studies at the University of East London. Her research interests are in cultural theory, memory studies and psychoanalysis. Her previous publications include *Memory and Methodology* (editor, 2000) and she is currently completing *On Memory and Confession*, to be published by Routledge.

Katharine Hodgkin teaches in the School of Cultural and Innovation Studies at the University of East London. Her research centres on questions of autobiography, memory and madness, particularly in the early modern period. She has published several articles on these topics, including most recently 'The Labyrinth and the Pit' (*History Workshop Journal* 51, 2001), a study of madness in seventeenth-century autobiography.

ROUTLEDGE STUDIES IN MEMORY AND NARRATIVE

Series Editors: Mary Chamberlain, Paul Thompson, Timothy Ashplant, Richard Candida-Smith and Selma Leydesdorff

REGIMES OF MEMORY

*Edited by Susannah Radstone
and Katharine Hodgkin*

Routledge
Taylor & Francis Group

LONDON AND NEW YORK

First published 2003
by Routledge
11 New Fetter Lane, London EC4P 4EE

Simultaneously published in the USA and Canada
by Routledge
29 West 35th Street, New York, NY 10001

Routledge is an imprint of the Taylor & Francis Group

Typeset in Baskerville by Taylor & Francis Books Ltd
Printed and bound in Great Britain by MPG Books Ltd, Bodmin

British Library Cataloguing in Publication Data
A catalogue record for this book is available from the British Library

Library of Congress Cataloging in Publication Data
Regimes of memory/edited by Susannah Radstone and Katharine Hodgkin.
Includes bibliographical references and index.
1. Memory. I Radstone, Susannah. II. Hodgkin, Katharine, 1961–
BF371 .R36 2003
153.1'2–dc21   2002031934

ISBN 0–415–28648–4

CONTENTS

v

CONTENTS

CONTENTS

NOTES ON CONTRIBUTORS

Paul Antze teaches in the Division of Social Science and in the Graduate Programmes in Anthropology and Social and Political Thought at York University, Toronto. He is a former President of the Canadian Association for Medical Anthropology and currently a member of the Editorial Board of *Ethos: The Journal of Psychological Anthropology*. He has written widely on the culture of psychotherapeutic movements and has a special interest in psychoanalysis, both as a tool for the analysis of culture and as a cultural phenomenon in its own right. His recent work has emphasised the cultural uses of trauma and dissociation, especially as seen in the multiple-personality movement. He is the co-editor, with Michael Lambek, of *Tense Past: Cultural Essays in Trauma and Memory*.

Jill Bennett is a senior lecturer in art theory at the University of New South Wales. She has published widely on visual culture in a range of areas including contemporary art practice, pornography, medieval painting, and theories of affect and trauma. Her essays have appeared in journals such as *Art History* and *Signs*. She has curated a number of exhibitions, including *Telling Tales* (Sydney, 1998, Graz, 1999), addressing the subject of personal and cultural trauma. She is co-editor (with Rosanne Kennedy) of *World Memory: Personal Trajectories in Global Time* (Palgrave, forthcoming) and is currently writing a book on trauma, conflict and visual art.

Tony Bennett is Professor of Sociology at the Open University in the United Kingdom. His current interests focus on questions of culture and governance with especial reference to museums, cultural diversity policies, and the history and theory of cultural policy. His publications include *Formalism and Marxism*; *Outside Literature*; *Bond and Beyond: The Political Career of a Popular Hero* (with Janet Woollacott); *The Birth of the Museum: History, Theory, Politics*; *Culture: A Reformer's Science*; *Accounting for Tastes: Australian Everyday Cultures* (with Michael Emmison and John Frow) and *Culture in Australia: Policies, Publics, Programmes* (co-edited with David Carter).

Stephan Feuchtwang is a senior research associate of the Department of Anthropology, London School of Economics. He has been engaged in research on popular religion, rural politics and social support arrangements in mainland

China and Taiwan since 1966. Together with a close colleague Wang Mingming, who is in Beijing University, he has recently completed a book, *Grassroots Charisma: Four Local Leaders in China* (Routledge, 2002). He is now engaged on a comparative project called 'The Transmission and Recognition of Grievous Loss' that is an empirical exploration in China, Taiwan, Berlin and London of the recognition of loss, which in Chinese cosmology and possibly elsewhere is pre-figured in the category of ghosts but demands something more than traditional ways of dealing with ghosts. An outline of this theme has been published as a chapter in S. Radstone (ed.) *Memory and Methodology* (Berg, 2000).

Karl Figlio is a psychoanalytic psychotherapist and Associate Member, London Centre for Psychotherapy. He is also Professor and Director, Centre for Psychoanalytic Studies, University of Essex. His recent publications include *Psychoanalysis, Science and Masculinity* (London: Whurr, 2000; Philadelphia: Brunner-Routledge, 2001); 'Historical Imagination/Psychoanalytic Imagination', *History Workshop Journal* 45, 1998.

Katharine Hodgkin teaches in the School of Cultural and Innovation Studies, University of East London. Her research centres on questions of autobiography and memory, particularly in the early modern period, and she has published various articles on these topics. She has also edited *Women, Madness and Sin in Early Modern England: The Autobiographical Writings of Dionys Fitzherbert* (Ashgate, 2003), an edition of an early seventeenth-century manuscript.

Michael Lambek is the author of *Human Spirits: A Cultural Account of Trance in Mayotte* and of *Knowledge and Practice in Mayotte: Local Discourses of Islam, Sorcery and Spirit Possession*, as well as editor of *Tense Past: Cultural Essays in Trauma and Memory* (with Paul Antze), *Bodies and Persons: Comparative Perspectives from Africa and Melanesia* (with Andrew Strathern), and *A Reader in the Anthropology of Religion*, among other works. His book *The Weight of the Past: Living with History in Mahajanga, Madagascar*, which elaborates the ethnographic material presented in his essay, is in press with Palgrave. He teaches anthropology at the University of Toronto and is a Fellow of the Royal Society of Canada.

Esther Leslie is a lecturer in the School of English and Humanities at Birkbeck, University of London. She is the author of *Walter Benjamin: Overpowering Conformism* (London: Pluto Press, 2000) and *Hollywood Flatlands: Animation, Critical Theory and the Avant-garde* (London: Verso, 2002). She is involved in the editing of three journals: *Historical Materialism*, *Radical Philosophy* and *Revolutionary History*, and has also edited and contributed to a collection called *Mad Pride: A Celebration of Mad Culture* (London: Handsell, 2001). Her essays have appeared in a number of books, including *Material Memories: Design and Evocation*, edited by Marius Kwint, Jeremy Aynsley and Christopher Breward (Oxford/New York: Berg, 1999), *Walter Benjamin's Philosophy: Destruction and Experience*, edited by Peter Osborne and Andrew Benjamin (Manchester: Clinamen Press, 2000), *The Body Politic: The Role of the*

Body and Contemporary Craft, edited by Julian Stair (London: Crafts Council, 2000) and *The Philistine Controversy*, edited by Dave Beech and John Roberts (London: Verso, 2002). She translated Georg Lukács' *A Defence of History and Class Consciousness: Tailism and the Dialectic* (London: Verso, 2000). Her writings appear regularly in *Things*, and she has also written in *New Formations*, *Act*, *New Left Review*, *Journal of Design History*, *Inventory*, *De-*, *Dis-*, *Ex* and *Mute*. Her current research investigates the philosophical and aesthetic implications of industrial colour chemistry in nineteenth- and twentieth-century Germany.

Constantina Papoulias has just completed a PhD thesis at the University of East London and is currently teaching at the University of Oxford. Her thesis 'The Making of a Cultural Psyche: Memory between the Humanities and the Social Sciences in Post-war America' dealt with the relationship between the current efflorescence of memory studies and earlier formulations of memory in psychology and sociology. Her research interests include investigating the interdisciplinary trajectories of theoretical concepts, with particular emphasis on embodiment and affect.

Susannah Radstone teaches in the School of Cultural and Innovation Studies at the University of East London. Recent publications include *Memory and Methodology* (editor, Berg, 2000); 'Autobiographical Times', in Tess Cosslett *et al.*, *Feminism and Autobiography* (Routledge, 2000); 'The War of the Fathers: Trauma, Fantasy and September 11th', in Judith Greenberg (ed.), *Trauma at Home* (University of Nebraska Press, 2003). She recently compiled, edited and introduced a dossier, 'Trauma and Screen Studies', *Screen*, 42(2), 2001. She is currently completing *On Memory and Confession: The Sexual Politics of Time*, to be published by Routledge.

Bill Schwarz teaches in the Department of Media and Communications at Goldsmiths College. His *Memories of Empire in Twentieth-century England: Unfinished Histories of Decolonisation* appears in 2003. He is an editor of *History Workshop Journal*, *New Formations* and *Cultural Studies*.

Richard Terdiman teaches in the Departments of Literature and the History of Consciousness at the University of California, Santa Cruz. His books include *Dialectics of Isolation; Discourse/Counter-discourse: The Theory and Practice of Symbolic Resistance in Nineteenth-century France* and *Present Past: Modernity and the Memory Crisis*. His *Body and Story: The Enlightenment, Postmodernity, and the Demands of Theory* will appear in 2003.

William N. West is Assistant Professor of English at the University of Colorado at Boulder, where he teaches early modern literature. He is also the author of the article on memory in *The Oxford Encyclopedia of Rhetoric* and has recently completed *Theatres and Encyclopedias in Early Modern Europe* (Cambridge University Press, 2002) on conceptions of knowledge and performance in the sixteenth and seventeenth centuries. He is currently working on a book about the uses of confusion in the drama of Shakespeare's time.

PREFACE AND
ACKNOWLEDGEMENTS

Regimes of Memory and its companion volume *Contested Pasts* have been some five years in the making. The seeds of both were sown during a research discussion day held in the Department of Cultural Studies (as it then was) at the University of East London, in 1997. At that meeting, it emerged that we shared an interest in memory, though coming at it from different places and directions and theories. Katharine Hodgkin had a background in research on autobiographical writing (especially early modern), and a general interest in questions of history and memory, as well as history and psychoanalysis. Susannah Radstone worked on cultural theory, psychoanalysis, literature, film and contemporary history, and was already actively involved in research on memory. A further seed was Raphael Samuel's brief presence as a professor in the department, setting up a history research centre that would undoubtedly have been a focus for work drawing on and developing his seminal work on history and memory. His death interrupted that project, along with much else. But for the department as well as personally it seemed a valuable thing to hold some sort of event that would acknowledge that work, and remember him. Susannah Radstone, meanwhile, in the throes of editing an interdisciplinary volume on memory and finding links to work going on in Canada and the USA, was keen to build on those links, and initiate a wider conversation on the subject.

The first outcome of this convergence of interests and wishes was an international interdisciplinary conference, 'Frontiers of Memory', held at the Institute of Education in September 1999. The response to our early calls for papers was disconcertingly large, and over the months that followed, as we worked through and selected from a continuing flood of abstracts, we found ourselves increasingly intrigued by the overview we were acquiring of work on memory in the late 1990s, and by the emphases and the absences these abstracts suggested. We wanted the conference to be as open as possible to interdisciplinary work; we were interested in work about past and present, space and time, objects and fantasies. It quickly became clear that, although we were not going to have as many papers from historians as we had hoped, a vast number of people were working on traumatic and Holocaust memory; this pattern is reflected on further in the Introduction to *Contested Pasts*. The conference was also firmly based in humanities subjects, in part no doubt a consequence of where it had been publicised; we had few contributions from psychology or geography, for instance, despite the significant work on memory going on in both these fields. Nonetheless, by the time we had managed to select some 100 papers from the 300 or more abstracts we were offered, it was clear that memory was indeed an immensely motivating and topical subject, drawing contributors from many parts of the world and from many different disciplines, as well as some from outside the academy. The theme of memory seemed to make possible an engagement with both personal and intellectual preoccupations in a way that remains rare in academic work.

The conference itself was a large and successful event, and we quickly proceeded to the even more difficult task of selecting from those 100 papers twenty or so with the aim of publication. Inevitably there were many deserving papers left out; and, as the volumes took shape, the agendas and the priorities we had initially envisaged shifted somewhat. Thus the eventual publications have moved quite a long way away from the original conference, and the changed titles of these two volumes reflect that distance, although certain themes and interests have remained constant.

In choosing essays for this volume and its companion, our main aim was innovation: we were looking for papers that would do something new with memory, whether through cutting-edge theory, or interesting and unusual applications of more familiar approaches, or indeed both. In addition, an important part of our aim was to bridge what still too often appears as a divide between 'history' and 'theory'. Our different fields of interest cover a great deal of the ground addressed by memory work – from autobiography and oral history to trauma and film, from heritage to psychoanalysis – and our historical and theoretical approaches are differently balanced. Nonetheless, for both of us it would be impossible to think about memory simply taking it as a given: to work with memory must entail asking questions about memory itself, how it is conceived in different cultural and historical contexts, and how to understand its extraordinary discursive prominence today. Precisely because of its interdisciplinary breadth, memory as a concept throws light on the unquestioned assumptions and the internal workings of the various disciplines in which it comes to be positioned. 'Memory' as it is mobilised by oral historians is not necessarily identical with 'memory' in the writings of film theorists; different priorities and problems come to the fore. By juxtaposing work from different fields we hope that these two volumes will help us to think across boundaries – as Luisa Passerini suggests, to make dangerous liaisons.

It would have been hard for us to imagine, on that research day in 1997, that the next five years would lead to such a sustained and productive and exhausting engagement with the topic we identified almost casually. Our first thanks should perhaps go to one another, for what has been a collaboration – an intellectual pilgrimage – of exceptional interest, as well as friendship, encouragement and mutual support. But we have many other thanks to give as well.

We owe thanks first to our department (now part of the School of Cultural and Innnovation Studies at the University of East London), and to Mike Rustin, then Dean of Faculty, for giving us encouragement and underwriting the initial conference, despite the constant anxiety about how much money we might be about to lose! Many thanks also to Tina Papoulias, at the time Susannah Radstone's research student, for a great deal of assistance during the planning of the conference – for much of the time during this period we were effectively a triumvirate; and to Joan Tremble and her team for taking over much of the burden of administering the event. Their efficient support kept us sane at various critical points. *History Workshop Journal*, of which Raphael Samuel had been a founding editor, very kindly funded the conference reception; our thanks to the editorial board for buying us lots of wine. We also remember with great gratitude and pleasure the participants, both those who gave papers and those who did not. We thank them all for their time and energy, their enthusiastic responses in discussion, and their good temper when things went wrong. We are only sorry that we couldn't publish a wider range of the papers given; so many merited wider circulation, and we hope by now they have found other homes.

For our contributors, it has been a long haul since the conference, and we are very grateful to them all for staying with us, and for their patience over the many and complex delays. We thank also the editors of Memory and Narrative, in whose series the two volumes are appearing, for their support; we are delighted to be in such excellent company as the previous volumes in this series.

Finally, personal thanks. From Katharine Hodgkin, thanks to Vian Vali, for (as she suggested I put it) leaving me alone while I am working. The conference and the books have been in the background for half her life, and she has tolerated the consequent parental distractions with impressive patience and good humour, not to mention charm. Thanks also to Abbas Vali; I owe more than he knows to his sustaining presence, as well as to his intellectual rigour.

From Susannah Radstone, thanks to Julia Boutall for helping her keep on track, and to Annette Kuhn, Claudia Lank, Clare Palmer, Sara Radstone and Amal Treacher for friendship and encouragement.

The authors and the publisher would like to thank the following for permission to reprint material:

'The Other Inside: memory as metaphor in psychoanalysis' is reproduced here with permission from *POIESIS: A Journal of the Arts and Communication*, Volume Three, 2001, EGS Press, Toronto, Canada.

Parts of 'Absent-minded professors: etch-a-sketching academic forgetting' originally appeared in *Hollywood Flatlands: Animation, Critical Theory and the Avant-Garde* (Esther Leslie, Verso, 2002) and is reproduced here with kind permission of Verso.

Parts of 'Memory in a Maussian universe' originally appeared in *The Weight of the Past* (Michael Lambek, Palgrave, 2003) © Michael Lambek. Reprinted here with permission of Palgrave Macmillan.

REGIMES OF MEMORY: AN INTRODUCTION

Susannah Radstone and Katharine Hodgkin

> Regime: a manner, method or system of rule or government; a system or institution having widespread influence or prevalence.
>
> (OED)

The continuing growth of interest in memory in the contemporary West, both inside universities and in the wider culture, is a phenomenon that has been widely debated in recent years.[1] This present-day fascination with memory, which might be likened to the 'discursive explosion' around sex that Michel Foucault traced from its beginnings in the seventeenth century,[2] raises problems for those struggling to understand memory's meanings or its contemporary prominence, as this volume attempts to do. In his chapter in this volume, Michael Lambek highlights this difficulty by arguing that 'in making "memory" the object of study, we run the risk of naturalizing the very phenomenon whose heightened presence and salience is in need of investigation' (p. 211). Lambek continues by asking 'how can we understand memory without enlarging its discourse? How do we acknowledge the salience of memory without contributing to either its objectification or romanticization?' (p. 211). Any volume focused on memory, including this one, clearly runs these risks, to which might be added the risks of making essentialist, universalistic or monolithic claims about memory. Nevertheless, our hope is that this volume's concern with what we are calling *regimes* of memory – its primary concern with the 'outside', rather than the 'inside' of memory, and with epistemological rather than onto-logical questions – might mitigate such risks by foregrounding studies whose field of enquiry is not memory's essence nor its ontology, but discursive *productions* of 'memory'.

This volume focuses, then, less on memory as an object whose inner workings are to be studied, and more on 'memory' as a concept. *Regimes of Memory* discusses the 'work' memory has done and continues to do in, amongst other things, the production of subjectivity and of the public/private relation. This volume suggests, however, that the specificities of regimes of memories' knowl-edge/power relations cannot be equated with, say, the regimes of subjectivity with which they are associated. Instead, it proposes that a study of regimes of

1

memory might complicate as well as simply deepen our understandings of related regimes – for instance, of subjectivity, of history, or of the mind.

In this volume, memory's meanings and purviews emerge as historically and geographically varied and debatable. The essays collected here pay particular attention to shifts and modulations in what we call 'figurations' of memory: those images, analogies or representations of memory that have been devised in attempts to generate understandings of memory's 'inside' workings and constitution. It is through analyses of figurations of memory, this volume contends, that something can be gleaned of regimes of memory – of the kinds of knowledge and power that are carried, in specific times and places, by particular discourses of memory. These essays focus, then, on these particular 'productions' of memory. But in pointing to what historical or contemporary figurations of memory 'forget', exclude, render unthinkable or make marginal, these essays remember, also, that all productions of memory are also productions of what memory is not, and that such inclusions and exclusions constitute a politics of memory discourses.

Histories of memory

Histories of memory/histories of the subject

If it is accepted that 'we are made of our memories',[3] that memory makes us, then it follows, as Fentress and Wickham have pointed out, that 'a study of the way we remember is a study of the way we are'.[4] In this sense, historical studies of memory are intimately and indissociably linked with histories of subjectivity, and shed light on historical variations in conceptions of subjectivity and experience. Memory, that is, like subjectivity, means different things and is understood in different ways at different times. At the same time, however, histories of memory also reveal that what are sometimes taken to be contemporary, or even new, debates about subjectivity have roots that stretch far back in time.

In contemporary memory studies, the focus falls not only on individual, private memory, but on historical, social, cultural and popular memory, too. Theorists speak with apparent ease, indeed, of the collective or social domains of memory. This contrasts strikingly with the early modern period, in which memory was the refuge of the individual and where the relation between that individual memory and the public sphere appeared fraught. As we go on to discuss further below, the question of the *meaning* and the determinants of this theoretical 'expansion' of memory from the individual to the social or collective is a fascinating one that can only be touched on here, but it is clearly a question that invites further study. Some have welcomed this expansion of memory, associating it with a new, less elitist and more democratic relation to the past.[5] Perhaps, indeed, the expansion of memory might be taken to signal a postmodern melting of boundaries between individuals – a suggestion that might find support in theories of memory transmission, and prosthetic memory, for instance.[6] Others might suggest, however, that the expansion of memory signals the atrophy of the public sphere and the theoretical difficulty of conceiving of social or collective life and experience outside the terms of an accretion of individuals – a position taken up in this volume by Michael Lambek.

The history of memory is indissociably linked, then, with the complex story of the emergence on to the historical stage of a bounded, coherent self who comes to be understood as the 'container' or possessor of memory. The distinction of an 'outside' of happenings and an 'inside' of their remembrance is inextricably connected with the emergence of this bounded subject. A study of the paradoxes associated with a figuration of the self as a container of memory reveals particularly starkly the difficulties inherent in attempts to conceptualise the bounded self's relation to the social. This history of subjectivity, which has by no means been settled or agreed upon, and which is linked to debates concerning the emergence of the discrete subject taking place in autobiographical studies and history, is too complex to be rehearsed in any detail here. Yet it is nevertheless clear that what is at stake here are two related questions about the emergence of this 'bounded' subject. The issues concern when and how this boundedness emerged. Moreover, what is also at issue here is the question of the figuration of a qualitative *difference* between that public 'outside' and memory's particularity and specificity – though this difference between 'outside' and 'inside' may have only later come to be associated with subjectivity, and with that uniqueness of self and of experience associated with possessive individualism[7] that emerged from the seventeenth century onwards. Memory's difficulties are linked, then with the question of how that 'gap' between memory's 'private' inside and its public 'outside' might be bridged.

Moreover, although there is clearly a thread of connection between histories of memory and histories of subjectivity, it cannot therefore be assumed that figurations of memory have straightforwardly supported the emergence of a coherent and bounded sovereign subject. What emerges, indeed, is a far more complex mapping. Memory is associated with coherent, bounded and sovereign subjectivity. Yet memory emerges, at points, as that which *undermines* that very conceptualisation of the subject. This is one of the insights provided by William West's study of early modern memory. West explains that:

> Memory, for the thinkers of the Renaissance and earlier, was the seat of identity; while reason made one human, it was memory that made one a particular individual…. Memory was the refuge of the individual – one's own memory as well as others' were the mysterious sources from which identity issues, tantalizingly almost present, frustratingly elusive, and above all, thoroughly and irreducibly private.
>
> (this volume: p. 62)

Between the fourth and the sixteenth centuries in Europe, memory's importance to intellectual practices led to the development of ways of improving and

3

supplementing natural memory. By the time of the fifteenth and sixteenth centuries in Europe, memory had already been imagined for centuries as a space of thought containing imaginary objects. Intellectual pursuits demanded highly developed memory skills. Deft practitioners of the 'arts' of memory remembered many such memory objects, each associated, perhaps, with several memories. By the sixteenth century, however, questions began to be raised concerning the nature and status of the knowledge carried by objects of 'artificial memory'. The questions posed here implicitly refer back to the issues raised in Plato's myth of the cave[8] and locate memory's problematic within the ancient but still pertinent question of the truth-value of images, representations, mimesis. The objects of memory, which had previously been construed as providing a secure basis for coherent identity, now began to emerge as objects which required the *pre-existence* and the continued presence after death of an interpreting subject. In the absence of such a subject, memory begins to appear as that which can dismantle, rather than support, that self-possessed individual.

The essays in this volume suggest, moreover, that the ambiguity of the relation between regimes of memory and constructions of the self-possessed subject continued into the eighteenth and nineteenth centuries, and continued to be linked to the question of the relation of the bounded self with the social. Tony Bennett's chapter discusses the relation between the emergence, in the West, of organicist theories of memory and the development of the nineteenth-century evolutionary museums. He stresses the support lent to notions of sovereign subjectivity by a model of memory that constructs the individual body as a container in which the past is remembered. In this figuration, the person – and then, later, the body – becomes conceived of as 'a storage system in which all that had gone before is retained for retrieval in the present' (p. 48) In placing all that had gone before *within* the organism, this figuration of memory arguably struggled to resolve the tension between the bounded self and its social history. However, this figuration of memory simultaneously inscribed a dominant version of the history of Western civilisation, since it constituted a ranking system in harmony with the imperialist thrust of the nineteenth century (particularly British and French) West. From the perspective of organicist theories of memory, the Western, imperial subject could be viewed as the end-point, or fruition, of those earlier stages of development located at once elsewhere and within the subject. In this sense, the 'possessiveness' of the individual extends beyond even 'the whole of history', as the Western individual of the late eighteenth and nineteenth century comes to be understood as a possessor or container of all previous stages of human development.

Yet, as psychoanalysis soon came to see, the 'possession' delivered by this figuration of 'organicist' and archaeological memory is double-edged, for the coherence and sovereignty of the (imperialist, Western) subject balances only precariously upon its own 'primitive' and/or infantile substratum – a substratum that could rise up and 'possess' its possessor. As West's discussion of early modern memory reveals, these instabilities emerged early. They hinged on the incongruence between writing and space as metaphors of memory, and on the need for interpretation of even the *apparently* transparent objects of artificial memory. If artificial memory understood its objects as *material*, these objects' *meanings* were nevertheless opaque to all but their possessor. Thus the apparent transparency of apparently material 'objects' of memory is called into question, once attention is turned to the subjects, rather than the objects, of artificial memory. For what emerges in that move, argues West, is a subject whose instability pivots on the opacity (to others) of the affects and meanings linked to those objects. Once again a regime of memory appears to founder on, or at least be put in tension by, the difficulty of the relation between the 'bounded' self and of the social. What is particularly striking about the early modern regime of memory described by West is that its contradictions pivot on an incommensurability between the subject's private sphere of affective memory traces and personal meanings, and the wider public sphere of reading and interpretation. Perhaps one might argue, then, that, certainly from the fifteenth century onwards, a lack of fit between figurations of the private individual and figurations of the public sphere made itself felt within the contested field of regimes of memory, and that this incongruity hinged, in particular, on questions of the ontology of memory's 'contents'. These objects, which might be conceived of by their possessor as both transparent and material, nevertheless become opaque traces requiring interpretation within a wider public sphere.[9]

In the nineteenth century, organicist figurations of memory arguably constituted one attempt to resolve the ambiguity between the individual and the social by emphasising the body's relation to a *shared* 'species memory'. This was a regime of memory that sustained a politics of imperialism and of individualism: the positioning of Western man as the container and summation of all that had gone before clearly works in the interest of imperialist discourse. But its 'insertion' into the body of the 'developed' Western subject of all previous stages of 'species memory' produces and displays in public a version of the individual as an exemplar, repository and *possessor* of memory, though in this case the memories possessed by the body are *shared* body memories, rather than those of the individual's private and unique experience. Here, then, the possession of shared memory paradoxically supports a particular figuration of subjectivity: possessive individualism.

That figurations of *shared* memory need not *necessarily* work to support possessive individualism is the central tenet of Michael Lambek's account of spirit possession in Madagascar. Lambek's comparative study of Western regimes of memory and Malagasy Sakalava spirit possession reveals the historical specificity and the non-inevitability of the relation between memory and possessive individualism naturalised in the West. On Lambek's account, Sakalava memory practices offer an alternative to Western modernity's regimes of memory. This alternative disrupts the binary oppositions of past/present, public/private, history/memory and self/other central to Western memory discourses. Lambek's study insists on the historically contingent nature of the relations between memory and subjectivity naturalised in the West and contends that 'conceptualizations of memory and history are dependent on conceptualizations of social persons' (p. 202).

Michael Lambek's argument concerning history/memory and conceptualisations of the subject refutes the argument that the conceptual divide between 'memory' and 'history' emerged alongside the rise of literacy and the loss of an earlier oral culture within which spoken memories were handed on from one generation to the next. Contesting arguments that draw a divide between societies of orality/memory and of literacy/history, Lambek argues, rather, that regimes of memory and their histories are intimately associated not with regimes of representation and their histories, but with regimes of *subjectivity* – in particular, of construals of social personhood. In certain societies, argues Lambek, the modern Western divide between history and memory does not pertain *not* because these societies remain rooted in an oral, memory culture, but because their figurations of subjectivity are not modelled according to modern Western divisions between self/other, past/present and individual/social.

Histories of memory/technologies of representation

One way of approaching the history of regimes of memory, then, is by studying their relation to the history of subjectivity. Yet other chapters in this volume remind us that, notwithstanding Lambek's argument, there is a relation between conceptualisations of memory and technologies of representation. An alternative approach to the study of how memory has been understood and deployed at different times, then, focuses on the analogies that have been made between memory and media technologies. Such a study might begin with analogies between memory and language.

The question of memory's relation to *language* is not identical to that of memory's relation to the orality/literacy divide. For what is at stake in debates about memory and language – whether spoken or written – is the opacity, the non-transparency, and the arbitrariness of language as a medium for remembrance.

William West's study of early modern memory reveals that since early modern times, memory has been conceived of as a storage space *and* as an internal writing. The associations West points to here between, on the one hand sight, unmediatedness and transparency and, on the other, writing, mediation and opacity produce ambiguities and incongruities that arguably underpin all future regimes of memory. For instance, Tony Bennett's chapter reveals that, in nineteenth-century figurations of organicist memory, relations between memory as storage system and as writing, as visual and as textual, were complex. Theories of organicist memory relied on analogies with sophisticated technologies of visual interpretation that were being developed at the time by archaeologists and scientists: 'the body was conceived ... as itself a storage and retrieval device in which the past was "remembered", albeit that the memories coded into the body needed to be *deciphered* by the evolutionary scientist ...'. (p. 46, emphasis added).

As Tony Bennett goes on to explain, this new conception of memory was closely associated with a new depth structure of vision – with the idea, that is, that vision could go below the surface and penetrate hidden strata – and with the concern within archaeology and geology to make the hidden visible by developing 'new principles of legibility in which reading became a matter of deciphering the relationships between the successive layers of meaning which lie beyond the visible surface of the present' (p. 47). What is striking about this formulation is the way that it straddles metaphors of memory as an organic, *material* storage system *and* as writing. This new way of visualising memory depended, argues Tony Bennett, on a revised understanding of the palimpsest as a surface that retained all impressions yet offered itself constantly as a clean surface upon which new inscriptions could be made. One interesting aspect of this conceptualisation of memory is the way that practices associated with digging up and making visible objects from a buried storehouse become collapsed together with practices concerned with writing and reading. In this move, an attempt is arguably made to bridge the divide between the domains of the experiential and of the non-experiential, of sight and affect on the one hand, and of language and mediation on the other. The tension between these domains remains evident in all future analogies between memory and technologies of representation in general and of the visual in particular.

Esther Leslie's discussion of modernity, modernism and memory reveals the continuing salience of analogies between memory and optical devices and technologies to early twentieth-century regimes of memory. Like Tony Bennett, Leslie points to the ways in which new visual technologies could serve as metaphors for an understanding of memory concerned with both its 'surface' invisibility or absence and with its deep visibility or presence. Leslie emphasises in particular the growing significance to modernism and to Freud of that negation or 'wiping' present in the revised understandings of the palimpsest discussed by Tony Bennett. In Freud's analogies between memory and the 'mystical writing pad', what becomes evident, then, is memory's duality: the simultaneous 'wiping' of memories from a continually cleaned surface as well as their retention. It was by analogy with new technologies of the visual that these figurations of memory evolved.

Leslie's concern with modernism and with central figures including Benjamin and Freud reveals that analogies between memory and modern visual technologies could be deployed to suggest memory's subversive potential. The analogy between organicist memory and the palimpsest identified by Tony Bennett arguably supported a version of organicist memory in keeping with the imperial west. But memory's association with Freud's 'mystic writing pad' or with an 'optical unconscious' associated, by Walter Benjamin, with new technologies of the visual such as photography and film, could reveal, rather, traces of that which *had been* repressed. The association between memory and possessive individualism appears to suggest complicity between regimes of memory and dominant power relations. Here, however, the potential of regimes of memory to undermine as well as support those power relations is revealed. For Benjamin, the activities and social relations of past generations (and of childhood) leave their traces on each new generation – traces that are 'ready to burst out and scatter the fragile consensus of the present' (p. 178). Leslie argues, moreover, that, for Benjamin at least, the relations between memory and power cannot be equated with the 'forced' forgetting of domination, for what 'civilisation' repressed, for Benjamin, is the 'originary sense of the *trace*' (p. 180, emphasis added). Leslie explains that, for Walter Benjamin, traces – memory traces – were indexical and mimetic. Historical activity *imprints* itself and leaves material traces. Memory's status as organic or as technical is held in tension rather than opposed in Leslie's account of modern aesthetics.

On Leslie's account, late nineteenth- and early twentieth-century technologies of the visual become ways of modelling memory. While the idea that technology debases memory continues to mark discourses of memory, technologies also provide the means for modelling memory at any one time. Moreover, as Leslie demonstrates, the study of the relation between memory and technology can move beyond revealing how memory has been conceptualised to show how, for certain modernist writers, seizing hold of new technologies of memory (metaphorical or actual) provided the grounds for impassioned and politicised positions on memory's relation to how the future might be envisioned.

Leslie's account of modernist figurations of memory, and, in particular, of Walter Benjamin's radical theories, returns us to those broader tensions between understandings of memory as having an unmediated relation to direct experience and memory as having a highly mediated relation to such experience. In the early modern period, there was a tension between memory as 'storage space' for objects associated with individual memory and the difficulty of interpreting these memories in the public sphere. What appeared to be 'material' and unmediated memory emerged, in the public sphere, one might say, as mediated writing. This is a tension that continues to echo through modernist theories of memory. Benjamin's 'traces' are at once material *and* social. For Benjamin, memory operates through mimesis and indexicality: historical activity *imprints* on the mind as a knife leaves its scratches on a tin plate. Benjamin's writings contest, then, any arbitrariness or even mediatedness of the relation between activity and memory: activity leaves material traces (which may then be repressed by civilisation) and these (repressed) traces are remembered, for instance in the body's ritual movements in dance. If these traces remain hidden, this is neither due to their idiosyncratic ties to private and individual memory nor to the arbitrariness of writing's relation to actuality, but to civilisation's repression of the links between traces and social activities – links that might sunder the hold of particular power relations.

Modernity's regimes of memory differed in their figurations of memory's relation to 'external reality' and in their understandings of the nature of the

8

correspondence that pertains between memory and actuality. While Benjamin emphasised a relatively direct mimetic and indexical correspondence between the trace and actuality, Freud's theories of psychical life emphasised a more mediated or, as some would see it, even tenuous relation between memory traces and 'happenings'.

Memory and mediation

Much research into memory remains haunted by the idea that memory's correspondence to and registration of external reality or experience is particularly direct or immediate. This is a position that can be contextualised and historicised by a study of regimes of memory. The history of debate concerning memory's 'transparency', and its relation to 'actuality' is too complex and detailed to be addressed adequately here and would demand a full-length study to do it adequate justice. Such work can begin to ask how and why ideas of memory's immediacy and directness emerged and can move on to question the political, philosophical and epistemological stakes of such ideas. But it confronts a complex picture.

Questions concerning memory and mediation arguably became of particular salience in the nineteenth century, although such questions of course have a long history; we have already seen how in the sixteenth century the idea that memory could offer unmediated access to experience or to external reality was already being challenged. In the nineteenth century, memory's direct or mediated relation to experience was very much at issue, though accounts of modernity offer divergent understandings of the positions taken on these issues by key nineteenth-century writers. While for Andreas Huyssen, writers including Benjamin, Freud, Baudelaire and Proust associated memory with a radical alternative to history and with a utopian space,[10] for Richard Terdiman, writers such as Freud and Proust were concerned, rather, with freeing the present from memory's intractable hold. Modernity's memory crisis might best be understood, then, as 'the site within which modernity's equivocations found their most pressing expression'.[11] Though memory may have been associated in this period with history's 'other', and with uncontrollable upsurges of a past from which modernity had 'broken', in the nineteenth century conceptions of memory as mediated, as elusive and almost impenetrable 'writing' had gained ground. Whether modernity *revealed* memory to have always been thus mediated, however, or whether, rather, modern memory had become sundered from a premodern immediacy and directness of relation to experience remained very much at issue.[12] Although nineteenth-century debates about memory and mediation are particularly complex, there are nevertheless two pointers that can be offered for those wishing to study these issues in greater depth. First, on Richard Terdiman's compelling account, nineteenth-century debates concerning memory and mediation made themselves felt as a crisis concerning the capacity of representations to offer access to external reality. In his book *Present Past*, Terdiman argues that the nineteenth-century 'crisis' concerning the relationship between representations and external reality can 'be construed as the memory crisis seen from within the latter's own cognitive restrictions'.[13] Second, for the period of the late nineteenth century onwards, it is within the field of psychoanalysis that debates concerning memory's mediated relation to 'reality' can most easily be charted (though one should perhaps guard against regarding psychoanalysis as exemplary of all other disciplinary domains). As Karl Figlio's chapter demonstrates, psychoanalytic perspectives complicate the relationship between memory and external reality by proposing that (for object relations, in particular) remembering is a form of phantasying in which relations to internal objects are continually worked over and revised. Chapters in this collection by Paul Antze, Constantina Papoulias and Karl Figlio remind us that the debate in psychoanalysis concerning memory's relation to past happenings remains very much alive and fraught.

As we have seen, this tension, which for West stretches as far back as Plato, continues to shape regimes of memory. It is upon this slippery ground – a ground more familiar, perhaps, in debates on post-structuralism and postmodernism – that the seeds have been sown for contemporary debates concerning the meanings of memory and its relation to external reality.

Contemporary regimes of memory

A focus on *regimes* of memory runs counter to the main tendencies within contemporary memory studies, where, under the impact of post-structuralism and postmodernism, the major focus has been on memory's capacity to destabilise the authority of the 'grand narratives' with which History[14] has become associated. While History has become negatively associated with the 'public', and with 'objectivity', memory has become positively associated with the embedded, with the local, the personal and the subjective.[15] There are several aspects to this positive valuation of memory. First, for historians, in particular, memory studies have been utilised in order to retrieve that which runs against, disrupts or disturbs dominant ways of understanding the past. Influenced by Foucauldian or Gramscian writings on popular memory, [16] oral historians and others have seized upon memories in order to contest official accounts of 'the happened'. Memory has also been valorised by historians and others for its capacity to run against universalising, monolithic generalities. Memory's locatedness and its particularity are in line with postmodernist critiques of grand narratives and History. The fraughtness of the relation between memory and history that emerges here has been much discussed and debated and is a central theme of our companion volume, *Contested Pasts*.[17] One of *Regimes of Memory*'s contributions to this debate is to suggest that the conceptual opposition between memory and history may depend on how the social person is conceptualised. As we have seen, Michael Lambek argues that if persons are understood as 'personages', as in some sense bearers of their predecessors and their social roles rather than being seen exclusively as individuals, then the memory/history distinction becomes untenable. Thus, to an extent, the contemporary Western opposition between memory and history can be understood to be linked to the rise of possessive individualism and the history of selfhood within which an increasingly sharp divide became instituted between the individual and the social.

Finally, memory has been positively valued and deployed as that which bears traces of that which cannot enter discourse or representation. On this account, the unspeakable or the unwitnessable makes its incognisable mark on the mind as traumatic memory, or in the body, as embodied memory (trauma theory), leaving traces that can only be read (if at all) through belated witnessings.

Contemporary scholarly interests in memory converge, then, in seeing memory as possessing the potential to contest public 'regimes' of History and of official narratives of the happened. So to speak of regimes of *memory* runs counter to or at least renders equivocal the claims of such tendencies, for it insists that both history and memory are 'regimes' in a number of senses: that is, that what is understood as history and as memory is produced by historically specific and contestable systems of knowledge and power and that what history and memory produce as knowledge is also contingent upon the (contestable) systems of knowledge and power that produce them. This is of course not to deny that memory may contest history, but it is to insist that neither memory nor history is 'outside' systems of knowledge and power. Although the following chapters do lean towards seeing particular figurations of memory as contestatory of other regimes of knowledge, the aim of the present volume is not to celebrate memory as contestatory or subversive of other established systems of knowledge, but rather to focus on the construction of regimes of memory themselves and their relation to understandings of history, of subjectivity, of the mind and of the social.

Questions concerning memory, mediation and the past continue to inflect contemporary discussions of memory. Recent positive evaluations of memory which link it with the subjective, the local and the particular shift the balance away from emphasising memory's *mediatedness*. This was a risk posed by the quests by radical oral historians of the 1960s and 1970s for what had been hidden from history. This risk was speedily identified and corrected in some historical work, and particularly in the seminal work of historians such as Luisa Passerini and Alessandro Portelli, who studied the relation between memories and literary and cultural narratives.[18] In such work, the idea that memory's representations are 'less mediated' than those of history is countered by the insight that memory is mediated differently, rather than less.

A powerful tendency within contemporary memory studies seeks out sites within which a relatively unmediated or 'authentic' order of memory continues to survive. On this account, these 'survivals' exist in the interstices of modern debased, silenced, or 'archivised' modes of memory. Central to these tendencies within memory studies is the concept of the body. In *Contested Pasts*, Luisa Passerini suggests that unspeakable, lost or hidden memories may survive

11

through generations in silent bodily gestures and movements.[19] Here, the bodily survival of memory is associated with its public silencing. Contemporary, debased, technologised or media-based memory may be counterposed to individual or social memories that are remembered *in* the individual body – as gesture, as habit or as the indecipherable traces of trauma. Michael Lambek's study of Sakalava spirit possession goes so far as to suggest, even, that more than one person's memory may be borne in one body.

Alternatively, contemporary 'archival' memory may be counterposed to the survivals, in certain sites, or locations,[20] of what had been an 'organic' mode of memory that sustained collective bonds within a community or social body. As Tony Bennett points out, this latter opposition extends or metaphorises the opposition between archival or representational memory and embodied memory by extending the idea of the body to that of the 'organic' community. Tony Bennett's chapter suggests, moreover, that the idea that memory can be carried in organic mechanisms has its origin in nineteenth-century *regimes* of memory. The section in this volume titled 'Believing the Body' explores this area in greater detail.

Memory, authenticity and recognition

The question of memory's relation to authenticity and recognition is currently being explored in relation to three modes of memory: representation, affect and practice.

Currently the notion that memory is constituted through representation is widely accepted. Yet to speak of memory as representation does not necessarily imply that the relationship between memory and experience is therefore inauthentic. These questions concerning memory, representation and authenticity are being researched, in particular, in relation to the various media that may be taken to constitute memory sites. As Esther Leslie's chapter in this volume shows, this is a field of study that was arguably anticipated by Walter Benjamin's writings on memory, photography and film. In the wake of such work, and influenced in no small part by debates concerning postmodernism and the media,[21] there is now a fast-growing debate concerning the ways in which the specific representational modes of particular media may *sustain* memory, rather than simply contribute to its atrophy or debasement (see essays by Robert Burgoyne, Graham Carr, Chris Healy and Janet Walker in *Contested Pasts*). What is particularly interesting about these studies is the positions they offer on questions concerning memory, mediation, authenticity and recognition. As the following two examples show, debates concerning Holocaust memories have contributed to the intensity of discussions concerning memory, mediation and authenticity, since to speak of Holocaust memory is to touch on issues of denial, the loss of witnesses and even the incapacity to remember. In this volume, Stephan Feuchtwang suggests that for Binjamin Wilkormirski, who did not experience it directly, the Holocaust nevertheless provided a memory prop through which he could recognise his own different yet devastating experiences of loss in childhood. Wilkomirski's consequent 'fictional' Holocaust autobiography then became a 'memory prop', argues Feuchtwang, for those seeking recognition of their own *actual* Holocaust sufferings. To put this more sharply, Feuchtwang's chapter suggests that, in the case of the memoirs and autobiographies that he discusses, the question of the directness of correspondence between a memory and historical actuality appears to be beside the point, where questions of authenticity and recognition are at stake. Similarly, Janet Walker's chapter on film and memory in *Contested Pasts* suggests that a memory may be true to an *experience*, while being historically inaccurate – again complicating the question of memory, authenticity and mediation. Importantly, what also emerges in both these examples is an approach that foregrounds the relation between memory, representation and affect.

Although the Holocaust has come to hold a central place in discussions of memory and authenticity, these questions have always been central – and much debated – within the field of psychoanalysis. In his chapter in this volume Paul Antze suggests that holding strictly to an understanding of memory's bond with actual past happenings, as some contemporary psychological theory insists that we should, may offer only a reductive account of the richness of human subjectivity. For Antze, the 'memories' through which we recognise ourselves are better understood as 'scenes' constructed through mental processes that he compares to metaphorisation. Yet these 'scenes', while not constituting actual representations of the past, are nevertheless the core of ourselves – the base of our own self-recognitions. So, once again, contemporary theory suggests a highly nuanced relation between memory, representation and recognition, while arguing that the recognitions that we make are nevertheless 'authentic'.

In several of the chapters in this volume, affect emerges as the conduit of recognition. Under the influence of a renewed interest in theorists such as Gilles Deleuze, research on affect in general is a fast-developing field currently making itself felt in the area of memory studies, particularly in relation to trauma. Jill Bennett's chapter in this volume exemplifies this work by suggesting that the visual media may prompt recognition of one's own or another's past experience not via representational but via affective memory. This suggestion arguably returns us to a regime of memory current in early modern times, for as William West explains in this volume, the imaginary objects of early modern 'artificial memory' were freighted with immensities of affect. It was the affective qualities of those objects, indeed, that rendered them memorable.

Finally, several chapters in this volume draw attention not only to the pairings of memory and representation, or memory and affect, but to memory and practice/performance. As Constantina Papoulias's chapter points out, this 'turn to practice' is a current trend in the humanities more generally. For theorists interested in practice, the concept offers a way of studying cultural exchange and transmission outside the confines of 'textual theory'. At the same time, theories of practice and performance suggest not the fixities of identity and regimes but the transience and the fluidity of bodies, of contingencies and of lived experience. The chapters in this volume by Paul Antze, Stephan Feuchtwang, Michael Lambek and Tina Papoulias demonstrate the wide range of application of concepts of practice and performance to the study of memory. Though concepts of practice/performance are deployed in each of these chapters, there is no shared agreement that memory practices are more 'authentic' than representational or affectual memory. Nor is it simply argued that regimes of memory that deploy the concept of practice have a more authentic or truer grasp of memory's ontology than those that do not.

Thus Stephan Feuchtwang's chapter, which is concerned, in part, with the recognitions of loss by means of memory prompts that may have only a highly nuanced relation to lived historical actuality, goes on to explore the religious, juridical and cultural processes through which recognition of loss is sought, pointing to the ritual/performance aspects of these processes. Paul Antze's critique of neuro-cognitive psychology foregrounds the centrality of practice to this currently influential theory. Antze explains that neuro-cognitivism's distinction between declarative and procedural memory rests on a distinction between memory as representation and memory as embodied practice, and, as we have seen, for Antze, the focus on embodied practice produces a psychology with a reductive and shallow grasp of human psychical life. This is a theme developed also by Constantina Papoulias, who outlines a critique of recent work within cultural studies, political science and social theory which approaches memory as practice. In the new psychological and cultural theories discussed by Papoulias, memory is conceived of as material social practice rather than as mental faculty, and as inhering in inter-mental, rather than intra-mental, processes: in intersubjective relations, in talk. But Papoulias goes on to argue that, although the focus of this research on inter-mental processes appears to challenge the hold of individualism, its rejection of Freudian and Laplanchian psychoanalysis's emphasis on desire's disruption of the subject leaves the coherence of that subject in place.

Finally, Michael Lambek suggests that the performance of spirit possession in Madagascar constitutes a practice between the modern West's distinct categories of memory and history – a practice that demonstrates that Sakalava people inhabit a liminal space between their past and their present. The temporality of the Sakalava people's performance of spirit possession may not conform, then, to the linear temporality of western history – a thought that brings us to a more general consideration of memory and time.

Memory and time

We have already seen that one way of approaching the study of regimes of memory is by way of regimes of subjectivity. Another fruitful approach to the study of regimes of memory charts their relation to regimes of temporality. Thus, while we argued earlier that one way of perceiving the development of the memory/history divide is by reference to the construction of a mode of subjectivity founded on a divide between 'inside' and 'outside', it is also possible to suggest that the memory/history divide is linked, certainly since the eighteenth century, with the alignment of history with the development of a linear, progressive temporality. Memory, one might argue, is that which complicates or refuses to sit within that temporality.

Time is a historical construct. The conceptualisation of temporality, that is, as linear progression from the past to the present and future is historically and culturally specific.[22] The project of charting the relationship between these domains is a vast one. In this volume discussion focuses in the main on the period from the late eighteenth century to the present. Tony Bennett's chapter demonstrates that newly emergent conceptualisations of temporality were central to the production of an organicist memory supportive of modern conceptualisations of history as progress. He points out that all times are ever-present in the evolutionary museums he describes, and associates the temporality of those evolutionary museums and of organicist memory with geological time, in which all past strata are continuously present. This geological time is linked, perhaps, to 'environmental time', which is, as Bill Schwarz explains in this volume, one of the three orders of historical temporality identified by the historian Fernand Braudel. Schwarz's chapter on memory and temporality takes as its starting point Braudel's categorisations of historical time, and moves on to suggest that historians need also to attend to the temporality of memory. But the question of whether temporalities of memory can be embraced by historiography, or whether they are in fact contradictory is a moot one. Modernist conceptions of memory might be regarded as contradictory, of modern regimes of temporality, tied as they were to constructions of history as linear progress. It is within psychoanalytic figurations of psychical temporality that the incongruence between the temporalities of memory and the linear temporality of history can most clearly be grasped. In this volume, this theme comes to the fore in Karl Figlio's chapter, which is concerned with the contrast between the secular, modern linear time of history and the temporality of memory/fantasy as it emerges in Freudian and object-relations psychoanalysis.

One insight provided by essays in this collection, however, is that it would be a mistake to consider the temporality of memory as itself single or homogeneous. Stephan Feuchtwang's chapter points to the different temporalities of the different recognising authorities through which victims seek recognition of their memories and losses. The temporality through which religion remembers and recognises loss diverges, that is, from the temporality of judicial remembrance.

Feuchtwang's chapter is concerned also with questions of survival: how memories of loss can survive when the props that support recall of what has been lost have been catastrophically destroyed. This question of 'survival' is intimately tied to questions of the temporality/ies of memory. Indeed the very concept of survival suggests the existence of different temporalities: that which survives in memory has survived beyond its own 'proper' time in actuality/history. This question of the relation between the temporality of memory and the concept of survival is raised in Schwarz's discussion of Althusser's consideration of the unevenness of development. The question of survival is central, too, to discussions of the temporality of traumatic memory, since, as Jill Bennett's chapter shows, contemporary figurations suggest that such memories *remain* ever-present in the mind, though in an area dissociated from consciousness. This is interesting for what it shows about the relationship in figurations of memory between regimes of time and of space. The idea that something may survive in the present though in another place recurs also in Tony Bennett's discussion of nineteenth-century organicist memory, for, as he explains, in this formulation, 'the past and present became contemporary with each other, but separated spatially, thus what was far away from Euro-American metropolitan centres became fashioned as their prehistory' (p. 49). Tony Bennett's chapter shows that in organicist memory, space became reconfigured as time – that which was far away became fashioned as Western man's prehistory.

An important aspect of the shift from modern to contemporary figurations of memory reverses the transposition identified by Tony Bennett. Whereas, in modernity, figurations of memory foregrounded questions of temporality, contemporary figurations emphasise rather issues of spatiality. In postmodernist theory, indeed, the relationship between time, memory and space identified by Tony Bennett is reversed; for, as much postmodernist theory has argued, in the postmodern world, time becomes reconfigured as space, but at the same time, the space between places and people becomes of only minor significance. This argument, most commonly referred to as 'time/space compression', [23] fore-grounds the impact of new electronic communications technologies on the experience of time and space. In postmodernism, these systems are argued to have overcome the temporal delays to communication previously caused by distance, making possible almost instantaneous communication across even the vastest distances. In his chapter in this volume, Richard Terdiman argues that postmodern time/space compression provides an accurate analogy for the ordinary workings of memory. The seemingly effortless, atemporal leaps across and between domains accomplished, for instance, by search engines are leaps, argues Terdiman, that memory has been accomplishing throughout history. Everyday life, he concludes, is finally catching up with the psyche. Terdiman's considera-tion of the similarities between the leaps across space as well as time accomplished by memory and by the Internet bring us to the question of memory and space more generally.

Memory and space

As Richard Terdiman's chapter demonstrates, figurations of memory mobilise more complex spatial metaphors than that of the simple storage space. Terdiman's discussion of memory and the postmodern concerns itself, in partic-ular, with cities – with Los Angeles, a city 'without depth, in effect *without memory*' (p. 189) and with Cieszyn, a Polish town loaded with memory. Meanwhile,

Constantina Papoulias asks '(w)hat happens when the market place and the town square replace the head as the spatiality through which memory is imagined ...?' (p. 114). A consideration of the figure of the city can shed light on shifting representations of memory. One starting point for a study of spatial regimes of memory and the city might be Walter Benjamin's *Arcades Project*, his huge and recently translated study of memory and the arcades of nineteenth- and early twentieth-century Paris. The fascinating figure of memory and the city can also be approached through Freud's discussion, in *Civilisation and its Discontents*, of the 'general problem of preservation in the sphere of the mind'.[24] Freud reaches for the figure of the city to illustrate his thesis that 'in mental life nothing which has been formed can perish – that everything is somehow preserved ...'.[25] He suggests that this difficult idea might be illustrated by imagining a walk through 'the Eternal city' of Rome:

> Now let us, by a flight of the imagination, suppose that Rome is not a human habitation but a psychical entity with a similarly long and copious past – an entity, that is to say, in which nothing that has once come into existence will have passed away and all the earlier phases of development continue to exist alongside the latest one. This would mean that in Rome the palaces of the Caesars and the Septizonium of Septimus Severus would still be rising to their old height on the Palatine and the castle of S. Angelo would still be carrying on its battlements the beautiful statues which graced it until the siege by the Goths. But more than this. In the place occupied by the Palazzo Caffarelli would once more stand – without the Palazzo having to be removed – the Temple of Jupiter Capitolinus.... Where the Coliseum now stands we could at the same time admire Nero's vanished Golden House.[26]

This passage has been quoted at length since it illustrates well the difficulty Freud faced in attempting to convey the idea of the preservation of memory traces in the mind. Indeed, having asked his readers to accompany him on this walk through an imaginary Rome, Freud is immediately forced to acknowledge that the figure will not sustain the idea he wished to convey:

> There is clearly no point in spinning our phantasy any further, for it leads to things that are unimaginable and even absurd. If we want to represent historical sequence in spatial terms we can only do it by juxtaposition in space: the same space cannot have two different contents. Our attempt seems to be an idle game. It has only one justification. It shows us how far we are from mastering the characteristics of mental life by representing them in pictorial terms.[27]

Having found his metaphor wanting, Freud rejects it completely, pointing out that the metaphor of the city is a priori unsuited for a comparison of this sort, since whereas the mind's capacity to preserve memory traces for unlimited duration depends upon the mind remaining undamaged, cities always and inevitably bear the marks of demolition and replacement.[28]

Freudian models of memory and the mind are frequently referred to as depth models. This notion of the depth model tends to be associated with temporality rather than with spatiality, but depth is in fact a spatial, rather than – or as well as – a temporal term. The concept of depth is linked to archaeological excavations, and to the mind's 'burying' of past experiences in underground or hidden spaces. It is a concept that recurs frequently in modern figurations of memory, and is discussed in this volume in chapters on psychoanalysis and memory by Paul Antze, Karl Figlio and Constantina Papoulias, as well as in Tony Bennett's discussion of nineteenth-century organicist memory. Yet what Freud's mobilisation of the imaginary city of Rome suggests is that the concept of 'depth' does not adequately capture the figuration of memory that he struggles for. As Freud points out, it is not possible to pictorially (or spatially) represent the idea of two different contents in one space. Perhaps, indeed, Freud's invocation of images of a Rome in which all remains intact demonstrates the difficulty of attempting to theorise memory in relation to *both* time and space.

If the model of the city cannot do justice to contemporary regimes of memory, time and space, perhaps the figure of the journey offers greater potential for modelling these relations. As William West shows us, already in early modern times map-making journeys were associated with the making of memory. Yet, as Richard Terdiman shows, the metaphor of the journey – a metaphor associated with both time and space – has life in it yet. For Terdiman, indeed, it is the metaphor of the journey – be it of physical bodies or of electronic information – that captures best the leaps and jumps characteristic of memory itself.

The essays collected in this volume constitute, together, a journey through figurations of memory in which certain themes repeatedly emerge: memory's relation to space and time, to affect and to representation, to conservation and to transformation, to the individual and the social, to history, to experience and to external reality. Yet what also emerges in this volume is a skeletal history of regimes of memory. A careful reading of the essays collected here can reveal, therefore, that critiques of *contemporary* regimes of memory resonate with older figurations. For example, contemporary theories of affective visual memory revise understandings of memory associated with early modern practices of artificial memory. Moreover, although figurations of memory are historically specific and changing, the break between older and newer figurations of memory may be less thoroughgoing than it appears. Indeed, accepted truths about *memory* may actually shed light on *regimes* of memory. For where regimes of memory are concerned, what appears to have been transformed or forgotten may actually have been preserved, and it is only through careful historical and comparative analysis of regimes of memory that the stakes of these forgettings and rememberings can be revealed.

The contents of this volume are divided into five parts. Part I, 'Believing the body' concerns itself with debates about the possibility of embodied memory. Tony Bennett's chapter argues that the very idea of embodied memory has its origins in eighteenth- and nineteenth-century regimes of memory associated with a depth structure of vision and with evolutionary museums. For Tony Bennett, all ideas about and theories of memory – even the idea of embodied memory – are produced by regimes of power and knowledge. Jill Bennett's chapter suggests, rather, that there is a register of memory that is both embodied and non-representational. Affect memory, she proposes, is carried in the body, and may be transmitted via art practices. Drawing on the concept of the witness, and on the suitability of visual icons as storehouses of memory, Jill Bennett proposes that photography, in particular, may act as a conduit for affect memory. In this section then, what is at stake is the question of whether there *can be* memory carried in the body, carried in the organism, and transferred between bodies, or whether the very *idea* of such embodied memory arises from a particular regime or discourse concerning memory.

In Part II, 'Propping the subject', the focus shifts to the ways in which the sustenance of subjectivity may be associated with particular relations to 'props' of recall. Stephan Feuchtwang's chapter is concerned with the relation between props of recall and catastrophic loss. His essay identifies how props of recall may ward off disintegration and sustain a sense of self, in the face of such loss, as well as providing the means for various modes of public as well as personal recognition of loss. Yet, as Feuchtwang argues, the personal recognition of loss, at least, need not necessarily be tied to any direct correspondence between props of recall and actual historical experience. William West's chapter is concerned with the functioning of 'objects of memory' in early modern times. During this period, memory was 'artificially' enhanced through the construction, in the mind, of memory objects to which could be attached several different memories. West points out, however, that, by the sixteenth century, there was a growing sense that the memories attached to such objects remained opaque within a public sphere that lacked knowledge of the associations to which these objects made reference. Thus, in early modern times, memory props, which were envisaged as the supports of the self, became its undoing.

Part III, What memory forgets: models of the mind' is concerned with the regimes of memory circulating in some of the newer and most current psychological and cultural theories. Both Paul Antze's and Constantina Papoulias's chapters suggest that the centrality currently accorded to memory in certain theories within psychoanalysis, psychology and the social sciences screen important aspects of previous psychoanalytic understandings of the subject. In short, what both chapters propose is that what these regimes of memory screen is psychoanalysis's most radical precept: that the subject is radically other to itself, driven by fantasies and desires of which it has only the most limited awareness. The question of why current and influential regimes of memory within the academy should have moved so far away from this precept is a compelling one that invites further enquiry.

Part IV, 'What history forgets: memory and time' is concerned with two aspects of the relation between history, memory and time. Bill Schwarz's chapter suggests that, although history is the study of past/present relations, the study, that is, of historical time, up until now, historians have retreated from the study of memory as the lived dimension of historical time. Looking at the work of the historian Fernand Braudel, the Marxist theorist Louis Althusser and the author Virginia Woolf, Schwarz's chapter goes on to propose how historians might begin to approach history's 'fourth dimension'. Karl Figlio, too, is concerned with the task of the historian. His concern is not, however, with the problem of how to integrate into history the study of memory. Rather, Figlio is intent on revealing that historical enquiry is always, unbeknownst to itself, unconsciously caught up with memory. Figlio's understanding of memory is informed by object-relations psychoanalysis, which sees memory in relation to phantasy relations to internal objects. These relations permeate the historian's quest, he suggests. Thus the chapters in this section are both concerned with relations between history and memory, the difficulty of consciously addressing memory as the lived dimension of history, and the difficulty of addressing those phantasies/memories that unconsciously drive the historian's pursuit of knowledge of the past.

Part V, 'Memory beyond the modern', comprises three chapters that complete this volume's journey through memory with considerations of alternatives to modern Western regimes of memory. Esther Leslie's chapter focuses on the modernisms of the late nineteenth and early twentieth centuries. During this period, new understandings of memory were developed by means of analogies with optical devices and new technologies of the visual. These modernist figurations of memory foregrounded memory's complex relations with consciousness and with forgetting. Leslie goes on to contrast modernist analogies between memory and optical devices with postmodernist analogies between memory and digital technology. At the heart of her chapter is a foregrounding of modernism's belief in the mediated relation between actuality and memory trace. Richard Terdiman's chapter focuses more centrally on postmodernist analogies between memory, electronic communications and the rapid political transformations that are arguably constitutive of postmodernity. In postmodernity, suggests Terdiman, everyday experience is catching up with memory. Yet, like Leslie's, Terdiman's chapter concludes by suggesting that remembering memory's relation to conservation as well as to transformation might militate against the radical relativism of postmodernist thinking. Finally, Michael Lambek's chapter describes a regime of memory that falls beyond the reach of modern, Western constructions of subjectivity and memory. Describing practices of spirit possession in Madagascar, Lambek suggests that the romantic objectification that arguably characterises Western regimes of memory is tied to possessive individualism. In the culture he describes, memory as a 'thing' possessed does not exist. Instead, he suggests, in spirit possession can be found a mode of intersubjectivity in which the past and the present commune and in which the history/memory divide does not pertain.

Notes

1 For a discussion of the authority vested in memory in earlier times, see Brian Smith, *Memory*, London: Allen and Unwin, 1966. See also James Fentress and Chris Wickham, *Social Memory*, Oxford: Blackwell, 1992, p. 8; Edward Casey, *Remembering: A Phenomenological Study*, Bloomington: Indiana University Press, 1987, p. 11. For a longer discussion of both memory's contemporary centrality in humanities research and of the wider cultural fascination with memory see Susannah Radstone, 'Working with Memory: An Introduction', in Susannah Radstone (ed.) *Memory and Methodology*, New York and Oxford: Berg, 2000.
2 Michel Foucault, *The History of Sexuality: Volume 1*, Harmondsworth: Penguin, 1981, p. 17.
3 Edward Casey, op. cit., p. 290.
4 James Fentress and Chris Wickham, op. cit., p.7.
5 Raphael Samuel, *Theatres of Memory*, London: Verso, 1994.
6 Alison Landsberg, 'Prosthetic Memory: *Total Recall* and *Blade Runner*', in Mike Featherstone and Roger Burrows (eds) *Cyberbodies/Cyberpunk: Cultures of Technological Embodiment*, London: Sage, 1995, pp. 175–89.
7 C.B. MacPherson, *The Political Theory of Possessive Individualism*, Oxford: Oxford University Press, 1962.
8 Plato, *The Republic*, Book vii, 514–18. Plato's discussion of the myth of the cave differentiates betweeen different degrees of enlightenment. He describes the progress of enlightenment by means of an allegory. Prisoners tied in a cave lit by firelight, first see only the shadows cast by artificial objects. Enlightenment consists in seeing the objects themselves, then the fire, then the real world and finally the sun.
9 My argument here is informed by Richard Terdiman's *Present Past: Modernity and the Memory Crisis*, Ithaca, NY and London: Cornell University Press, 1993. Terdiman's thesis is that the nineteenth-century West (particularly France, and Europe more generally), experienced a memory crisis in which 'the very coherence of time and of subjectivity seemed disarticulated' (p. 4). Terdiman goes on to suggest that what is generally considered to be modernity's crisis of representation arises as the flattened form in which the memory crisis was able to appear to a culture intent on coming to terms with its own isolation from history. The crisis of representation can thus be construed as the memory crisis seen from within the latter's own cognitive restrictions (p. 7).
10 Andreas Huyssen, *Twilight Memories: Marking Time in a Culture of Amnesia*, London: Routledge, 1995, p. 6.
11 Susannah Radstone, 'Working with Memory', op. cit., p. 5.
12 Ibid., pp. 2–9.
13 Richard Terdiman, *Present Past*, op. cit., p. 7.
14 The use of the capital 'H' here is common amongst 'new' historians who wish to signal the difference between dominant versions of the past delivered by history as grand narrative, and other historical accounts. For accounts of theories of 'new' history, see, for instance, Keith Jenkins, *Re-Thinking History*, London: Routledge, 1991 and *The Postmodern History Reader*, London: Routledge, 1997.
15 Susannah Radstone, 'Screening Trauma: *Forrest Gump*', in Susannah Radstone (ed.) *Memory and Methodology*, op. cit., p. 84.

16 Michel Foucault, 'Film and Popular Memory', in *Foucault Live (Interviews 1966–1984)*, New York: Semiotext(e), pp. 89–106; Centre for Contemporary Cultural Studies, *Making Histories: Studies in History Writing and Politics*, London: Hutchinson, 1982.

17 Katharine Hodgkin and Susannah Radstone (eds) *Contested Pasts*, New York and London: Routledge, 2003.

18 Luisa Passerini, *Fascism in Popular Memory*, Cambridge: Cambridge University Press, 1987; Alessandro Portelli, *The Death of Luigi Trastulli and Other Stories: Form and Meaning in Oral History*, Albany: State University of New York Press, 1991.

19 Luisa Passerini, 'Memories Between Silence and Oblivion', in Katharine Hodgkin and Susannah Radstone (eds) *Contested Pasts*, op. cit.

20 Pierre Nora, *Les Lieux de mémoire*, 7 vols, Paris: Gallimard, 1984–93.

21 Here, the seminal text is Fredric Jameson's 'Postmodernism, or the Cultural Logic of Late Capitalism', *New Left Review* 146, 1984, pp. 53–92. In that essay, Jameson argued that postmodern media and, in particular, film, were suffused by a pastiche and nostalgia that substituted for a truly historical consciousness. For Jameson, postmodernism is simply incapable of grasping or remembering historical reality, and postmodern subjects are condemned to a schizophrenic existence, bereft of memory and any sense of continuity through time. These ideas have been developed and challenged from many directions, both within and outside postmodernist theory. Studies of memory and the media, in particular, have sought both to develop these ideas and to challenge them by suggesting that to describe contemporary media-ted memory as 'inauthentic' or debased may be to ignore both the complexities of the relation between the media, representation and memory and the potential of media-ted memory for transmitting and sustaining memory.

22 For an accessible introduction to the history of time see G.J. Whitrow, *Time in History: Views of Time from Prehistory to the Present Day*, Oxford and New York: Oxford University Press, 1988. For a discussion of the modern politics of time see Peter Osborne, *The Politics of Time: Modernity and Avant-Garde*, London: Verso, 1995.

23 David Harvey, *The Condition of Postmodernity*, Oxford: Blackwell, 1989.

24 Sigmund Freud, 'Civilisation and Its Discontents', in James Strachey (trans.) *The Standard Edition of the Complete Psychological Works of Sigmund Freud*, vol. 21, London: Vintage Press, [1930] 2001, p. 69.

25 Ibid.

26 Ibid., p. 70.

27 Ibid., pp. 70–1.

28 Ibid., p. 71.

Part I

BELIEVING THE BODY

Introduction

Susannah Radstone and Katharine Hodgkin

This section is concerned with the possibility of embodied memory – of memories that are carried in the body and that may be transmitted *between* bodies, even across generations. As Tony Bennett's introductory remarks make clear, this is a topic that touches on wider questions that are being debated outside as well as inside the academy, and that have immediate political resonance. For to speak of memories that are carried in the body and that may be passed on through the generations touches on debates between those who believe in the possibility of genetic or biological inheritance, versus those for whom character and disposition, whether individual or collective, are shaped, in the main, by cultural and environmental forces.

The two chapters that follow have certain themes in common. They both foreground the significance of the visual in relation to the passing on or construction of memory. Both chapters, too, are concerned with memory *transmission*. Jill Bennett suggests that photography may transmit affect memory, while Tony Bennett discusses organicist theories of evolutionary transmission between the generations. Yet these two chapters take up very different positions on the question of embodied memory.

Jill Bennett's chapter is about the transmission of what she calls bodily 'affect memory' – a mode of memory that she distinguishes from representational memory. She argues that affect associated with past experiences may be transmitted to others, particularly through the visual media. Conversely, Tony Bennett argues that all ideas concerning embodied or organicist memory have their origins in eighteenth- and nineteenth-century regimes of memory that reached their apogee in the evolutionary museum. For Tony Bennett, the idea of embodied or organicist memory serves as a limit-case for an argument concerning the imbrication of *all* ideas about and theories of memory – even the notion of a mode of memory buried in the body – with regimes of power and knowledge. Even the idea that memory can be carried in the body, argues Tony

23

Bennett, is produced by a 'regime' of memory, the politics of which invite analysis. For Jill Bennett, on the other hand, affect memory can itself be disruptive of regimes of knowledge and can transmit that which cannot be represented in written language. Here, she focuses on affects linked to sexual abuse, and through an analysis of the affectual qualities of the photographs she discusses, demonstrates that the feelings that surround such abuse may be far more complex and ambivalent than writings on sexual abuse tend to suggest.

Jill Bennett's chapter focuses on the transmission of traumatic affect through photographic practices, and suggests that affect may be drawn on directly by an art practice aimed at regenerating sensation so as to produce an encounter in the present. She argues that experience that cannot be spoken may nevertheless be registered visually, producing visual icons in the mind's eye. As Jill Bennett herself points out, these ideas concerning affect, memory and visual iconography have a long history; such ideas underpinned the medieval understanding of the mnemonic function of art. This was a conception of art not as aiming to reproduce the world – art as representation – but as registering and producing affect. As William West's chapter in this collection demonstrates, early modern memory practices stressed visuality and spatiality, and counterposed the direct experience of visual icons with the mediations of language and representation. The poetics of sense memory involved not speaking of but speaking out of a particular memory or experience. The beginnings of an unravelling of this regime of memory in early modern times is the subject of his chapter. Jill Bennett's chapter suggests, however, that the medieval notion of art as registering and producing affect – a conception that preceded the Renaissance stress on art as representation – might now be ripe for revision, since it dovetails with many of the most powerful and influential trends in current humanities research in the fields of memory, trauma and representation. She substantiates this proposal by arguing that visual icons provide the most effective means of storing and retrieving memories, since the eye can function as a mute witness. This concept of the witness is central to contemporary theories of trauma and testimony, and, in this regard, Jill Bennett's work touches on wider debates in the humanities concerning trauma and representation.[1] However, the most influential work in this field has, up until now, been informed by revisions of Freudian or Lacanian psychoanalysis.[2] Jill Bennett's essay takes a fresh departure by theorising the transmission of traumatic memory not in relation to psychoanalytic concepts, but via the work of Gilles Deleuze, whose writings on affect have yet to be fully explored in the field of traumatic memory, and whose work, she argues, subverts the opposition between thought and sensation that has shaped so much previous thinking on memory.

Jill Bennett's chapter follows Charlotte Delbo in distinguishing between two modes of memory: ordinary representational memory versus sense memory, which registers the physical imprint of an event. This is a distinction which is taken up in this volume in Paul Antze's critique of current developments in psychology, which identify similar modes of memory. For Antze, the notion of a psychical process that does not make use of associations akin to linguistic tropes produces an understanding of the human being which is overly deterministic and impoverished. But Jill Bennett suggests, rather, that an attention to modes of memory that by-pass representation may offer a fuller and more adequate account of human experience. Jill Bennett's chapter raises a key question about the relationship beween affect memory and (visual) language. She raises the possibility of non-representational memory that is transmitted via photographic images. Yet these images also make meaning by means of visual signs. A fascinating field is opening, then, for the investigation of the relation between the meaning-making of (visual) languages and affect memory.

Like Jill Bennett's chapter, Tony Bennett's contribution to this section is concerned with memory, the body and the visual. Whereas Jill Bennett's focus falls on memory transmission through photography's spectatorial relations, however, the focus of Tony Bennett's chapter is the new depth structure of vision that emerged in the nineteenth century. This new structure of vision arguably informed archaeological theory and practice and the construction of the evolutionary museum. Drawing on novels of the period to show how particular eighteenth- and nineteenth-century regimes of memory were evolving, Tony Bennett's chapter discusses the idea of organicist memory as it developed in the eighteenth and nineteenth centuries and was put on display in nineteenth-century evolutionary museums.

Theories of organicist memory suggest that all previous stages of an organism's development are simultaneously present, layered within that organism. When applied to the human species, this theory suggests that the human body carries within it layered memories of its development from prehistory to the present. Tony Bennett goes on to suggest that it was the development of a new depth structure of vision, particularly within archaeology, that produced the idea that all the layers of the past are simultaneously present below the ground surface. This idea could then be extended to the human organism itself, to produce an archaeological construction of the person as an entity comprised of successive layers. This idea of simultaneous presence touches on the issues of memory and temporality discussed in this volume's introduction; as Tony Bennett points out, the temporality of memory constructed in the evolutionary museum is one of the simultaneous existence of all past moments.

Tony Bennett's central thesis is that it was only when evolution was made *perceptible* (as in the nineteenth-century evolutionary museums) that it became possible to see the long pasts that theories of organicist memory placed within the body as a set of memory traces. In other words, for Tony Bennett, the idea of organicist memory emerged out of a *construction* of human prehistory and history as evolutionary – a construction that depended upon the development of a particular regime of vision: '(i)t is because this is so', argues Tony Bennett, that 'it is … imperative to view the notion of an organic memory carried in the body … as an effect of the evolutionary museum's functioning as an evolutionary accumulator in which all pasts are stored and rendered simultaneously present' (p. 51).

The significance of this argument lies, in part, in its rebuttal of the idea that embodied memory lies outside culture, outside regimes of power and knowledge. The idea that memory traces may be carried in the body is an idea, of course, that is aligned with those geneticist theories of human behaviour, ethnicity and sexuality that are currently being mobilised both within and outside the academy. Tony Bennett insists, however, that the very *idea* of memory carried within the body arose out of particular museum and archival practices that were tied to specific regimes of power and knowledge. For Tony Bennett, then, there is *no* conception of memory that lies outside systems of power/knowledge – that lies, that is, outside specific regimes, or ways of thinking and understanding the world. Jill Bennett, on the other hand, seems to suggest, rather, that bodily affect memory by-passes or precedes systems of representation.

Notes

1   For an introduction to debates about trauma and screen studies see Susannah Radstone (ed.) 'Special Debate on Trauma and Screen Studies', *Screen* vol. 42(2), 2001, pp. 188–216.
2   The most influential work in this field includes Cathy Caruth, 'Introduction to Psychoanalysis, Culture and Trauma', *American Imago*, vol. 48(1), 1991, pp. 1–12; *Unclaimed Experience: Trauma, Narrative and History*, Baltimore, MD: Johns Hopkins University Press, 1996; *Trauma: Explorations in Memory*, Baltimore, MD: Johns Hopkins University Press, 1992; Shoshana Felman and Dori Laub, *Testimony: Crises of Witnessing in Literature, Psychoanalysis and History*, New York and London: Routledge, 1992.

1

THE AESTHETICS OF SENSE-MEMORY

Theorising trauma through the visual arts[1]

Jill Bennett

> It is impossible to feel emotion as past.... One cannot be a spec-
> tator of one's own feelings; one feels them, or one does not feel
> them; one cannot imagine them without stripping them of their
> affective essence.[2]

There is a compelling logic to these words written in 1911 by the Swiss psychologist Edouard Claparède. Emotions are felt only as they are experienced in the
present; in memory they become ideas, representations, and representation
inherently implies distance, perspective. For Claparède, to represent oneself in
memory was to see oneself 'from the outside' as one might see another. 'My past
self', he wrote, 'is thus psychologically distinct from my present self, but it is …
an emptied and objectivised self, which I continue to feel at a distance from my
true self which lives in the present.'[3]

Claparède's refutation of emotional memory's possibility is partly influenced
by the work of William James, who argued that although we can remember
undergoing specific emotions, we cannot remember just how those emotions
felt.[4] However, wrote James, if emotions are not retrievable from memory, they
are *revivable*; hence, we don't remember grief or ecstasy, but by recalling a situation that produces those sensations we can produce a new bout of emotion.[5] So,
in other words, affect, properly conjured, produces a real-time somatic experience, no longer framed as representation.

This opposition between affect and representation also subtends early work on
trauma and memory. Pierre Janet argued that, in the normal course of events, experiences are processed through cognitive schemes that enable familiar experiences to
be identified, interpreted and assimilated to narrative. Memory is thus constituted
as experience transforms itself into representation. Traumatic or extreme affective
experience, however, resists such processing. Its unfamiliar or extraordinary nature
renders it unintelligible, causing cognitive systems to baulk; its sensory or affective
character renders it inimical to thought – and ultimately to memory itself.
Moreover, trauma is not so much remembered as subject to unconscious and

uncontrolled repetition: 'It is only for convenience that we speak of it as a "traumatic memory"', wrote Janet, 'The subject is often incapable of making the necessary narrative which we call memory regarding the event....'[6]

In this chapter, I want to consider the issue of the registration of affect as it relates to traumatic memory, not from a clinical or psychological perspective but from the point of view of art practice. The argument that trauma resists representation has continued to be made at different times in relation both to psychological process and to aesthetics. Bessel Van der Kolk, for example, has been particularly influential in reviving the work of Janet in order to argue that traumatic memory is of a 'non-declarative' type, involving bodily responses that lie outside verbal-semantic-linguistic representation.[7] In the humanities, the development of trauma studies in the USA in the 1990s has prompted a revaluation of modernist literary texts, and of poetry in particular, as forms of Holocaust or war testimony.[8] Such texts, rather than narrativising traumatic experience, are seen as bearing the imprint of trauma. To date, however, theorists of trauma and memory have paid relatively little attention to visual art. Yet the ways in which an artwork might evoke immediate affective experience suggest the possibility – for both artist and viewer – of 'being a spectator of one's own feelings'. This is not to argue that, through such a process, trauma enters the realm of representation. The value I think, of maintaining a distinction between narrative memory and traumatic memory is that it allows us to conceive of a realm of imagery that maps onto the latter. Rather than reducing itself to a form of representation, such imagery serves to register subjective processes that exceed our capacity to 'represent' them. A substantive category of memory, but also of image-making, is instituted by this process – a category in which affective experience is not simply referenced, but activated or staged in some sense. Theories of expression are inadequate to the task of understanding this mode of image production insofar as they regard the artwork as the transcription or deposit of a prior mental state. The imagery of traumatic memory deals not simply with a past event, or with the objects of memory, but with the present experience of memory. It therefore calls for a theorisation of the dynamic in which the work is both produced and received – a theory, in other words, of affect.

A useful reference point for conceptualising such a project is provided, in a literary context, by the French poet and Holocaust survivor Charlotte Delbo, whose work following her experience in Auschwitz is interesting not simply for its form and content as survivor testimony, but also for the fact that it institutes a category of memory that becomes at the same time an aesthetic category. This category, identified with the terms 'deep memory' and also 'sense memory', designates precisely the realm of affective memory that Janet regards as nameless – as outside memory proper.[9]

Like Janet, Delbo posits ordinary memory as properly representational; it is the memory connected with the thinking process and with words – the realm in which events are rendered intelligible, pegged to a common or established frame of reference so that they might be communicated to, and readily understood by, a general audience. But whereas Janet is concerned primarily with identifying cognitive process, Delbo extends the notion of ordinary or common memory to describe a social or popularly understood discursive framework, designated as the site where history is written. Common memory is thus not simply a form of narrative memory inherent in the individual subject but the language that enables such memory to be transmitted and easily understood. For Delbo, the writing of history in the language of common memory, its processing and presentation within an intelligible narrative framework, is of vital social importance. But at the same time, she realises that something integral to the experience of the Holocaust is lost when an essentially traumatic experience is consigned to history, when the imposition of a temporal frame establishes a distance from the present and effects a stripping of affect in Claparède's sense.

For Delbo, sense memory registers the physical imprint of the event. As such it is always in the present, though not continuously felt:

> Auschwitz is there, fixed and unchangeable but wrapped in the impervious skin of memory that segregates itself from the present 'me' ... everything that happened to this other 'self', the one from Auschwitz, doesn't touch me now ... so distinct are deep memory and common memory.[10]

Seen from the outside, Delbo's Auschwitz experience is the property of another self, much like Claparède's 'past self'. Delbo experiences these two selves as segregated, yet she also speaks of being in the grip of sense memory for periods of several days, during which time the physical pain of her trauma returns. Thus, the Auschwitz self, for all that it is discrete, retains a capacity to touch and affect, to trigger emotion in the present.

As the source of a poetics or an art, then, sense memory operates through the body to produce a kind of 'seeing truth' [11] rather than 'thinking truth', registering the pain of memory as it is directly experienced, and communicating a level of bodily affect. The art of sense memory might further be distinguished as a motivated practice. Radically different from timeless or transhistorical expressionism, it aims to constitute a language of subjective process (specifically of affective and emotional process) to complement history and to work in a dialectical relationship with common memory. Its production thus becomes a contingent and culturally situated practice – linked to social histories – that requires framing against a backdrop of cultural knowledge. [12] One could add to this that the distinctive feature of an artistic exploration of subjectivity is, as Foucault reminds us, that *ars*, unlike *scientia*, promotes open-ended enquiry; it can embrace the unknown, the abject, the amoral, the aberrant, the pornographic, not as pathology but as experience.[13]

The advantages of this kind of art practice may be seen in relation to the highly charged issue of child sexual abuse. Once unspoken and effectively denied, child abuse is now the subject of a certain amount of moral panic. Thus it tends to be figured in 'common language' in rather stark moral terms, the demonised figure of the paedophile representing the antithesis of the child victim who becomes, in turn, the cipher of innocence. This framework leaves little space for exploring the subjective experience of either perpetrator or survivor, both of which frequently confound moral categorisation. How can a survivor describe the experience of rape perpetrated by a loved one – or that of 'becoming sexualised' at an early age – from the perspective of an 'innocent'? And what of the abuser who is him (or her) self the survivor of abuse, a victim of the act s/he now perpetrates? For all that we might concur that the act of abuse can be represented categorically as an immoral act, the experience of being abused cannot be contained in the figure of the victim; survivors are necessarily *more* than passive victims of the acts of another in the sense that survivors live and continually negotiate the effects of abuse. To register and understand the nature of those effects, we need a form of imagery that proceeds from, or at least privileges, subjective experience. In other words, we require an approach that pursues the exploration of traumatic memory not as *scientia sexualis* in which moral or medical classification precedes representation, but as open artistic enquiry. This means not only circumventing classification, however, but moving outside a representational practice which aims to 'comment' on its subject matter, treating the event of abuse as a completed past action, towards a practice which sees the artwork as regenerating sensation so as to produce an encounter in the present. Yet, at the same time, such work does require a discursive framework; it operates, in other words, in concert with developing cultural awareness of the issue of sexual abuse.

Dennis Del Favero's *Parting Embrace*, a series of ten large type-C photographs, does not approach the experience of abuse from within a narrative or moral framework. Instead, it seeks to register the pain of abuse as physical imprint (see Figure 1). Constructed as an unfolding of memory, the imagery offers a vision from the body, embracing in the process a certain moral ambiguity. The artist says of this work that it incorporates not just the pornography and the violence of memories of abuse, but also an element of love or fantasy, and that these things are not always distinct; the affects of fear, humiliation, shock and so on, may be tied to the same objects as those of joy and excitement. Hence *Parting Embrace* actually divides through the centre: the first five images in the series constituting *Parting*, the last five *Embrace*. As the titles suggest, the second set of images, which are softer, and more diffused, cast memories in more positive, romantic hues than the more overtly disturbing and hard-core *Parting*.[14] Here, then, the mix of feelings, sensations and emotions that characterises the experience of abuse for certain survivors is privileged, at the cost of moral clarity. Part of what the imagery conveys is precisely a condition of confusion. In this respect the work does not aim to transcribe sense memory into common memory, but offers only fragments of memories written on to the body. These can be 'read' only in reference to the viewer's bodily sense. To see these images is to be moved by them – not in the sense that narrative engenders an empathic response through identification with characters, but in the more literal sense of inciting affect. Affective experience may be subsequently overlaid with empathy; conversely it may produce a negative response in a viewer in whom it fails to stimulate critical thought. Thus one could argue that such images need ultimately to be inscribed within the discourse of common memory so that the affective experience of viewing can be understood in relation to a larger set of political/moral issues. This does not imply that the imagery of sense memory can be reduced to representation or common memory; rather, as Delbo suggests, the two realms of memory need to work in a kind of dialectical relationship with each other. Nor does it imply that these works engender what Geoffrey Hartman has called a 'secondary trauma' in the viewer.[15] While it is certainly possible that a viewer might be disturbed by the work, the various affects that it produces do not simply combine to approximate an experience identifiable as 'trauma' or a specific emotional condition. Its aim is not to subordinate affective devices to didactic ends, but to stimulate thought in a different way. A particular conception of the relationship of visual signs to the body and to thought underpins this work.

Words, Delbo tells us, are on the side of thought: common memory, narrative memory. While clearly words can be put into the service of sense memory, vision has a very different relationship to affective experience, experience that – while it cannot be spoken as it is felt – may register visually. The eye can often function as a mute witness through which events register as eidetic memory images imprinted with sensation. We see this particularly in relation to childhood trauma where access to speech is limited, and there is something of the mute witness in Del Favero's portrayal of the boy who appears to cry in anguish (Figure 1).

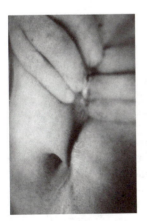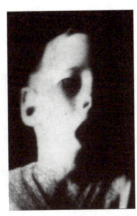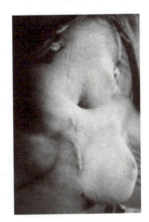

Figure 1   Dennis Del Favero, *Parting Embrace: Parting 1, Parting 2, Parting 3* (1997)

Source: Reproduced courtesy of the artist.

Visual artists and those who theorise about art and its function have long exploited this allegiance of sight to affective memory. The notion that visual icons were the most effective means of storing and retrieving memories, including those consisting of perceptions mediated through other senses, under-pinned the medieval understanding of the mnemonic function of art which held that religious imagery was effective in acting upon memory insofar as it could – like the *phantasm* or memory icon – act as a trigger, inciting an affective response.[16] The images developed from the late medieval period with the express function of inspiring devotion were not simply the 'Bible of the unlettered' in the sense of translating words into images. Rather, they conveyed the essence of Christ's sacrifice, the meaning of suffering, by promoting and facilitating an empathic imitation of Christ; those who engaged in self-mortificatory devotional practices such as flagellation hoped to come to know Christ through bodily *imitatio*. The conveyance of suffering through imagery in this context is possible only insofar as images have the capacity to address the spectator's own bodily memory, to *touch* the viewer who *feels* rather than simply sees the event, drawn into the image through a process of affective contagion.[17] Bodily response thus precedes the inscription of narrative, of moral emotion or empathy.

At work here is a conception of art, not as aiming to reproduce the world (the Renaissance conception of art as representation), but as registering and producing affect; affect, not as opposed to or distinct from thought, but as the means by which a kind of understanding is produced. This is a formulation that has some resonance with the aesthetics of Gilles Deleuze, which might be brought to bear on a theorisation of sense memory and its representation.

In his early work *Proust and Signs*, Deleuze develops the concept of the 'encountered sign', which he distinguishes from a recognised object insofar as it can only be felt or sensed.[18] The kind of affect the sign incites, however, is not opposed to the thinking process in the sense of supplanting critical enquiry with a kind of passive bodily experience; far from foreclosing on thought, it agitates, compelling and fuelling enquiry rather than simply placating the subject. In its capacity to stimulate thought the encountered sign is – according to Deleuze – superior to the explicit statement, for it is engaging at every level: emotionally, psychologically, sensually. The importance of this conception of the sign lies in the way it links the affective actions of the image with a thinking process without asserting the primacy of either the affective experience (sense memory) or repre-sentation (common memory).

Deleuze's focus, it should be noted, is always on creative production rather than reception, and in this regard what he says of the philosopher's compulsion is instructive. Attacking the notion of the philosopher as lover of wisdom, Deleuze reasons with Proust that critical enquiry isn't in fact motivated by love so much as by jealousy; he says the philosopher or truth seeker isn't a lover but a 'jealous man who catches a lying sign upon his lover's face' and in doing so 'encounters the violence of an impression'.[19] At this point the jealous man is forced by the violence of his own emotions to scrutinise the impression or sign which itself produces a set of affects – so that philosophy is not regarded as a dispassionate or neutral activity. Nor is it necessarily willed at the outset, for one may well be thrust into an encounter. 'Neither perception nor voluntary memory, nor voluntary thought gives us profound truth ...', says Deleuze: 'Here nothing forces us to interpret something, to decipher the nature of a sign, or to dive deep like "the diver who explores the depths".'[20] For Deleuze, as for Delbo, deep thought entails circumventing conventional thought and moving into darker regions; it is also motivated by an affective connection. But, most importantly, the affective encounter becomes the means by which thought proceeds and ultimately moves towards deeper truth. It is thus also integral to the composition of an artwork, as Deleuze outlines in particular in his work on the painter Francis Bacon.[21]

Deleuze effectively subverts the opposition between thought and sensation, arguing – at times somewhat wilfully – that whereas philosophers think in concepts, artists think in terms of sensations. Sensation is generated through the artist's engagement with the medium, through colour and line in the case of the painter, so that it is not the residue of self-expression, or a property of some prior self, but emerges in the present, as it attaches to figures in the image. 'Sensation is what is being painted,' writes Deleuze, 'what is being painted on the canvas is the body, not insofar as it is represented as an object, but insofar as it is experienced as sustaining this sensation.'[22]

Painting is thus essentially non-referential; sensation is less subject matter than *modus operandi* as the emphasis shifts from expression to production, from object to process. A Deleuzian framework does not therefore allow us to theorise art as a transcription of a psychological state. But this may be of the essence insofar as sense memory is about tapping a certain kind of process; a process experienced not as a remembering of the past but as a continuous negotiation of a present with indeterminable links to the past. The poetics of sense memory involve not so much *speaking of* but *speaking out of* a particular memory or experience – in other words, speaking from the body *sustaining sensation*.

While Deleuze's argument turns on a reading of one figurative painter (Bacon), contemporary art has its own history of the senses, or tradition of engagement with process and affect, in which various means of presenting the body *in extremis* have been explored. Such works might be understood as being about sensation to the extent that they stage the body undergoing sensation, but also to the degree that they incite an affective response in the viewer. To engage with this kind of work is always in some sense to feel it viscerally.

As one example, I cite Marina Abramovic's 1975 performance, *The Lips of St Thomas*, in which Abramovic sits at a table, eats a kilo of honey, drinks a litre of wine, cuts a 5-point star into her stomach with a razor blade, whips herself until she can no longer feel pain, and finally lies on ice blocks for thirty minutes. The most enduring image from this performance is that of the incised star.[23] Despite its status as image, the body, here the ground of inscription, was not, to use Deleuze's terms, represented as an object but rather experienced as sustaining sensation.

33

But if Abramovic the artist experiences the body – or the artwork – in this manner, what of her audience? Seeing sensation for an audience surely entails feeling or, at the very least, experiencing a tension between an affective encounter with a real body in pain and an encounter with the body as image or ground of representation. As Abramovic focuses on sustaining the act of incision until the nominal star form is completed, the star promises to emerge as an object, with some meaning or purpose other than as site of pain, even though, as it appears, the flow of blood spoils the clean lines and obscures its shape. But ultimately one cannot perceive the star except as wounding process. Even as one reads the figure, one winces or squirms, forced into an affective encounter with the image.

The refusal of other meaning here conjures up Kafka's image of a torture machine from *In the Penal Colony*, in which a harrow writes for twelve hours on the body of a condemned man, incising a script into his flesh. In excruciating pain the man finally comes to determine the text's significance, just before he is impaled completely. The machine operator says:

> Enlightenment dawns on the dullest. It begins around the eyes. From there it spreads out. A spectacle that might tempt one to lay oneself under the harrow beside him. Nothing further happens, the man simply begins to decipher the script, he purses his lips as if he were listening. You've seen that it isn't easy to decipher the script with one's eyes; but our man deciphers it with his wounds.[24]

To be a spectator in this instance does not yield true understanding, but the rather Catholic image of revelation is (supposedly) so enticing that it tempts one to lay oneself under the harrow. This is exactly how Christian imagery tradition- ally operates, the spectacle of crucifixion promoting an *imitatio Christi* or practice of bodily mortification that in turn will yield its own enlightenment. Revelation proceeds from bodily affect; the stigmatic does not read his or her wounds but *feels* their true meaning. Truth is revealed to the body, never to the onlooker, except as the spectator is 'touched' by the image and, through a process of contagion, induced to become the image. The becoming implied in this pre-modern concept of imitation (as in *imitatio Christi*), entails precisely taking on the pain of the other; seeing from the body so that one *sees truth* in a more profound way. And this is what the art of sense memory must achieve by touching the viewer, bringing him/her into contact with the image. Sense memory doesn't just present the horrific scene, the graphic spectacle of violence, but the physical imprint of the ordeal of violence: a (compromised and compromising) position to see *from*.

Hence the image of pure affect in Kafka: the Darwinian sounding description of the external features of the body undergoing revelation ('it begins around the eyes' and proceeds with a pursing of the lips ...).[25] We see enlightenment, but we don't see the cause; we see fear in the figure of the boy with open mouth in *Parting Embrace*, and we see the scream with Bacon (Francis Bacon paints the scream, not what causes the scream, it has been said).[26]

34

If thinking in sense memory is a mode of thought like the artist's (the painter's, the performance artist's), the idiom of which is sensation, it does not reflect on past experience – though it is undoubtedly motivated by such experience – but rather registers the lived process of memory at a specific moment. The art of sense memory, then, does not make a claim to represent originary trauma – the cause of the feeling – but to enact the state or experience of post-traumatic memory. Cathy Caruth in her reading of Freud's *Beyond the Pleasure Principle*, emphasises that:

> trauma is not locatable in the simple violent or original event in an individual's past, but rather in the way that its very unassimilated nature – the way it was precisely *not known* in the first instance – returns to haunt the survivor later on.[27]

Traumatic memory is, in this regard, resolutely an issue of the present.

Australian photomedia artist Justin Kramer worked for a long time on the experience of child sexual abuse. His memory images relating to this experience were always vivid with no 'pain' associated with them, so that one might argue they were ultimately 'stripped of affect', easily rendered within 'common' or representational language. For Kramer, his sense memory comprised not these accessible screen images of scenes from his childhood, but a lived bodily response to trauma. In 1995 he began to experience a new set of physiological symptoms: blackouts, disorientation, vertigo, a fear of falling to which his response was always to seek out a chair. Although unconnected in his conscious mind with the photographic memories of abuse, these symptoms were in some sense experienced by Kramer as his memory of abuse, as his body's response to prior events. He began to make photographic images documenting physiological symptoms, visualising sensations. Acting out slapstick performances in which he balances precariously on a chair (echoing the features of some of Bacon's paintings), the artist produces the source material for a set of images of a body in tumult.

In 1996, Kramer was diagnosed with a tumour in the right temporal lobe of his brain. Although it was successfully removed, Kramer continues to experience the sensation or aura that it produced. He continues to live its symptoms in what he describes as 'the manner of a phantom limb', his memory haunted by the former presence of the tumour as it is haunted by the memory of abuse. Was the tumour somehow connected to his abuse? Is it a symptom? – he asks. But these are not questions his work can answer. The work is itself about the failure of thought to connect. It is, indeed, an *enactment* of this failure. It is not about the past so much as a haunting of the body; haunting in Blanchot's sense when he says: 'What haunts is the inaccessible which one cannot rid oneself of, what one does not find and what, because of that, does not allow one to avoid it. The ungraspable is what one does not escape.'[28]

One can argue with Deleuze's disciplinary distinctions when he talks about the differences between philosophy and art, but the advantage of disciplinary specification is that it enables us to ask what art can do that philosophy can't, what art can do that psychology or psychoanalysis can't, what sense memory can see that common memory or conventional language can't. The answer might be that the art of sense memory does not analyse the process or the symptom; it cannot theorise the links between traumatic memory and originary trauma. But in presenting the process of memory as 'sign' it registers the affective experience of memory, enacting a process of 'seeing feeling' where feeling is both imagined and regenerated through an encounter with the artwork.

Deleuze says one must ask of a work of art not 'What does it mean?' but 'How does it work?', so the question becomes, how is 'seeing feeling' achieved, how does it yield information to the body? But crucially there remains the question Deleuze is less concerned with – but which is always a factor in performance work – of how precisely sensation is encountered by the viewer.

Delbo said that her Auschwitz self was encased in the skin of memory so that it could not touch her now. But the skin of memory is notoriously permeable – particularly the skin of traumatic memory, which is at once 'tough' and 'impervious' (Delbo's words), but also broken, ruptured and scarred. In dreams, she wrote:

> Sometimes ... it bursts and gives back its contents.... I see myself again ... just as I know I was ... and the pain is so unbearable, so exactly the pain I suffered there, that I feel it again physically, I feel it again through my whole body, which becomes a block of pain.... It takes days for everything to return to normal, for memory to be 'refilled' and for the skin of memory to mend itself.[29]

It is no coincidence that the image of ruptured skin recurs throughout the work of artists dealing with sense memory, in the details from *Parting Embrace*, for example.[30] If the skin of memory is permeable, then it cannot serve to encase the past self as other. It is precisely through the breached boundaries of skin in such imagery that memory continues to be felt as a wound rather than seen as contained other. One might say also, that it is through the breached boundaries of *memory* that *skin* continues to be felt as a wound rather than seen as contained other, or as 'past other' in Claparède's sense; it is here in sense memory that the past seeps back into the present, becoming sensation rather than representation.

How do we know then, that what is happening in sense memory (which is, after all, in the present) is not really happening to us now – if, indeed, there is such a bleed, and if affect cannot be contained within representation?

Sara Chesterman, a student of mine with no surface skin sensation on 90 per cent of her body, once told me that now she couldn't feel her body and had only her brain interpreting what she saw, she found this entirely inadequate for viewing.[31] You need to feel to see images, she said, and in particular you need to feel to know that what is visibly occurring before you is not actually happening to your own body.

Chesterman now relies on her brain to tell her what is happening to her body, so that if she burns her leg her brain knows this only by seeing the skin damage.

36

Conversely, however – and this was the surprising thing to me – when she sees other bodies in pain she finds herself more rather than less connected to these other bodies because she cannot readily dissociate herself from the site of pain. For this reason, she explains: 'my experience of thrillers and horror films becomes so intense that it becomes almost unbearable'. In other words, sensory images designed to hit the nervous system are experienced not as 'stripped of affect' but with an added intensity of affect felt not on the skin but internally, as a deeper more invasive process. By-passing the surface response (galvanic skin response) this viewer has a depth reaction, which may also involve autonomic functions such as fluctuations in heart rate and breathing, visceral sensation and so on. Such responses, although autonomic, are, as Brian Massumi notes, usually associated with expectation and entail some kind of narrative identification: a level of personal identification that renders the image all the more compromising.[32] Lacking skin sensation as the first line of defence, this viewer finds the image goes straight to the core – or heart – of her in quite a literal sense.

But what was missing? How do other people – people who take for granted surface skin sensation – watch movies that depict people undergoing extreme bodily sensations, or watch Abramovic? And how does the skin protect us from the intensity of this experience? The answer for Chesterman lies in the squirm:

> When people watch films they squirm. I think that the physical act of squirming is one of feeling one's own body, it is an act of distancing the sensual experience being depicted – a way of feeling your own body and sending messages to the brain.

Although the squirm is a recoil, a moment of regrouping the self, it is also the condition of continued participation, the sensation that works with and against the deeper level response, which on its own is 'unbearable'. The squirm lets us feel the image, but also maintain a tension between self and image. It is part of a loop in which the image incites mimetic contagion acted out in the body of the spectator, which must continue to separate itself from the body of the other. And it is this function that enables one to see feeling as the property of another, and simultaneously to feel it – or at least to know it as felt. The squirm is in essence, then, a moment of seeing feeling – the point at which one both feels and knows feeling to be the property of an other. It is a trivial unwilled response that, in terms of spectatorship, can constitute an experiential link between affect (sensation in the present) and representation.

This kind of affect is, I suggest, a crucial part of the process by which the sign unfolds to the viewer as corporeal, sensing, emotional subject – and is ultimately 'thought through the body' to borrow a phrase from the painter Francesco Clemente.[33] And we should take it seriously, for as Deleuze says, 'voluntary thought' is not what leads us to profound truth. Philosophers may differ on this, of course, but in the area of traumatic memory, where we would rarely choose to go, and where 'unknowability' is the key motif, there perhaps is no better guide.

Notes

1 A shorter version of this essay is published in F. Kaltenbeck and P. Weibel (eds) *Trauma und Erinnerung* (Trauma and Memory: Cross-cultural Perspectives), Vienna: Passagen Verlag, 2000, pp. 81–95.
2 E. Claparède, 'La Question del la "mémoire" affective', *Archives de Psychologie* 10, 1911, pp. 361–77, 367–9; quoted and discussed in R. Leys, 'Traumatic Cures: Shell Shock, Janet and the Question of Memory', Paul Antze and Michael Lambek (eds) *Tense Past: Cultural Essays in Trauma and Memory*, New York: Routledge, 1996, pp. 103–45, 113–14.
3 Claparède, op. cit., p. 368; Leys, op. cit., p. 113.
4 W. James, *Principles of Psychology*, 3 vols, ed. F.H. Burkhardt, F. Bowers and I. Skrupskelis, Cambridge, MA and London: Harvard University Press, 1981 (1890); see Leys, op. cit., for discussion of James in relation to Claparède.
5 See Leys, op. cit., p. 95.
6 P. Janet quoted in B. Van der Kolk and O. Van der Hart, 'The Intrusive Past: The Flexibility of Memory and the Engraving of Trauma', in C. Caruth (ed.), *Trauma: Explorations in Memory*, Baltimore, MD and London: Johns Hopkins University Press, 1995, pp. 158–82, 160.
7 Van der Kolk, op. cit. For an overview see also Ruth Leys, *Trauma: A Genealogy*, Chicago: University of Chicago Press, 2000, esp. p. 7. Leys develops a sustained argument against the notion that trauma stands outside representation, critiquing both Van der Kolk and cultural adaptations of this work such as Cathy Caruth's.
8 See especially Shoshana Felman's discussion of Paul Celan in S. Felman and D. Laub *Testimony: Crises of Witnessing in Literature, Psychoanalysis, and History*, New York and London: Routledge, 1991.
9 C. Delbo, *Days and Memory*, trans R. Lamont, Marlboro, VT: Marlboro Press, 1990; C. Delbo, *Auschwitz and After*, trans R. Lamont with an introduction by L. Langer, New Haven, CT: Yale University Press, 1995; for further discussion see L. Langer *Holocaust Testimonies: The Ruins of Memory*, New Haven, CT: Yale University Press, 1991, pp. 1–38.
10 Delbo, op. cit. 1990, trans. and quoted in Langer, op. cit., 1991, p. 5.
11 On the use of the phrase 'seeing truth' see ibid., p. xv.
12 The exhibition project *Telling Tales* (curated J. Bennett and J. Dunn) explored how languages of sense memory are developed by artists against the background of 'common language', history and popular discourse, as, for example, in relation to the recent history of Aboriginal people in Australia, where the lived effects of the past are frequently disavowed. See English/German exhibition catalogue, J. Bennett and J. Dunn, *Telling Tales*, Ivan Dougherty Gallery, College of Fine Arts, University of New South Wales, 1988.
13 M. Foucault, *The History of Sexuality, vol. 1: An Introduction*, trans. R. Hurley, New York: Random House, 1978 (1976).
14 This interpretation is developed further in my essay for the exhibition catalogue, *Parting Embrace*, Mori Gallery, Sydney and Milan, 1998.
15 Geoffrey Hartman, 'Tele-suffering and Testimony in the Dot Com Era', in Barbie Zelizer (ed.) *Visual Culture and the Holocaust*, New Brunswick, NJ: Rutgers University Press, 2000, pp. 111–24, 117.
16 See M. Carruthers, *The Book of Memory: A Study of Memory in Medieval Culture*, Cambridge: Cambridge University Press, 1990. On the production of affect in relation to visual imagery see J. Bennett, 'Stigmata and Sense Memory: St Francis and the Affective Image', *Art History* 24(1), 2001, pp. 1–16.
17 The notion of 'affective contagion' is drawn from the work of the psychologist Silvan Tomkins; see Eve Kosofsky Sedgwick and Adam Frank (eds) *Shame and its Sisters: A Silvan Tomkins Reader*, Durham, NC and London: Duke University Press, 1995.

18 Gilles Deleuze, *Proust and Signs*, trans R. Howard, New York: Georges Braziller, 1972 (1964).
19 Ibid., p. 163.
20 Ibid., p. 164.
21 *Francis Bacon: Logique de la sensation*, Paris: Éditions de la Différence, 1981.
22 Quoted in Daniel W. Smith, 'Deleuze's Theory of Sensation: Overcoming the Kantian Duality', in P. Patton (ed.) *Deleuze: A Critical Reader*, Oxford: Blackwell, 1996, pp. 29–56, 45, from Smith's unpublished translation of Deleuze's, *Francis Bacon*, op. cit.
23 The inscription of the star was repeated in *Biography* in 1992, when Abramovic re-enacted highlights of her life. The documentation of this work has also had a considerable afterlife.
24 Franz Kafka, *In the Penal Colony*, trans M. Pasley, Harmondsworth: Penguin, 1992, p. 31.
25 Darwin describes the physiological symptoms of affects in *The Expression of the Emotions in Man and Animals*, a work glossed and developed by Silvan Tomkins in his four-volume study *Affect, Imagery, Consciousness*; see Kosofsky Sedgewick and Frank (eds) op. cit.
26 See Smith, unpub. trans. of Deleuze's *Francis Bacon*, op. cit., p. 42.
27 C. Caruth, *Unclaimed Experience: Trauma, Narrative, and History*, Baltimore, MD: Johns Hopkins University Press, 1996, p. 4.
28 Maurice Blanchot, *The Gaze of Orpheus*, ed. P. Adams Sitney, trans. L. Davis, New York: Station Hill, 1981, p. 84.
29 C. Delbo, *La Mémoire et les jours*, Paris: Berg International, 1985; trans. and quoted by Langer, op. cit., pp. 6–7.
30 See Bennett and Dunn, op. cit., for further examples related to the experiences of abuse, grief and Aboriginal family memory.
31 I am indebted to Sara Chesterman for her insights and for permission to quote from an unpublished student assignment. All subsequent citations are from that source.
32 Brian Massumi, 'The Autonomy of Affect', in Patton, op. cit., pp. 217–39.
33 See 'Francesco Clemente', interview with G. Politi, *Flash Art*, April–May 1984, p. 1.

2

STORED VIRTUE

Memory, the body and the evolutionary museum

Tony Bennett

When I recently visited the justly famous District 6 Museum in Capetown I was assailed by a white prehistoric archaeologist who – for reasons I struggled to fathom – went to great lengths to persuade me that the human genome project would help to clarify the confused politics of race and identity in South Africa by at last giving identity a fixed genealogy anchored in the subterranean history of the body. The very suggestion seemed out of place in an institution that is committed to repairing a fractured sense of local identity through a culturally fabricated form of remembering. By reassembling the fragments of a shattered history, the District 6 Museum aims to restore a thread of connection between the vibrant multicultural community that District 6 had once been, before its inhabitants were removed to the townships and their homes razed to the ground, and that which, as the area is rebuilt, it might once again become. How, I thought, could the archaeologist's view of the relations between the body, memory, race and identity be of help here? For it implied that, once they had been assigned a molecular ancestry, people would wake up and remember who they really were, and had been all along, quite independently of any cultural fashioning of the relations between memory and identity. Yet the currency of such conceptions is not limited to white fantasists. There is also a strong tendency, in current critiques of anti-essentialist conceptions of race and identity, to ascribe racial identity to a shared memory rooted in the ancestral history of the body. Paul Gilroy comments on this in his criticism of Elizabeth Alexander for interpreting a 1994 Whitney Museum exhibition of artistic representations of black males to suggest that the flayed and mutilated black bodies on display reflected 'a "text carried in the flesh" composed of "ancestral" memories of terror', thereby evoking a 'shared racial memory'.[1] How, Gilroy asks, can there be an active politics of memory if the 'bottom line' of black identity is lodged within 'the memory tape carried in those black cells'?[2]

Figurations of memory that locate it within the body inevitably imply a devaluation of other forms of remembering as inauthentic, and therefore politically debased, coinage. John Frow identifies the consequences of this in the terms used by Pierre Nora to contrast history and memory.[3] For Nora 'true memory' is that

40

which has 'taken refuge in gestures and habits, in skills passed down by unspoken traditions, in the body's inherent self-knowledge, in unstudied reflexes and ingrained memories'.[4] By contrast, Frow argues that the passage of memory through history renders it 'archival' in its reliance on the materiality of writing and representation. In thus being severed from any collective psychologically or bodily grounded mechanisms of transmission that might vouchsafe its rootedness in a connected past, history as memory can only offer what – viewed from the perspective Nora advocates – Frow calls 'the empty traces of a lost plenitude'.[5] A similar devaluation of history is involved, Frow argues, whenever its evidently fabricated nature is contrasted with forms of remembering that are said to arise out of forms of collective memory that function organically as a part of the social tissue of specific groups or movements. Emile Durkheim's account of collective memory and some contemporary socialist and feminist traditions of oral history, in which oral testimony is validated as authentic through its relation-ship to an originating community, are among the examples of this kind of operation that Frow cites.

The opposition that is at work here is profoundly disabling. In automatically preferring forms of remembering that are inscribed in the body or in the organic consciousness of a particular collectivity, these approaches diminish the political significance that ought properly to attach to the analysis of the different institu-tional and technological forms in which memory is socially organised. For Frow is surely right in suggesting that this is where the real issues lie. 'To speak of memory as *tekhnè*, to deny that it has an unmediated relation to experience,' he argues, 'is to say that the logic of textuality by which memory is structured has technological and institutional conditions of existence.'[6] This entails, he continues, an emphatic denial that memory is or ever can be carried by organic mechanisms – whether these are physiological or psychological, individual or collective, in conception – and an insistence on its necessarily fabricated nature, as the result of particular practices of recall which depend on specific technolog-ical conditions provided by 'storage-and-retrieval devices and sites such as books, calendars, computers, shrines, or museums'.[7] Quite so. But if this point is taken, the following questions also arise: what are the mechanisms, the mnemonics, through which organicist conceptions of memory are said to operate? And what are the technological conditions of these mnemonics?

With questions of this kind in mind, I argue in what follows that the bodily mnemonics echoed in the formulations of contemporary theorists like Pierre Nora derive their originating rationale and intelligibility from the practices of evolutionary museums.[8] My purpose is to deny the conditions that organicist accounts of memory presuppose by showing how those accounts depend on precisely the kinds of technological and archival conditions which serve as the degraded counterpoint to their own claims to authenticity. For it was only in relation to the archival form of the evolutionary museum – and associated tech-nical and representational devices – that a practice of memory carried in the body was made both thinkable and do-able.

41

Time, death and the museum

A key factor informing the ways in which museums operate as technologies of memory concerns the relationships they organise between the living and the dead, and how they insert these relationships into the flow of time. This is the central perception of Didier Maleuvre, who, in an argument reminiscent of Frow's, takes issue with the tradition of analysis (derived from Quatremère de Quincy[9] and running through Adorno[10] to, more recently, the work of Douglas Crimp[11]) which views the art museum as a mausoleum for art which, in detaching works of art from their originating cultural contexts, severs their connections with tradition and effective memory. The museum permits the objectification of history only at the cost of abstracting the objects it contains from the flow of living history; it preserves the past only by petrifying it, making it an object of intellectual observation and analysis rather than a living force carried into the present through its active inscription in 'real' historical forces. Here, in summarising his discussion of Quatremère, is how Maleuvre puts the matter:

> Deprived of experiential content, the museum objects are mere vessels of dead knowledge, of alienated contemplation. The museum thereby testifies to modernity's failure to preserve the past unmaimed. Abstracted from any context, stripped of living history and shrouded with scholarly history, artifacts lie in the museum as corpses in an ossuary.[12]

The connections between this tradition and organicist conceptions of memory of the kind proposed by Pierre Nora are clear. In both cases, it is the fabricated and archival qualities of the museum (and other technologies of storage and retrieval) that are regretted as representing a fall from the plenitude that is said to characterise those ways of knowing and remembering that are prompted by cultural artefacts when they remain at the centre of ongoing, continuous traditions of lived experience. Drawing on Hegel, Maleuvre gives this argument short shrift by showing that, to the contrary, it is only through their detachment from an immanent tradition that cultural artefacts can become the objects of self-conscious theoretical attention – and, by the same token, objects of contention – in a properly historical cultural politics, one orientated to the new histories that such artefacts acquire through their mobile and changing inscriptions within museum practices.[13] I shall, however, leave this aspect of his discussion to one side here, for what he goes on to say about the relations between death, time and memory in the museum lays down a better set of markers for the argument I want to develop.

Maleuvre turns to Balzac's *The Wild Ass's Skin* to explore these relations, treating the episode in which Raphaël visits 'the old curiosity shop'[14] as a critical commentary on the formative rationality of the modern museum that was under development, just across the river, at the Louvre. As 'a living illustration of the museum's repudiated ancestry', but one which, at the same time, incorporates elements of the museum's new rationality, the old curiosity shop 'is both a critique of the museum's present, which it reflects from across the Seine, and a historical critique of the museum, of which it dredges up the repressed ancestry'.[15] As such, Maleuvre suggests, it offers 'an image of how the past is lost: *how history is lost in its very preservation*'.[16] This critique is carried by Balzac's representation of the curiosity shop as a liminal space in which things – and the visitor – are installed ambiguously between life and death, the present and the past:

> Pursued by the strangest of forms, by fabulous creations poised on the confines between life and death, he walked along as in the enchantment of a dream. Indeed, in some doubt as to his own existence, he felt himself at one with these curious objects: neither altogether living nor altogether dead.[17]

The pact Raphaël enters into by accepting the wager of the Ass's Skin provides the main narrative device through which this relation between the living and the dead is played out. The more his wishes are granted, the more Raphaël withers and atrophies, as his life is precipitated toward the form of objecthood represented by the museum object, which is able to preserve and represent the past only because it has been extracted from the flow of history. Maleuvre puts the point as follows:

> Balzac's museum lays out the place of conflict between the domineering dead and the beleaguered living. Conflict is conceivable only if the two parties stand in mutual alienation. In order for the past to be inimical to the present, as it is to Raphaël, it cannot appear to be integrated with the present. Historical consciousness must have gone from an integrated, homogenous sense of historical continuity to a splintered state of separation. What used to flow into the present like a generative stream of age-tested wisdom (and likened historical knowledge to soothsaying) is now dammed up as something alien and threatening. The museum piece is a bit of historical consciousness that has cut itself off from its source in traditional time. It embodies the rootlessness of modern consciousness. Behind Raphaël's fight to the death with the collectibles – a fight that comes to a head in the Skin – stands alienated history.[18]

If this echoes Quatremère's critique of the museum, it also differs from that critique in the respect that, as Maleuvre goes on to argue, the past out of which the museum object is thus wrested is seen as a result of that act of wresting itself. 'The historical past does not precede its transplantation in the present: history is precisely the recognition that the past does not exist outside of the reminiscing present.'[19] And it is in view of this that the modern museum, in its aspiration to represent the totality of the past, stands opposed to, and destroys the possibility of, organicist forms of memory. To the extent, as Maleuvre puts it, that 'everything is absolutely recalled, as on Judgement Day,' then so also 'nothing is remembered, because everything is inextricably present'.[20] Or, more fully:

> Balzac's collection makes it difficult to go on nursing the image of the past as a homogeneous continuum rolling into the present. To the historical consciousness aware that the past does not exist diachronically but synchronically in the moment of its being remembered, the beginning of the world and the immediate past appear synchronously. History is not a road winding through the thicket of historical events; it is the flash of remembrance in which all historical layers exist simultaneously.[21]

The conditions of memory that emerge from Maleuvre's account are thus, as in Frow's view, inescapably archival and representational. So far so good. However, I want to push Maleuvre's argument – which focuses mainly on the art museum – a step further. For the distinctive potentialities of the modern museum as a new kind of memory machine only become fully clear when the art museum is placed in the context of its relations to other types of museum. We must also therefore take into account the mid- to late nineteenth-century developments in evolutionary thought which made it possible for the museum to articulate a distinctive set of relations between cultural history and – as a new set of objects – geological and natural history. This, too, is clear in Balzac's curiosity shop, whose logic – at first site a random one – exhibits an increasingly proto-evolutionary aspect the more closely Raphaël looks at it. Striking him initially as 'a chaotic medley of human and divine works' in which the 'beginnings of creation and the events of yesterday were paired off with grotesque good humour',[22] Raphaël's route through the galleries subjects this apparently random miscellany to a disciplinary ordering, as he moves from the frameworks of archaeology and art history to those of anthropology and geology, thereby inscribing cultural history in the deeper and newly fabricated pasts of a proto-evolutionary conception of time. His glance – subject, initially, to an archaeological and art-historical organisation – at first takes in the whole of the ancient world, and is led from there, through a series of stages (Moses and the Hebrews, imperial and Christian Rome, the medieval period, the dawn of Indian and Chinese civilisation) to culminate in the Renaissance. His gaze then becomes anthropological-cum-historical as, prompted by objects recalling past ways of life (of Flemish workers, Cherokee hunters, and medieval chatelaines), he 'made all the formulas of existence his own' so that 'the tread of his own footsteps echoed within himself like far-off sounds from another world, like the roar of Paris heard from the top-most towers of Notre-Dame'.[23] But it is only in being subjected to a geological gaze that Raphaël's historical vista is stretched beyond the cultural realm to encompass the immense reaches of time that had been newly installed in the museum – not at the Louvre but at the *Muséum d'Histoire Naturelle* – as a result of Georges Cuvier's palaeontological reconstructions of extinct forms of life. As a consequence, 'the flash of remembrance in which all historical layers exist simultaneously'[24] is extended back beyond the time of human memory:

> As one penetrates from seam to seam, from stratum to stratum and discovers, under the quarries of Montmartre or in the schists of the Urals, those animals whose fossilised remains belong to antediluvian civilisations, the mind is startled to catch a vista of the milliards of years and the millions of peoples which the feeble memory of man and an indestructible divine tradition have forgotten and whose ashes heaped on the surface of our globe, form the two feet of earth which furnish us with bread and flowers.[25]

Balzac finishes this passage with the question: 'Is not Cuvier the greatest poet of our century?'[26] This recalls an earlier passage, in which Raphaël's encounter with the 'ocean of furnishings, inventions, fashions, works of art and relics made up an endless poem'[27] which, since it did not spontaneously cohere as a totality, he had to call on the poet within him to complete. But it is only Cuvier's poetry, in which 'dead things live anew and lost worlds are unfolded before us', that provides the perspective from which such completion can be undertaken, as it becomes possible to 'imagine the shape of the past history of the universe in a sort of retrogressive apocalypse'[28] in which human life, 'crushed as we are under so many worlds in ruins', becomes part of a 'nameless infinity, which is common to all spheres and which we have baptised as TIME'.[29]

It is from this pitiless perspective of geological time, in which we are destined 'to become, for future generations, an imperceptible speck in the past', that 'we are become as though dead'.[30] And it is from the dejection he experiences as a consequence of this 'phantasmagoric panorama of the past'[31] that Raphaël's thoughts turn once again to the suicide he had been contemplating before entering the curiosity shop. As the night draws on, however, his melancholic reflections are interrupted by the appearance of the master of the shop, a centenarian occupying the twilight zone between life and death. As the keeper of the collection, moreover, the master duplicates its structure to the degree that he has himself become a storehouse of all that it contains:

> 'Since my mind has inherited all the forces which I have not misused, this head of mine is still better furnished than my showrooms are. Here,' he said, tapping his forehead, 'here are the riches that matter. I spend beatific days letting my intelligence dwell on the past; I can summon to mind whole countries, vistas of beauty, views of the ocean, the faces that history has transfigured. ... how could one prefer all the

disasters of frustrated desires to the superb faculty of summoning the whole universe to the bar of one's mind?'[32]

Stored virtue

It is in the light of the symmetry evident here between the organisation of the collection and that of the person, as storehouses in which the past accumulates, that I want now to look at the relationship between the evolutionary museum and the practices of memory which depended on just such an archaeological construction of the person. However, this archaeological construction of the person as an entity comprised of successive layers took a number of different forms depending on how those layers were construed – sometimes as bodily, sometimes as cultural, sometimes as psychological, and sometimes as all three at once. Laura Otis provides a useful means of entry into these questions in her account of what she calls 'organic memory', a pervasive late nineteenth-century metaphorical construction of the relations between body and memory which 'placed the past *in* the individual, *in* the body, *in* the nervous system'.[33] In this conception, the past is viewed as a force that has deposited itself in the body, leaving a set of residues or traces there, so that the individual is a summation of the whole history that had preceded him or her. This conception was most coherently developed in those schools of evolutionary thought where Jean Baptiste Lamarck's law of the inheritance of acquired characteristics was viewed in conjunction with Ernst Haeckel's law that ontogeny recapitulates phylogeny. If the former provided a means whereby changes induced in the organism as a result of its adaptation to its changing environment could be transmitted to the next generation, the latter contended that all of the changes which had thus been stored in the body were recapitulated in the history of the single organism as it progresses from egg cell to full maturity. That said, these arguments had a much broader currency: Darwin's concept of pangenesis, for example, provided a toe-hold within Darwinism for an account of the transgenerational transmission of acquired characteristics that was to prove influential in many applications of Darwinism to the social and political field.[34]

Perhaps the most significant consequence of this conception was that it provided a means through which the new pasts that had been fabricated within the recently constructed horizons of prehistory were able to enter into the field of memory. No longer limited to what had been passed down through oral tradition, writing or other storage and retrieval systems, the reach of memory was now dramatically extended by being stretched backwards in time to encompass the much deeper pasts that had been written into the body. As a consequence, the body was conceived in a new light, as itself a storage and retrieval device in which the past was 'remembered', albeit that the memories coded into the body needed to be deciphered by the evolutionary scientist for this bodily mnemonics to be translated into a practice of conscious recollection. Alternatively, this decipherment could be undertaken by the cultural anthropologist or the psychoanalyst; for, as Otis shows, this conception of the body was one which – through a process of metaphorical extension – was applied to other fields of thought. It provided a template, in anthropology, for an understanding of culture as itself a storage and retrieval system, and, in psychoanalysis, for a layered conception of the organisation of the psyche in which the mind of each and every individual bore the impress of the whole historical development of the species and, in some formulations, of pre-human evolution. By 1895, Otis argues, Miguel Unamuna's metaphor of a lake bottom for culture, describing a process through which layers of cultural development had been progressively sedimented one on top of the other, had acquired an almost universal currency, albeit that the mechanisms of transmission from one period to the development to the next were sometimes conceived biologically, sometimes in terms of the cumulative momentum of tradition, sometimes in terms of institutional mechanisms, and sometimes in terms of all three of these factors acting in combination.[35] For Freud, similarly, the memory traces left by the archaic heritage of biological evolution were a means of bridging the gap between individual and group psychology, enjoining the psychoanalyst to bring to the surface of conscious recollection both the heritage of ancestral impressions and the individual experience that had been added to this heritage. For Jung, finally, the body was so much the summary of the accumulated deposits of the past that it was theoretically possible 'to "peel" the collective unconscious, layer by layer, until we came to the psychology of the worm, and even of the amoeba'.[36]

This new conception of memory was closely associated with a new depth structure of vision. Kate Flint throws useful light on this in her discussion of the ways in which the relationships between the past and present associated with this organic conception of memory were articulated with 'a vocabulary of surface and depth, of the hidden and revealed, of dark and of light'.[37] This new depth structure for the organisation of vision derived from the practices of archaeology and geology which, in their concern to make the hidden visible, developed new principles of legibility: reading became a matter of deciphering the relationships between the successive layers of meaning which lie behind the visible surface of the present. Focusing on the study of glaciation as a case in point, Flint cites as an example of this archaeological or depth-structure of vision James Forbes's 1843 image of a glacier as 'an endless scroll, a stream of time, upon whose stainless ground is engraven the succession of events, whose dates far transcend the memory of living man'.[38] Archibald Geikie proposes a similar way of seeing in his 1858 text *The Story of a Boulder*, when, having cut into the surface of a riverside boulder with his geological hammer, he summarises the layered vistas of the past that his subsequent excavations bring to view as 'the memorials of bygone ages, traced in clear and legible characters on the boulder'.[39]

It is, however, in the increasingly prevalent understanding of human memory as a palimpsest that these new ways of thinking and visualising the past and its relations to the present are most clearly brought together. Flint takes as her prompt here Freud's account of the preservation, in each successive archaeological layer in the development of Rome, of elements from the preceding layers, which he takes as a metaphor for a view of mental life in which 'the primitive is ... commonly preserved alongside of the transformed version which has arisen from it' and in which 'nothing which has once been formed can perish'.[40] However, this way of visualising the organisation of the mind depended on a revised understanding of the palimpsest that had been undertaken earlier in the century, principally, according to Josephine McDonagh, in the work of Thomas De Quincey. Conceived initially as 'a piece of vellum whose surface had been erased of inscription for re-use', it was only late eighteenth-century developments in chemistry that, in enabling the recovery of former inscriptions, transformed the palimpsest from its earlier conception as – once scraped – a *tabula rasa*, into that of an archaeologically layered entity, capable of generating practices of reading in which 'ancient texts, formerly considered lost, were excavated from the forgotten depths of these manuscripts'.[41] McDonagh goes on to indicate how the imagery of the palimpsest was subsequently extended to the field of evolution by providing a means of visualising the person as a storage system in which all that had gone before is retained for retrieval in the present:

> The palimpsest editor, like the other nineteenth-century archaeologists, searched for the origins of life and society by uncovering a history that could inform the present. Just as contemporary scientific developments enabled former inscriptions to be recalled, thereby giving the palimpsest a history it had never before had, so too did contemporary evolutionary sciences give people a history, a past from which they had evolved as physiological, psychological and social beings. And the palimpsest offered a convenient way of figuring such a process, for as the surface is always wiped clean, successive generations might make new inscriptions which would always be retained and joined together by the retentive function of the palimpsest.[42]

The relationship between this new imagery of the palimpsest and new understandings of the person as an evolutionary storehouse is clear in Walter Bagehot's conception of 'stored virtue'. This served as a summary of his account of the means – partly moral and cultural, partly natural and biological – through which the skills and aptitudes acquired in one generation are carried through to the next, to be deposited there as a cumulative inheritance which, in turn, as a civilisational imperative, awaits further development and cultivation. The lynchpin of this account is Bagehot's concept of 'the connective tissue of civilisation', through which skills acquired through repetition and social training are, in being imprinted on the nervous system, thereby transmuted into a physical inheritance that is transmitted – via an inherited nerve element – from one generation to the next. This 'subtle materialism', as Bagehot calls it, thus provides for 'a physical cause of improvement from generation to generation ... which enables each to begin with some improvement on the last'.[43] If, as Bagehot argues, the 'body of the accomplished man has thus become by training different from what it once was, and different from that of the rude man', this is because it has become 'charged with stored virtue'.[44] Lodged in the body, this is carried forward to the next generation, via a practice of bodily mnemonics, as an inheritance that is simultaneously biological, cultural and social.

The layered self and the practice of memory

'No universal history leads from Savagery to Humanity,' Theodor Adorno once argued, 'but certainly there is one leading from the stone catapult to the megaton bomb.'[45] Adorno's contention is, at one and the same time, a summary and a devastating critique of the basic grammar of the evolutionary ethnology museum in which weaponry – alongside tools and other artefacts – was typically arranged in evolutionary sequences both as a means of visualising and as standing in for the development of civilisation. The same was true of peoples who – whether in the form of their skeletal remains or as live exhibits in international exhibitions or other living ethnology displays – were arranged in developmental stages so that they were, as Bernard McGrane puts it, 'seen as coming before and after one another, as earlier and later than one another, like the linear and serial museum arrangement of rock, stone axe, flint knife, iron knife, bow and arrow, rifle, cannon, and atomic missile'.[46] The mutually reinforcing logic that is evident in ethnological arrangements of the relations between people and things was also underpinned by the application of a similar logic in the fields of geology, palaeontology and natural history where – in evolutionary arrangements of the sequence of the rocks, of the evolution of the horse from extinct to extant species, or the development of human crania and skeletons from their simian origins – the whole of prehistory was arranged as a prelude to the evolution of man. In this way, the grammar of evolutionary displays, as articulated across geological, palaeontological, natural history and ethnological or anthropological exhibits, served to accumulate the whole of the past and deposit it in the present.

However, McGrane makes a more arresting point when he observes that the 'nineteenth century's temporal scale of development was everywhere contemporary with itself; it was everywhere simultaneous with itself'.[47] This was so in the case of ethnology, he argues, because different peoples were believed to pass through fixed and identical stages of development at different velocities with the consequence that 'past and present became contemporary with each other'.[48] It was this variability in the *speed* but not the *course* of progress that was attributed to different peoples and races that made it possible, in the context of Euro-American colonialism, for what was far away from Euro-American metropolitan centres to be fashioned as their prehistory. Africa, Australia, parts of the Americas – all of these, at one time or another, did service as 'living museums' where, so it was argued, the prehistoric still survived as an integral component of the present. Nor was this 'simultaneity effect' limited to ethnology, where the concept of survivals received its most developed articulation, especially in Edward Tylor's *Primitive Culture*.[49] It was equally true of natural history, where, to take Ann Moyal's formulations as an economical summary of a complex process, the 'unnatural monsters' which, from the perspective of Enlightenment systems of classification, seemed to abound in Australia were subsequently re-assigned to new positions as 'living fossils', and – in the process – integrated into an order of nature which, now that it had been evolutionised, no longer afforded any spaces for either the monstrous or the marvellous.[50]

In his *Science in Action*, Bruno Latour cites the natural history museum as one of his primary examples of the ways in which centres of calculation are constituted first and foremost through the activity of collection. For it is the organisation of collections that facilitates the 'mobilisation of worlds' in the sense of making it possible for things collected from diverse distant locations to be assembled in one place and thereby make possible the construction of a 'universal' knowledge. He puts the point as follows:

> The zoologists in their Natural History Museums, without travelling more than a few hundred metres and opening more than a few dozen drawers, travel through all the continents, climates and periods.... Many common features that could not be visible between dangerous animals far away in space and time can easily appear between one case and the next! The zoologists *see new* things, since this is the first time that so many creatures are drawn together in front of someone's eyes ...[51]

The same was true of ethnological collections during the period of 'armchair anthropology', when museums supplied the principal institutional setting for anthropological practice.[52] For it was only the acquisition of diverse artefacts from different peripheral locations and their accumulation in metropolitan collections that made it possible for things, and thereby peoples, to be arranged in evolutionary sequences leading from the simple to the complex, the past to the present.

Thomas Huxley's 1865 essay 'On the Methods and Results of Ethnology' offers a telling example of the new things and relations that were made perceptible as a result of the conjoined effect of the operations of evolutionary natural history and ethnology museums. In taking his reader on a 'progress along the outskirts of the habitable world',[53] Huxley converts earlier conceptions of those outskirts as a zone of wildness into an account of progressive human and technological evolution. Starting in Australia and Tasmania and moving thence to New Zealand and the Americas before working his way back through Asia and the Middle East, to Africa, Europe and the Mediterranean, Huxley converts space into time. He summarises his findings by proposing an 'Ethnological chart' which, with the Pacific Ocean as its centre, 'exhibits an Australian area occupied by dark smooth-haired people, separated by an incomplete inner zone of dark woolly-haired Negritos and Negroes, from an outer zone of comparatively pale and smooth-haired men, occupying the Americas, and nearly all Asia and North Africa'.[54] But it is the way in which he arrives at this chart that is of interest. For this depends on a comparative analysis of both anatomical characteristics and the evidence of cultural artefacts – and a reading of the relations between the two – which allows movement through space to also become movement through evolutionary time. The 'brief voyage'[55] from Tasmania to New Zealand brings about a change from the 'long and narrow' skulls of the Australians, and their 'dark, usually chocolate-coloured skins; fine dark wavy hair, dark eyes, overhung by beetle brows; coarse, projecting jaws'[56] to the long skull, wavy-to-straight hair and brown skin of the Maori, for example. Cross to the Americas, and (except for the Fuegians and Esquimaux) skulls become wide and high, the hair is straight, and the skin 'various shades of reddish or yellowish brown'.[57] But each step in this journey is also one of technological and cultural progress – from the absence of cultivation, metals, pottery, fabrics, bow and arrows and anything more sophisticated than bark canoes among the 'Australian tribes' to the Maoris, Polynesians and Micronesians who 'cultivate the ground, construct houses, and skilfully build and manage outrigger, or double canoes; while, almost everywhere, they use some kind of fabric for clothing'[58] and thence to the sometimes 'remarkable degree of civilisation'[59] in the Americas with animal husbandry, pottery, textiles and metals all in evidence. It was not from the 'outskirts of the habitable world', however, that these evolutionary relations of similarity and difference were made evident. This depended on anatomical remains and arte-facts being collected together in metropolitan centres of calculation, where – by placing things acquired from various distant locations side-by-side – new rela-tions were made perceptible and actionable.

And it is only when evolution is made perceptible in these ways that it becomes possible to see – and so also to think, practice and perform – those long pasts that had allegedly become coded into the body as a set of memory traces. It is because this is so that it is possible – indeed, imperative – to view the notion of an organic memory carried in the body (or in a collective unconscious, or whatever similar mechanisms might be proposed) as an effect of the evolutionary museum's functioning as an evolutionary accumulator in which all pasts are stored and rendered simultaneously present.[60] In the case of the art museum, it will be recalled, Didier Maleuvre argues that it is the museum that organises the historical consciousness of modernity precisely by extracting objects from the flow of time, and, by reassembling them all together, making all pasts synchroni-cally present. 'History', to repeat his argument, 'is not a road winding through the thicket of historical events; it is the flash of remembrance in which all histor-ical layers exist simultaneously.'[61] The evolutionary museum considerably extended the reach of this apparatus. It deepened and extended the layers of the pasts that it accumulated, and made these available for a practice of memory that was inscribed in the body. Like the person, the body was now fashioned as a thoroughly archaeologised entity, with a series of sequentially layered pasts stored up within it for retrieval by way of a bodily or psychoanalytic mnemonics that stretched the reach of memory beyond writing and effective tradition into the depths of prehistory.

For John Frow, to recall an earlier part of my discussion, any sense that, in Pierre Nora's terms, authentic remembering is carried 'in the body's inherent self-knowledge, in unstudied reflexes and ingrained memories' is to be countered by an insistence that all memory is necessarily archival and technical, as a result of its reliance on the materiality of writing and representation and the technologies in which such practices are conducted. My point has been that any belief in organic memory is itself the result of conditions which are archival and technical in precisely this sense. And my purpose – writing at a time when such conceptions are present not only in essentialist forms of racial reasoning, but also when molecular conceptions of memory have revived evolutionary conceptions of memory carried in the body[62] – has been to disable such beliefs by showing how, just as much as any other practice of memory, they depend on particular technical and archival conditions.

Notes

1 Gilroy, Paul (2000) *Against Race: Imagining Political Culture Beyond the Color Line*, Cambridge, MA: The Belknap Press of Harvard University Press, p. 263.
2 Gilroy, op. cit., p. 264.
3 See Nora, Pierre (1989) 'Between Memory and History: *Les Lieux de mémoire*', *Representations* 26, pp. 7–25.
4 Nora cited in Frow, John (1997) *Time and Commodity Culture: Essays in Cultural Theory and Postmodernity*, Oxford: Clarendon Press, p. 222.
5 Frow, op. cit., p. 222.
6 Ibid., p. 230.
7 Ibid.
8 Nora's views on this matter are echoed in quite a wide range of post-war French social theory. They are evident, for example, in the work of Henri Lefebvre and Michel de Certeau. See, for a discussion of the implications this has for their accounts of everyday life, Bennett, Tony (2003) 'The Invention of the Modern Cultural Fact: Toward a Critique of the Critique of Everyday Life', in Elizabeth Silva and Tony Bennett (eds) *Contemporary Culture and Everyday Life*, Durham: Sociology Press.
9 Quatremère de Quincy (1989) [1815] *Considérations morales sur la destination des ouvrages de l'art*, Paris: Fayard.
10 Adorno, Theodor W. (1967) 'Valéry Proust Museum', in *Prisms*, London: Neville Spearman.
11 Crimp, Douglas (1993) *On the Museum's Ruins*, Cambridge, MA: MIT Press.
12 Maleuvre, Didier (1999) *Museum Memories: History, Technology, Art*, Stanford: Stanford University Press, p. 16.
13 I have developed a similar perspective elsewhere: see the essay 'The Multiplication of Culture's Utility', in Bennett, Tony (1998) *Culture: A Reformer's Science*, Sydney: Allen & Unwin; London: Sage.
14 Balzac, Honoré de (1977) *The Wild Ass's Skin*, Harmondsworth: Penguin Books, p. 33.
15 Maleuvre, op. cit., p. 205.
16 Ibid., p. 207.
17 Balzac, op. cit., pp. 38–9.
18 Maleuvre, op. cit., pp. 269–70.

19 Ibid., p. 271.
20 Ibid., p. 279.
21 Ibid., p. 278.
22 Balzac, op. cit., p. 34.
23 Ibid., p. 38.
24 Maleuvre, op. cit., p. 278.
25 Balzac, op. cit., pp. 40–1.
26 Ibid., p. 41.
27 Ibid., p. 37
28 Ibid., p. 41.
29 Ibid., p. 42.
30 Ibid.
31 Ibid.
32 Ibid., p. 53.
33 Otis, Laura (1994) *Organic Memory: History and the Body in the Late Nineteenth and Early Twentieth Centuries*, Lincoln and London: University of Nebraska Press, p. 3.
34 A notable exception here is Huxley whose *Evolution and Ethics* took explicit issue with this aspect of the lingering influence of Lamarckian conceptions on the social and political wings of evolutionary thought. See Huxley, Thomas H. (1968) *Man's Place in Nature and Other Anthropological Essays*, New York: Greenwood Press.
35 Otis, op. cit., pp. 96–7.
36 Jung, in Otis, op. cit., p. 209.
37 Flint, Kate (2000) *The Victorians and the Visual Imagination*, Cambridge: Cambridge University Press, p. 140.
38 Flint, op. cit., p. 129.
39 Geike, Archibald (1858) *The Story of a Boulder, or Gleanings from the Note-Book of a Field Geologist*, Edinburgh: Thomas Constable and Co., p. 258.
40 Freud, Sigmund (1969) *Civilisation and Its Discontents*, London: Hogarth Press and the Institute of Psycho-Analysis, pp. 5–6.
41 McDonagh, Josephine (1987) 'Writings on the Mind: Thomas De Quincey and the Importance of the Palimpsest in Nineteenth-century Thought', *Prose Studies* 10, p. 210.
42 McDonagh, op. cit., p. 212.
43 Bagehot, Walter (1873) *Physics and Politics: Or Thoughts on the Application of the Principles of 'Natural Selection' and 'Inheritance' to Political Society*, London: Henry S. King & Co, p. 8.
44 Ibid., p. 6.
45 Adorno in Gardiner, Michael E. (2000) *Critiques of Everyday Life*, London and New York: Routledge, p. 77.
46 McGrane, Bernard (1989) *Beyond Anthropology: Society and the Other*, New York: Columbia University Press, p. 102.
47 Ibid., p. 102.
48 Ibid., emphasis in the original.
49 Tylor, Edward (1871) *Primitive Culture*, 2 vols. London: John Murray.
50 Moyal, Ann (1986) *A Bright and Savage Land*, Ringwood, Victoria: Penguin Books, p. 131. For fuller discussions of the respects in which evolutionary thought entailed a redefinition and relocation of the monstrous precisely by finding a place for it within the new evolutionary order of nature as, necessarily, a stage in a developmental sequence see Richards, Thomas (1993) *The Imperial Archive: Knowledge and the Fantasy of Empire*, London: Verso, and Ritvo, Harriet (1997) *The Platypus and the Mermaid and Other Figments of the Classifying Imagination*, Cambridge, MA: Harvard University Press.
51 Latour, Bruno (1987) *Science in Action*, Cambridge, MA: Harvard University Press, p. 225.

52 See Stocking, George W. Jr (1995) *After Tylor: British Social Anthropology, 1888–1951*, London: Athlone.
53 Huxley, Thomas H. (1968) *Man's Place in Nature and Other Anthropological Essays*, New York: Greenwood Press, p. 234.
54 Ibid., p. 237.
55 Ibid., p. 225.
56 Ibid., pp. 222–3.
57 Ibid., p. 226.
58 Ibid.
59 Ibid., p. 227.
60 I have discussed this notion of the evolutionary museum as an evolutionary accumulator in more detail elsewhere: see Bennett, Tony (2001) 'Pasts Beyond Memories: The Evolutionary Museum, Liberal Government and the Politics of Prehistory', *Folk: Journal of the Danish Ethnographic Society* 43 (autumn).
61 Maleuvre, op. cit., p. 278.
62 See Rose, Steven (1993) *The Making of Memory*, London: Bantam Books.

Part II

PROPPING THE SUBJECT

Introduction

Susannah Radstone and Katharine Hodgkin

Given the immense swathe of time that separates the subjects of these two chapters, the extent of the ground they share is remarkable. Both are concerned with memory 'props'. William West discusses how, in early modern times, practitioners of artificial memory constructed vivid objects in the mind that supported a number of different memories. Stephan Feuchtwang enquires into 'props' of recall that aid in the remembrance and recognition of loss. Both chapters concern themselves with the relationship between subjectivity and memory – a relationship that emerges, in both cases, as interdependent and yet fragile. William West points to a breakdown, in the sixteenth century, of the belief that memory props could sustain the self. Stephan Feuchtwang, on the other hand, points to the subject's reliance on props of recall for sustaining a sense of self, and considers the devastating impact that follows the loss of such props. Both chapters take as their primary focus works of literature. William West discusses how the faltering of memory's support to subjectivity is registered in the poetry of John Donne and Edmund Spenser, and how the faltering of memory's relation to national unity marks the historical writings of William Camden; Stephan Feuchtwang discusses Binjamin Wilkomirski's 'fictional' Holocaust memoir, *Fragments* and Leon Wieseltier's memoir concerning his father's death, *Kaddish*. Both chapters, too, are concerned with memory and affect: William West points out that what made memory objects memorable was the affect with which they were charged, while Stephan Feuchtwang explores both how feelings associated with catastrophic loss may be articulated to the self through identification with unexperienced events, and the feelings in play in institutional processes of recognition-seeking.

The two chapters in this section focus on historical moments separated by 400 years. William West's chapter is concerned with early modern 'artificial memory'. His discussion, although it begins in pre-modern times, focuses on the sixteenth century, exploring the particular practices devised to acknowledge and try to improve on memory's fragility. To augment memory and act as a bulwark against forgetting, practitioners of the arts of memory had, since classical times, constructed memory objects which they placed in imaginary spaces within the mind. These brightly coloured and striking objects were memorable to their 'possessors' due to their personal and private associations. Yet, as West goes on to argue, during the sixteenth century the relationship between subjectivity and memory objects began to break down. Up until then, it had seemed that memory formed the basis of the person: memory told pre-modern selves who they were. But, by the sixteenth century, it became evident that 'artificial memory' relied on props that required a *pre-existent* subject for whom they made meaning. As West points out, this raised the problem of where subjectivity comes from if not via objects. A tension revealed itself at the heart of this configuration of memory, argues West, between giving objects meaning in the mind to constitute a memory that confers subjectivity and the question of where the subjectivity comes from that moulds the memory props in the first place. West points out that it is not simply the personal nature of the associations that renders memory objects opaque to others. There is a tension that runs through this figuration of memory, between the immediacy and transparency of seeing objects in the imaginary space of the mind, and the mediation and opacity associated with the ways those objects make meaning. In short, West argues that memory objects were 'written' and that their interpretation required a knowledge of the language in which they were written – yet this was a language known only to the maker of the memory objects:

> To condense the memory images so that one image embraces a whole concept, the practitioner is advised to use puns and idiosyncratic associations. The images ... are not naturalistic, but representational, and thus need to be decoded like hieroglyphs.... Thus, from the outset, the images of memory are not purely mimetic, not wholly experiential; they partake of the abstraction of language. (p. 63)

The revelation that memory could not sustain subjectivity, as had been supposed in pre-modernity, was a particularly threatening one, due to the relation between memory and ethics: as West points out, the role of memory was to support the self and guarantee immortality.

That the sixteenth-century faltering of faith in memory's relation to subjectivity could have wider resonances is pointed to by West's discussion of the 'chorography'; a written account of a journey through localities. In 1586, Camden published a chorography of England that used as sources not chronicles but monuments, thus transforming the whole of England into a vast memory space. In this sense, one might argue that Camden's chorography anticipated Pierre Nora's recent, seminal study of the memory places of France, *Les Lieux de mémoire*.[1] Yet what Camden discovered, argues West, is that his chorography revealed anything but a unified nation, for the landscape and monuments through which he sought to fix the nation's identity turned out to have shifting and unstable meanings, and multiple or absent histories. Thus the faltering of belief in memory's capacity to support the self also problematised the unity of the nation and national identity. In short, then, West's chapter demonstrates that the instabilities that follow from the fragility of the relation between memory and subjectivity, and which are sometimes assumed to characterise only contemporary Western experience, have a long history.[2]

Stephan Feuchtwang's chapter is about the part played by props of recall in the personal and public recognition of catastrophic loss. He asks what happens if, through catastrophe, victims lose many or all of those props of recall that sustain a sense of self in everyday life – home, friends, family – and argues that in such cases, recognition of this loss is sought. Recognition acknowledges that the seeker is a victim of loss. This identification then comes to stand in for all that has been lost. His chapter focuses in particular on the relation between the personal and interpersonal transmission of loss, and the conventions and institutions, including those of religion, history and the law, that commemorate loss. Feuchtwang outlines the specular nature of the relationship between victims and these recognition-granting authorities. In this relation, both the authority and the victim seek self-confirmation through their mutual and unstable encounter. Feuchtwang's central concern, then, is with the incommensurabilities and disturbances that permeate these relations, for he argues that the authorities that grant recognition and through which redemption is sought are themselves insecure and demand recognition from those who approach them. These institutions also deploy different systems of verification from each other and, most crucially, from the victims themselves.

As Feuchtwang goes on to explain, in law and in history, what claims to be testimony should be verifiable fact. Yet as Binjamin Wilkomirski, one of the authors he discusses, points out, there is a difference between legally accredited truth and the truth of a life. Feuchtwang develops this point by arguing that something that has not been experienced can become a memory prop for the self due to its correspondence to experience. But the efficacy of this prop breaks down when the institutions of the law, or of history, say, refuse to confer recognition. For instance, Binjamin Wilkomirski found recognition of his childhood experiences in the Holocaust. Yet public institutions refused him the recognition of his losses that he sought, because he had not actually lived through the experiences in which he recognised his own past. Thus his loss could not be transmitted to the public realm. In the public sphere, recognition demands that testimony be recognised as verifiable fact. The question of testimony and its relation to historical experience, and in particular to the experience of catastrophe, is one that has been the focus of much recent debate.[3] As Feuchtwang shows, where catastrophe is at issue, a memory's relation to accredited historical truth may be particularly complex (see Janet Walker in our companion volume, *Contested Pasts*).

Like West, then, Feuchtwang points to the problematisation of memory's relation to coherent subjectivity once recognition of props of recall is sought in the public realm. But Feuchtwang also reverses the direction of movement from that of private to public, to that of public to private, for he looks, too, at the impact of a historical loss on one person's personal mourning.

Feuchtwang's chapter touches on several themes that continually re-emerge in discussions of contemporary memory. First, he points out that the institutional granting of recognition of loss and of victim status leads ideally to the gradual giving up of that status. In practice, however, argues Feuchtwang, the demand for recognition and for victim status can become never-ending. This is a point that has been echoed by Paul Antze and Michael Lambek, who have argued that the politics of memory can become the politics of blame, and who have pointed to the link between the 'rise' of memory and the current shift in the West, from an emphasis on collective to individual suffering.[4] Perhaps, then, the dynamics towards which Feuchtwang points are related to memory politics' imbrication with identity and the personal: abdication from victim status is by no means straightforward.

Second, Feuchtwang's essay is concerned with the impact of catastrophic events, and here his chapter overlaps with the concerns of those theorists who have recourse to theories of trauma in order to describe that impact. Yet Feuchtwang's chapter takes another tack. Instead of deploying psychoanalytic or psychological theories to describe the impact of trauma, he offers two alternative perspectives on memory and the after-effects of catastrophe. First, Feuchtwang describes the various relations of correspondence that might pertain between what has been lost and props of recall. Second, he describes the complex relations of identification between victims and recognition-granting institutions. Though a focus on affect runs through both Feuchtwang's chapter and trauma theory, while trauma theory stresses memory's *absence*, Feuchtwang focuses rather on how the absence of props of recall is *negotiated* personally, interpersonally and between persons and institutions.

Both the chapters in Part II foreground specularity – the importance of the appearance of memory objects, on the one hand, and the processes of specularity in play in the recognition of loss, on the other. Both chapters, too, are concerned with ethics. William West discusses the role of memory objects in remembering those moral precepts that were understood to aid in the sustenance of virtue. In this sense, his chapter demonstrates that the idea of embodied 'stored virtue' that emerged in the nineteenth century, and that Tony Bennett discusses in Part I, Chapter 2, on organicist memory, had a long history. West points out, though, that in the sixteenth century, faith in artificial memory's capacity to sustain a sense of an individual's virtue in the public realm began to break down. Meanwhile, Stephan Feuchtwang's chapter is concerned with the ethical dimension of those public processes of recognition and judgement of the losses suffered by victims, and shows that here, too, the relation between the private and the public is a fragile one: whereas for West, it was the idiosyncrasy and opacity of memory objects that complicated their public interpretation, for Feuchtwang, it is the particular demands of the conventions and institutions that commemorate loss that may invalidate personal props of recall.

Both chapters, then, are very much concerned with the relationship between the personal, subjective relation to memory props and its 'translation' into the public sphere, and, in both cases, what emerges is that the sustenance of the subject by means of 'props' of recall may not survive the transition of those relations into the public sphere.

These questions about the 'translation' of private into public memory arguably touch on what some have called 'prosthetic memory'.[5] The term 'prosthetic memory' is usually associated with postmodernist theory, with the impact of technology on memory and with the possibility that film and, more recently, digital technology, might enable the 'implantation' of memories of unexperienced events. William West's chapter demonstrates, however, that what is generally taken to be an absolutely contemporary question has roots that stretch at least as far back as early modern times. For the problem memory objects presented to the sixteenth-century writers and poets West discusses was precisely the difficulty of their wider interpretation. Perhaps this is to stretch the point slightly, but what it does suggest is that already, in the sixteenth century, what was at issue was whether the private idiosyncrasies of memory might be made more widely available, or whether memory objects – associated, as they were, with personal experience – could only ever speak for their 'owners'. Stephan Feuchtwang's chapter puts questions about prosthesis and private/public memory transitions slightly differently, for his essay insists that an unexperienced event might be integrated into memory in order to sustain a sense of self. Feuchtwang argues that this was precisely the case for Binjamin Wilkomirski, whose 'autobiographical memoir' about his childhood experiences in Auschwitz was later revealed to be fictional. Feuchtwang argues that, for Wilkomirski, the Holocaust provided a prop of recall for his own differently catastrophic childhood. Yet problems emerge, once prosthetic memory is submitted for public recognition, for the institutions which confer such recognition – courts or historians, for instance – demand proofs that cannot be provided, and cannot recognise the 'truth' expressed through the identification with such props. Taken together then, the chapters in this section show that the question of the relation between memory, subjectivity and the public realm has a long history. Both chapters show that 'props' of recall both confer and undermine the coherence of the remember's subjectivity, and that this problem seems intractable in regimes in which the associated binaries of memory/history and personal/public hold sway.

Notes

1   Pierre Nora (ed.) *Les Lieux de mémoire*, 7 vols, Paris: Gallimard, 1984–93; for a selection of essays from this work in English, see Pierre Nora, *The Realms of Memory: The Construction of the French Past*, trans. Arthur Goldhammer, New York: Columbia University Press, 1997. For a recent introduction, in English, to the work of Pierre Nora, see Peter Carrier, 'Places, Politics and the Archiving of Contemporary Memory in Pierre Nora's *Les Lieux de mémoire*', in Susannah Radstone (ed.), *Memory and Methodology*, New York and Oxford: Berg, 2000, pp. 37–57.

2   Fredric Jameson's discussion of postmodern subjectivity suggests, for instance, that
     the 'failure' of memory and of the capacity to sustain a sense of continuity through
     time is a contemporary phenomenon; see Fredric Jameson, 'Postmodernism, or The
     Cultural Logic of Late Capitalism', *New Left Review* 146, 1984, pp. 53–92.
3   See Dori Laub and Shoshana Felman, *Testimony: Crises of Witnessing in Literature,
     Psychoanalysis and History*, New York and London, Routledge, 1992. For recent contri-
     butions to the discussion of testimony see *Cultural Values* 5(1), 2001, special issue on
     'Testimonial Cultures'.
4   Paul Antze and Michael Lambek, 'Introduction: Forecasting Memory', in Paul Antze
     and Michael Lambek (eds) *Tense Past: Cultural Essays in Trauma and Memory*, New York
     and London: Routledge, 1996, pp. xi–xxxvi.
5   Alison Landsberg, 'Prosthetic Memory: *Total Recall* and *Blade Runner*', in Mike
     Featherstone and Roger Burrows (eds) *Cyberspace/Cyberbodies/Cyberpunk: Cultures of
     Technological Embodiment*, London: Sage, 1995, pp. 175–89.

3

"NO ENDLESSE MONIMENT"

Artificial memory and memorial artifact in early modern England

William N. West

Hamlet:	My father – methinks I see my father.
Horatio:	O where, my lord?
Hamlet:	In my mind's eye, Horatio.

(Hamlet, I, ii, 184–5)

Hamlet's innocuous expression of nostalgia elicits a startled – perhaps a startlingly startled – response. We better understand Horatio's surprise: he has, after all, himself just come from seeing Hamlet's father unexpectedly on the battlements of Elsinore and is alarmed to find Hamlet seeing him elsewhere. But Hamlet is, it turns out, not seeing him elsewhere but *nowhere*, attending in memory to his father's flickering, ghostly image. What should perhaps startle us is Hamlet's easy comprehension of Horatio's surprised 'Where?' For Hamlet, the 'mind's eye,' memory, works precisely like ordinary vision. It takes place in a *where*, and confronts its objects as visual. Horatio's memory of sight is in an exterior, physical space; it is public, shared with Marcellus and Bernardo. In Hamlet's case, the sight of memory takes place within the private space of thought, here treated in metaphor as involving sight and space.

To imagine the memory as a space of thought containing imaginary objects was a widespread practice in fifteenth- and sixteenth-century Europe, as indeed it had been for centuries. In Book 10 of his *Confessions*, for instance, Augustine describes his memory as 'like a great field or a spacious palace, a storehouse for countless images,' as 'vast cloisters' or 'a great treasure-house.'[1] So important was memory to the varied intellectual practices of Europe between Augustine's time and Shakespeare's – legal rhetoric, literary composition, and scriptural mastery among them – that a set of rules and practices to supplement the natural memory was developed: the arts of memory or the 'artificial memory.' The arts of memory, originally part of training in rhetoric and later expanding to touch almost every intellectual field from preaching to medicine, systematized this metaphor: one's memory was imagined as a space that could be defined and then filled with the objects that one needed to recall, including, most importantly, the ethical and political precepts that could help one in leading one's life well.[2] These arts turned on two related but distinct ideas of how memory functions. The first is of memory as a kind of internal writing in the soul or heart; the second, memory as a kind of storage space for whatever is remembered. Both are as old as Plato, and both are still current – we *write* a file on to the hard drive of our computer or ask how much *space* is left on a floppy disk.[3] But writing and space as metaphors of memory are not fully congruent with one another. Spatialization, as in Hamlet's response, retains the authority of direct experience; ultimately the mind's eye, facing its imagined objects within their shared imagined space, is a pre-modern equivalent of virtual reality. Language or writing, on the other hand, can never be more than a form of recording. Hamlet and Horatio exchange descriptions of what they have seen within the non-experiential, non-mimetic realm of words, but to confirm Horatio's vision and Hamlet's memory, they must return to the battlements. Within this logic, the inscription of memory as language is shown to be a less desirable alternative to its spatialization. At the same time, the spatial and visual memory requires the supplement of language if it is to change private experience to public knowledge. On these terms, then, within the arts of memory there is a grudging allowance of narration into memory spaces. But this incongruity within the artificial memory, and its need for supplementation, is a place where its tenets, in early modern Europe, falter.

The underlying principles of the artificial memory are relatively straightforward.[4] The would-be memory artist remembered (or imagined) an organized space – houses or theaters were commonly suggested. Within this space, at regular intervals, he or she distributed images that would serve as prompts to the memory. Later, when the user wished to remember something, he or she would, in an act of literal re-collection, mentally retrieve the images in any order he or she desired. This schematic account, though, fails to render the *affective* qualities of this disciplined form of memory. Memory as a virtual space for each of our pasts, the theater of memory that replays the drama of our histories, the memory palace that holds and organizes the wealth of our experience in the form of imagined property – these images of memory are themselves so arresting that, in accord with their own theories of the memorable, they have veiled other less striking but equally important elements in this cultural history. Contemporary interest in the medieval and early modern arts of memory, in contrast to much of the work of scholars of more recent periods, has emphasized the *objects* of memory rather than its *subjects* – that is, critics have focused on the striking (and memorable!) images of angels, demons, and other figures that adorn early 'theaters of memory' rather than on the users of those spaces.[5] Premodern writers themselves, though, stressed the importance of personal affect in constructing an artificial memory, which produced meaning not systematically but idiosyncratically. Memory, for the thinkers of the Renaissance and earlier, was the seat of identity; while reason made one human, it was memory that made one a particular individual.[6] Modern critics have overlooked the full significance of the rememberer's subjectivity because, in a way, we have mirrored it –

reading over the images and spaces, we have overlaid the experience of moving mentally within them with our own traversal of them, and so have tended to see these spaces as static and fixed.[7]

The metaphor of spatiality is so central to pre-modern ideas of memory that memory's images and spaces were treated as virtual – that is, as if they were not metaphors at all, but things with independent existence. Memory spaces, our sources insist, should be of moderate size and well lit: too large a space, and the user had to travel too much (mental) distance between images; too dim, and he or she might overlook one of his or her images in the darkness. Images should not be too far away from the user, lest distance obscure the images (*Ad Herennium*, 3.19.32). Most crucially, to be easily remembered the images must be 'extraordinary': brightly dressed, violently active, or smeared with paint or blood, so that they produce a strong emotional effect on their deviser (3.22.35).

Although the images are treated as if they were visual, they are not simply mental copies of what one has seen; if they were, there would be no advantage to the artificial memory over the natural memory. Since, in the interests of brevity, one image must often stand for several concepts, these striking images must always be deciphered before they can be understood. To condense the memory images so that one image embraces a whole concept, the practitioner is advised to use puns and idiosyncratic associations. The images in the system described in *Ad Herennium* are not naturalistic but representational, and thus need to be decoded like hieroglyphs rather than viewed like photographs. Thus, from the outset the images of memory are not purely mimetic, not wholly experiential; they partake of the abstraction of language. Artificial memory, in spite of its fascinating images, is ultimately conceived of as a kind of writing without language, securing meaning within the unique subjectivity of its deviser. A memory system is a set of private cues to meaning rather than a legible code that can be systematically translated, and so, when it is given a material form, its individual particularities must be conventionalized, and perhaps even censored or circumscribed if they are to remain meaningful to a larger group. The *Ad Herennium* author recognizes that many images that appear vivid and memorable to one person are uninteresting to another. This seemingly offhand observation significantly differentiates artificial memory from similar symbolic systems. The images of memory are symbolic, but they are not part of a shared set of symbols; instead they are close to a private language, idiosyncratic and unsystematic. Because they are not simply mimetic, memory images must be created by their user rather than learned from a teacher or a book. Creating one's own memory images further anchored personal identity in the faculty of memory; it required that one combine private fantasies, perceptual stimuli, and intense feeling in a mental experience that was simultaneously physical, sensual, and emotional. While the images were stored in abstract spaces, the process by which memories were gathered, assembled, and brought to bear on the present was understood as itself a form of experience. Pre-modern remembering was holistic, linking intellect and feeling, past and present, subject and object. It thus recorded and secured, like writing and language, the unique meaning of its possessor – but it was unlike writing because the contents of the memory were not, and could not be, fully shared or publicized. The visual and spatial basis that was imagined to support the individual memory also protected it, as it were, from being shared and diffused. Memory was the refuge of the individual – one's own memory as well as others' were the mysterious sources from which identity issued, tantalizingly almost present, frustratingly elusive, and, above all, thoroughly and irreducibly private.[8]

In the sixteenth century, though, historians like William Camden and poets like Edmund Spenser and John Donne proposed a counter-theory for the workings of memory. In different ways, each of these writers took up the ideology of memory as virtually objective and ethical, as spatial and visual, often without explicitly recognizing it as an ideology. But for each of these writers – Camden as he recorded the historical geography of the English landscape, Spenser as he exfoliated a series of imagined inner spaces in his nationalist epic *The Faerie Queene*, Donne as he explored the use of memorial objects – the public writing of private memory called into question the effectiveness of the earlier memory systems, not as *practical* disciplines that might help one record facts in memory, but as the *ethical* discipline that they sought to be, the support of the self and its guarantee of immortality. In particular, they challenged the simple equation of memory with selfhood. For these writers, the brightly illuminated objects of the traditional arts of memory pointedly *fail* to memorialize what they are meant to recall in the absence of a unifying self that can organize them. They do not constitute a subject of memory, as in previous formulations; rather, they are remembered by such a subject and remain, in its absence, literally insignificant things.

William Camden's *Britannia* (1586) was the most ambitious of the chorographies of sixteenth-century England.[9] 'Chorography' was a short-lived but very popular genre that described the physical and historical structure of a single locality (a 'choros'), much like the equally popular and equally novel 'geographies' of Ortelius and others, which, as their name suggests, were writings of the world. Rather than relying on visual maps like the geographies, though, a chorography was often composed of written itineraries and routes across the territory, adorned with particular histories, points of interest, and local lore. Instead of presenting a generalized (and literal) overview of a place, a chorography recounted a path through it. In contrast to the geographical imagination that subordinated space to a single view, there could be as many chorographies as travelers, or indeed as travels. Camden's important decision in his chorography was to turn from chronicles and other narratives as sources, which he characterized as 'feigned fables, which it were vanity to recite, and mere folly to believe' (p. 34), to the 'incorrupt and ancient monuments' scattered over the countryside. Camden's treatment of English origins is specifically indebted to the idea of artificial memory because it is simultaneously historical and topographical; he attempts no survey of either history or land, but rather traces rivers, ancient roads, or county lines on their respective courses, using them as devices to recount historical events and to grasp some mediated whole. In effect, Camden's chorography tried to turn the entire realm of England into a vast memory space, using its natural features, cities, and ruins to recover the successive histories of settlement in England by the aboriginal Britons, and the subsequent invasions of Romans, 'English-Saxons,' Danes, and finally Norman French. The past, and the truth of English identity, is revealed by describing the lay of the land, which itself reveals a fissured and hybrid past, remains of various cultures lying haphazardly spread over the landscape. For Camden and his readers, to walk through Elizabeth's England is to recall a visible but usually unnoticed palimpsest of civilizations and events that have disappeared into the past and also been transmuted into contemporary England.

Richard Helgerson has suggested that large-scale chorographies and mapping projects were part of a clearly defined Tudor project to reconceive England along national lines as a kingdom unified under a single monarch. Although expanded from the imaginary realm of an individual's identity to a physical topography and a national identity, Camden's chorographic project is well within the means and aims of the artificial memory, as Camden himself realized. But Camden's results belie his apparent intentions. Rehearsing the landscape of England, Camden discovers, in contravention to his declared intention, not a unified Britannia, but one marked by all sorts of local difference and even incommensurability. Rivers change names; borders shift or are calculated differently; ruins have contradictory histories or sometimes no history at all. The narrative that Camden recounts suggests a breakdown of the simple passage from memory to identity, because no simple English identity, even a mediated or postdated one, emerges in the course of Camden's journey. Camden's *Britannia* reveals a significant oversight in the prevailing theories of artificial memory – an identity constituted through spatial memory of images does not construct a subject, but rather requires the pre-existence of a subject under whose gaze the scattered objects of memory can come to make sense. Part of the difficulty of Camden's text comes from the incommensurability of the subject who writes the work – Camden, who faithfully follows each disappearing trail and shifting border until it fades or changes, revealing through his scrupulous fidelity to the space he covers its ultimate lack of integrity – and the subject for whom the work is conceived – a royal subject, Elizabeth, whose imaginary eye can take in at a glance an apparent confusion of forms, names, times, regions. The princely overview corresponds to an ideal of artificial memory; Camden's text falls into narrative disarray, slipping any moment of full self-awareness.

Camden's chorographical project had parallels in both its nation-building and its critique of identity-memory to works in other genres as well. Edmund Spenser's *Faerie Queene* (1590) is explicitly an allegory of the paradoxes and challenges of possessing virtues appropriate to a Protestant state.[10] But its second Book also addresses some problems that face the traditional conception of a spatial, visual memory as the locus of identity. Book II begins with its knightly hero, Sir Guyon, discovering a dying woman and her child by a fountain. The striking *visuality* of the scene – and hence in this framework's terms its memorability – is repeatedly invoked: it is a 'sad pourtraict' (II.i.39.3), a 'pitifull spectacle' (40.1), an 'image …/ Of rueful pittie' (44.4–5) and 'of mortalitie' (57.2) – a perfect image for memory, in fact, since she serves to remind Guyon and the aged palmer who travels with him of their mortality and her commitment (as it turns out) to her chastity:

> That as a sacred Symbole it may dwell
> In her sonnes flesh, to mind revengement
> And be for all chast Dames an endlesse moniment.
>
> (II.ii.10.7–9)

Guyon encounters death in a form that requires its commitment to memory – the dead woman is preserved as a 'Symbole' literally inscribed 'In her sonnes flesh,' as Guyon and Palmer 'engrave' her body in the earth (II.i.60.1). But although it serves as an image of memory for Guyon to identify with, the image of the dead woman is also curiously lethal. As soon as he sees her, Guyon's

> hart gan wexe as starke, as marble stone,
> And his fresh blood did frieze with fearefull cold.
>
> (II.ii.42.2–3)

Guyon's sudden coldness and torpor mirror 'the stony cold' of the 'frozen hart' (46.5–6) of the dead woman, who becomes here not only a spectacle but his model. Furthermore, what Spenser, with his intentionally archaizing spelling, names Guyon's 'frieze' is both a becoming-frozen and a becoming-a-frieze – in short, the transformation of Guyon into a monument like that the woman leaves behind. Memory here paralyzes the living Guyon and the child, converting them into the form of an alien image that they must bear with them.

Here and throughout *The Faerie Queene*, Spenser's interest in memory focuses on what he calls a 'moniment' – a Latinate spelling that recalls the etymological meanings of both *preservation* and *threat*.[11] One threat is that which Guyon faces here – the threat of being first paralyzed by memory and then consumed by it. Memory here does not secure identity, as it was supposed to do, but erases and remakes it in the shape of something external to its rememberer. The second anxiety is a more curious one of simple oblivion. In the emergent idea of a 'moniment,' what is remembered is not merely imagined but really appears in the external world, only to be abandoned to a future that lacks the key to interpreting it. Spenser's 'moniments' are frequently contrafactual – that is, the word signals the absence of a suitable monument or even its erasure.[12] The word 'moniment' first appears in *Faerie Queene* in the myth of Hippolytus, whose dismembered body leaves 'no moniment' (I.v.38.9). Nearly a third of the word's subsequent occurrences point out similar absence of a moniment, and another third are moniments that record disaster or failure.[13] Even more strikingly, several references are to erased or illegible moniments. Later in Book II, for instance, another knight, Verdant, lies in a voluptuous post-coital daze in the Bower of Bliss surrounded by his now-unused arms, themselves a kind of moniment to his moral failure: 'And his braue shield, full of gold moniments,/ Was fowly ras't, that none the signes might see' (II.xii.80.3–4). What Verdant's shield memorializes is, in fact, nothing but its own loss of memory; instead of anchoring Verdant's identity either for himself or for those who come after him, it exposes only its own failure to serve as an adequate object of memory. In a sense, it can signal no more than its own forgetfulness.

These episodes dramatize the vicissitudes that can befall the artificial or spatial memory, and thus expose the threat inherent in this memory system. But in Book II Spenser also takes up the issue of memory proper with an extended allegory. At one point in the book, Guyon, together with the knight who will later become King Arthur, visits the House of Alma, a castle in the form of the human body. In the topmost tower – the head – Guyon and Arthur find three chambers that represent the three psychological faculties of Reason, Fantasy (or Imagination), and Memory. It is this last that interests us here:

> That chamber seemed ruinous and old
> And therefore was removed farre behind,
> Yet were the walls, that did the same uphold,
> Right firme & strong, though somewhat they declind;
> And therein sate an old oldman, halfe blind,
> And all decrepit in his feeble corse,
> Yet lively vigor rested in his mind,
> And recompenst him with a better scorse:
> Weake body well is chang'd for minds redoubled forse.

> This man of infinite remembrance was,
> And things foregone through many ages held,
> Which he recorded still, as they did pas,
> Ne suffred them to perish through long eld,
> As all things else, the which this world doth weld,
> But laid them up in his immortal scrine,
> Where they forever incorrupted dweld:
> The warres he well remembred of king *Nine*,
> Of old *Assaracus*, and *Inachus* divine.

> The years of Nestor nothing were to his,
> Ne yet Methusalem, though longest liv'd;
> For he remembred both their infancies:
> Ne wonder then, if that he were depriv'd,
> Of native strength now, that he them surviv'd.
> His chamber all was hangd about with rolles,
> And old records from auncient times deriv'd
> Some made in books, some in long parchment scrolles,
> That were all worme-eaten, and full of canker holes.

Amidst them all he in a chaire was set,
Tossing and turning them withouten end;
But for he was unhable them to fet,
A litle boy did on him still attend,
To reach, when ever he for ought did send;
And oft when things were lost, or laid amis,
That boy them sought, and unto him did lend.
Therefore he *Anamnestes* cleped is,
And that old man *Eumnestes*, by their propertis.
(II.ix.55.1–II.ix.58.9)

The chamber of Eumnestes is, transparently, a space of artificial memory, and at first glance, at least, it seems to fulfill its practical and ethical tasks admirably. First, its contents are apparently immortal; although outwardly both the chamber and its principal inhabitant Eumnestes ('Good Memory') are 'ruinous' and 'decrepit,' we are told that they retain the power to preserve their memory contents faithfully. Further, the disembodied memory that the chamber presents successfully makes the private realm of memory publicly available through its writing, at once memory contents and legible text.[14] Arthur and Guyon are able to enter into this alien memory space and read through someone else's memory in the form of the scrolls and books the chamber contains. The memories of Eumnestes' chamber are both lasting and transferable.

It is this promise of sharing memory, though, that disrupts the smoothness of the chamber's memorial performance. The space of the chamber as it is first described is disordered and as illegible as the covers of the books and scrolls it contains – these memory objects are at once perfectly visible and utterly incomprehensible. The possessors, whether Eumnestes or the two knights, cannot use it until its architectural space is replaced by the 'auncient booke, hight *Briton moniments*.' Space and vision cede to writing. Like the difference between Camden's *Britannia* and Elizabeth's England, a fragmented and fragmenting narrative stands in for the promised intuitive grasp of the whole. This fragmentation extends to the subject of memory as well. Judith Anderson neatly encapsulates the paradox of the written memory: 'Such resources may be accessible to individuals in time but always exceed their direct or specific experience.'[15] What, then, embodies the race or nation – or individual – by giving the memory a dwelling place within a subject? Between the determining contents of memory, eternal and still, and its dynamic unfoldings in narrative opens a gap. Eumnestes seems at first to be the subject of memory: he is the 'man of infinite remembrance,' and although at first Spenser leaves it uncertain whether this limitless memory is simply Eumnestes' recording of events in writing, he is later said to have 'remembred' – rather than recorded – the wars of Ninus and the infancies of Methusalem and Nestor. But what role, then, does Eumnestes' helper, the 'litle boy' Anamnestes ('Recall'), play? The artificial memory requires a self-possessed subject, but in this memory chamber, this seems not to be the passive and immobile Eumnestes, but the active

Anamnestes, not the apparent subject of memory, that is, but another agent who stands aside from what is remembered. What is remembered in the following canto of the *Faerie Queene* is also nothing of Eumnestes' own, but rather the double histories of Arthur's Albion and Guyon's land of Faerie. The remembering is thus as much theirs as Eumnestes' or Anamnestes'; at the same time, the past that in some sense belongs to Arthur and Guyon is discovered alienated from them in the memory of another, where they find it as if it were not theirs. In *Confessions*, Augustine spoke of going back into his own memory in search of a fact that he knew he had learned but could not remember, but there the single remembering subject is his own prompt, searcher, keeper. It is a strangely disturbing vision that Spenser offers, splitting the subject of memory into multiple ones, each intent on a different facet of recall. In place of the promise of the 'endlesse moniment,' Spenser's library offers infinite writing, and even this comes at the expense of 'endlesse exercise' (II.ix.59.2), feebleness and even acrasia for Eumnestes, and mediation and alienation for Arthur and Guyon, whose memories and identities are part of the contents of the chamber.

At the same time, the space and the writing in Eumnestes' chamber is completely absorbing. Arthur and Guyon view the interior of the self as an alien object and are transfixed by it, 'burning both with fervent fire' (II.ix.60.6) to read their own histories. The result of looking over these written moniments is much like the fascination and 'frieze'-ing of Guyon when he sees the murdered woman; when Arthur's book unexpectedly breaks off at the story of Uther, Arthur's own father

> that so untimely breach
> The Prince him selfe halfe seemeth to offend,
> Yet secret pleasure did offence empeach,
> And wonder of antiquitie long stopt his speech.
> (II.x.68.6–9)

Arthur is 'quite ravisht with delight' (69.1), seized and overcome by the 'secret pleasure' of discovering his own unrecognized memory outside himself. This ravishment and silencing of the subject in the face of the memory object, as should by now be clear, is for Spenser no epiphenomenon of memory, but its primary working. One of the ancient tales recounted by Arthur's book is that of Brutus, the legendary founder of the British kings, and the end of his royal line not through the fading of memory, but paradoxically by its unbated force. The last heirs of Brutus, Ferrex and Porrex, turn on one another in a struggle for Brutus's crown and the glory of his descent:

> Thenceforth this Realme was into factions rent,
> Whilest each of Brutus boasted to be borne,
> That in the end was left no moniment
> Of Brutus, nor of Britons glory aunchient.
> (II.x.36.6–9)

This is the threat of the moniment that entwines its ability to preserve. The memory of Brutus held in and by a subject erases all the objective moniments of Brutus; the erasure of the objective moniments of Brutus includes the subject himself, who is also a sign of Brutus's memory as well as its subjective bearer. What is left of Brutus's memory, held too fast, erases itself so that nothing remains.

But what if the object of memory proves more stubborn, resists its destruction more successfully? The seventeenth-century poet and minister John Donne explores memory and the objects of memory from a similar angle in two of his poems, 'The Funeral' and 'The Relic.'[16] These poems – in fact almost the same poem written from two different perspectives – seem to represent the same event, the burial of a man with a memorial bracelet of his lover's braided hair around his wrist. In Donne's imagination, the memorial object of the artificial memory becomes real and shared – the bracelet of hair passes, as it were, from its safe location in the mind of its wearer into the public eye, where it is subject to interpretation by a crowd of onlookers who do not know or understand its particular history or affective significance. 'The Funeral' comes earlier in the 1633 collection of Donne's poems in which both were first published and, from the standpoint of its treatment of memory, is the more traditional. The poem begins with the speaker's warning not to disturb the memorial artifact that, like its imaginary counterpart, he keeps to preserve his identity after death:

> Whoever comes to shroud me, do not harm
> Nor question much
> That subtle wreath of hair, which crowns my arm;
> The mystery, the sign you must not touch,
> For 'tis my outward soul ...
>
> (1–5)

The bracelet, the speaker's 'outward soul,' is an externalized representation of what it means to be the speaker. Unlike the more usual poetic epitaph, in which the speaker is imagined as already dead and posthumously addressing the living, Donne's speaker addresses his audience in a kind of proleptic epitaph, envisioning himself as dead in the future rather than the present, self-possessed now but contemplating his later absence. But the speaker of Donne's poem is preserved even as he announces his own disappearance in the form of the bracelet, his 'outward soul' and the sign of his continuing devotion, now and after his death, to the woman who gave it to him. This gift, however, is no benevolent one: the speaker speculates that the woman gave him the bracelet that he

> By this should know my pain,
> As prisoners then are manacled, when they are condemned to die.
>
> (15f.)

Like a conventional memorial artifact, the speaker's bracelet preserves an awareness of self for him, but it is one that is defined by its literal devotion to death, if not oblivion. The poem closes on a still more jarring note in the third and final stanza when the speaker acknowledges that although the bracelet serves him as a memorial of his lover and will serve his survivors as a 'Viceroy' for his absent soul, he is not entirely certain what significance it had for the woman it commemorates:

> Whate'er she meant by it, bury it with me
> For since I am
> Love's martyr, it might breed idolatry,
> If into others' hands these relics came ...
> (17–20)

The real danger in the poem is not, then, the speaker's death, but rather his double oblivion, his incomprehensibility to those who follow him in time and in fact his own failure to grasp his own identity ('Whate'er she meant by it,' which is his 'outward soul') from his memory-laden ornament. The speaker's lack of understanding is mirrored – as Guyon's stillness mirrored that of the dead woman in *Faerie Queene* – in his audience, which he imagines as falling into 'idolatry,' literally the mistaking of a likeness of a thing for the thing itself. Here, the speaker distinguishes his supposed erotic martyrdom from the spiritual martyrdom it mimics and parodies.

'The Funeral' ends on a note of closure that, in light of the indeterminacy that precedes it, seems forced and unconvincing. The absence of the woman who gave the speaker the bracelet allows the speaker to revalue the bracelet's meaning. Taking refuge in the hitherto unexploited discourse of misogyny, the speaker ends his poem with unanticipated decisiveness:

> 'tis some bravery,
> That since you would save none of me, I bury some of you.
> (23f.)

The speaker lends his voice coherence by concentrating his diffused emotions and impressions into a clearly articulated spite. In effect, he demands that the poem be read backwards and lent wholeness as a proclamation of a kind of poetic mutually assured destruction. It is a moment of strange triumph, where the speaker suddenly claims the right to re-assign meaning to his dead lover's hair, and 'bury' her as she erased him from her mind. Such certainty seems to be belied by the memory of statements of indeterminacy that begin each of the three stanzas: 'Whoever.... For if.... Whate'er....' But such certainty also props up the speaker's identity in a way that the memorial bracelet, with its illegibilities and uncertainties, apparently cannot. The poem dramatizes a struggle to determine the meaning of a particular memorial object. But even the threat of such a struggle seems to undercut the conventional role of the memory object as a prop for memory. If there is indeterminacy in meaning of the object itself, and if its meaning is determined rhetorically by the competing claims of the speaker and the woman rather than by some inherent symbolism, it is subject to the revisions of already constituted subjects acting upon it. What it cannot fully answer, then, is how such subjects – who ought to be in a sense *its* subjects, subject *to it* – could themselves be constituted. Their coherence, such as it is, must come from elsewhere – in this case, from a sense of vindictiveness seemingly unconnected and even opposed to the outward meaning of the bracelet.

'The Relic' begins, apparently, some time after 'The Funeral':

> When my grave is broke up again
> Some second guest to entertain ...
> And he that digs it spies
> A bracelet of bright hair about the bone,
> Will he not let us alone,
> And think that there a loving couple lies ...?
> (1–8)

In contrast to the almost triumphant ending of 'The Funeral,' where the speaker suddenly gains the power – even if abruptly and unconvincingly – to interpret the bracelet, 'The Relic' shows a speaker similarly shackled with 'a bracelet of bright hair about the bone' (6), but here helpless to prevent himself from being misunderstood:

> If this fall in a time, or land,
> Where mis-devotion doth command,
> Then he that digs us up will bring
> Us to the Bishop and the King,
> To make us relics; then
> Thou shalt be a Mary Magdalen, and I
> A something else thereby;
> All women shall adore us, and some men;
> And since at such times, miracles are sought,
> I would have that age by this paper taught
> What miracles we harmless lovers wrought.
> (12–22)

Unlike 'The Funeral,' in which the poem remains for the reader together with the 'subtle wreath of hair' which supports it, the speaker of 'The Relic' leaves behind him not the reassuring solidity and objectivity of 'a bracelet of bright hair about the bone' but only his poems – the readers must be taught 'by this paper' rather than the bracelet – and, in the end, no meaning. 'The Relic' seems to follow 'The Funeral' in time, as it does in space in the volume in which both were first printed. Rather than projecting his future absence, as in 'The Funeral,' 'The Relic' performs the erasure of the speaker's subjectivity in present and future perfect tenses. The speaker first suspends his present consciousness in the fiction of his future death, seeing himself as already dead and buried so that his 'grave is broke up again' (1) now, as he speaks. Rather than focusing on the moment of his death, though, the speaker here presents his death in the past. He speaks, then, not as one living now who will be dead, but as a kind of revenant speaking past his death in the future perfect. As in 'The Funeral,' the speaker's self-presentation takes a surprising turn in the last two lines of the poem, as his own recollected memory of having-been is suspended in the narrative of the incomprehensibility of his remains. Dead or alive, the speaker's voice fails him:

> All measure, and all language, I should pass
> Should I tell what a miracle she was.
>
> (33–34)

It is not the speaker's loquaciousness after death that startles here, which is after all a convention of epitaphic verse; it is the suspension in the *present* of the speaker's voice that is so startling. The speaker falls silent, stricken dumb or spoken out, and the poem trails off into the misunderstandings of the idolatrous relic-seekers. Such erasure is arguably a more total representation of self-annihilation than the traditional form of the epitaph, which preserves, however imperfectly, the speaker's voice and consciousness after his projected death. In 'The Relic,' Donne's voice is handed over entirely to those who come after and who fail to understand him; he becomes for his poetic heirs 'something else' (18) – another instance of mis-devoted idolatry.

What produces this erasure of subjectivity is the failure of artificial memory. 'The Relic' of the title becomes a stupid object of fascination rather than a part of an interpretable system of signs. In this poem, the thing does not support personal identity, but replaces it. As the speaker falls silent and the bracelet is misunderstood as a Christian rather than an erotic relic, the speaker's unique subjectivity – so strongly defined and marked in 'The Funeral' by his manacle – simply disappears. What is left behind in the narrative is an assortment of meaningless fragments of bright hair and bone that are misinterpreted by 'mis-devotion,' the 'idolatry' the speaker foresees and prevents in 'The Funeral.' The remainder that is the poem erases itself by denying its ability to speak accurately – what it wishes to say is already, like death itself, beyond all language and all measure. What Donne understands as 'mis-devotion' or 'idolatry' is what modern readers might better understand as fetishism – an emphasis on the thing itself that serves to shift its meaning into some meaningless but absorbing form. But this is effectively the alternative to memory: something remains – bright, fascinating – but it is something else.

What Camden, Spenser, and Donne each suggest, I argue, within the terms set out in the arts of memory, is pointedly the *failure* of memory to submit to a strict discipline. The artificial memory is presented as a hedge, a secure field for retaining and ordering past experience, and assembling from it a coherent identity that is both publicly recognizable and ultimately private. For each of these writers, the use of memorial objects within the artificial memory defeats these goals – the objects we are shown require further narration, or say otherwise than they ought, or say nothing at all. Without straying too far from the concerns of these early modern writers, we can begin to interrogate in light of their memorials our own intellectual relationships to memory. Memory, artificial or natural, pre-modern, modern, and now postmodern, presents a seductive field of exploration and a persistent problem to (now) more established academic disciplines. It grips us and hints at its riches. But it does not necessarily adhere to the rules on consistency and objectivity that we, and others before us, have laid down for disciplines and practices to follow. We must be wary of our attempts to sound it, lest in our idolatry we set up as an 'endlesse moniment' what is only – also? – 'something else thereby.'

Notes

This paper has veered through several different incarnations in its short lifespan. Recalling those, I want also to recall the people who, by their supportive criticism, made it possible to (re)write it: Kate Hodgkin and Susannah Radstone, for offering the occasion; the astonishing participants in Frontiers of Memory; and Jeni Williams, who sent me several long e-mails that forced me to rethink my premises.

1 Augustine, *Confessions* 10. 8, trans. R.S. Pine-Coffin, Harmondsworth: Penguin, 1961, pp. 214–16.
2 The history of artificial memory systems from the ancient world to the Renaissance is a vast field. The best introductions to the practices of artificial memory, especially its use of space and image, are Frances Yates, *The Art of Memory*, Chicago: University of Chicago Press, 1966; Mary Carruthers, *The Book of Memory: A Study of Memory in Medieval Culture*, Cambridge: Cambridge University Press, 1990; and Lina Bolzoni, *La stanza della memoria: modelli letterari e iconografici nell'età della stampa*, Turin: Einaudi 1995, Eng. trans. *The Gallery of Memory: Literary and Iconographic Models in the Age of the Printing Press*, trans. Jeremy Parzen, Toronto: Toronto University Press, 2001.
3 On these two images of memory from Plato to Heidegger, largely confined to the philosophical tradition, see David Farrell Krell, *Of Memory, Reminiscence, and Writing: On the Verge*, Bloomington: Indiana University Press, 1990.
4 In addition to the modern accounts of Yates, Carruthers, and Bolzoni, the canonical sources for the art of memory are the pseudo-Ciceronian *De ratione dicendi (Rhetorica ad Herennium)*, trans. Harry Caplan, Cambridge, MA: Loeb Classical Library, 1964, and Cicero, *De oratore* II. lxxxvi. 351–7, as well as Augustine's *Confessions*, Book 10, and sections of Quintilian.
5 One counterexample is Jonathan Spence's *The Memory Palace of Matteo Ricci*, Harmondsworth: Penguin, 1984, which uses the 'memory palace' of a seventeenth-century Italian Jesuit missionary to China to organize Spence's own biographical researches. The result is a highly speculative but fascinating attempt to understand Ricci and his worlds from the inside out.
6 See, for instance, Augustine, op. cit., pp. 208–11, who locates his sense of himself firmly in his memories – whether they stem from his experience or not.
7 Recently, Richard Lanham has suggested that the modern paradigm of reading as *looking over and picking out* is, with the increase of various computer and textual media that emphasize the graphic elements of writing, being replaced by a paradigm of reading as *flying into*, somewhat as in a video game. This image seems very apt for describing the affectivity of a memory system as well.

8 For a reading of early modern aristocratic subjectivity in very similar terms, see Patricia Fumerton, *Cultural Aesthetics: Renaissance Literature and the Practice of Social Ornament*, Chicago: University of Chicago Press, 1991.

9 On chorography in general, see Richard Helgerson's chapter on mapping in *Forms of Nationhood: The Elizabethan Writing of England*, Chicago: University of Chicago Press, 1992, pp. 105–47; on Camden in particular, see William Herendeen, 'Wanton Discourse and the Engines of Time: William Camden – Historian Among the Poets-Historical,' in Maryanne Horowitz, Anne Cruz, and Wendy Furman (eds) *Renaissance Re-readings: Intertext and Context*, Urbana: University of Illinois Press, 1988, pp. 142–56. My citations of Camden's *Britannia* are to Philemon Holland's translation of 1610, London: George Bishop and John Norton.

10 Citations, preserving Spenser's archaizing spelling but typographically modernized, are from *The Faerie Queene*, ed. Thomas P. Roche, Harmondsworth: Penguin, 1978.

11 Cf. Judith H. Anderson, '"Myn auctour": Spenser's Enabling Fiction and Eumnestes' "immortal scrine,"' in George M. Logan and Gordon Teskey, *Unfolded Tales: Essays on Renaissance Romance*, pp. 16–31, Ithaca, NY: Cornell University Press, 1989, pp. 25–6, citing the Roman scholar Varro, who links *manere*, remain, and *monere*, warn, to both *memoria* and *monimentum*.

12 Nor is this (ab)usage confined to Spenser. One might almost observe that the quintessential early modern literary monument is defaced or otherwise rendered incommunicative.

13 There are twenty-five appearances of 'moniment' or any of its grammatical forms in the *Faerie Queene*; eight are contrafactual monuments and seven more are monuments of catastrophe or death.

14 See Anderson, op. cit., p. 17, on Spenser's use of the fiction of the literary tradition as 'recorded memory.'

15 Ibid., pp. 19–20.

16 Quotations from these two poems are taken from *The Oxford Authors: John Donne: Selections*, ed. John Carey, Oxford: Oxford University Press, 1990.

4

LOSS

Transmissions, recognitions, authorisations

Stephan Feuchtwang

When someone dies and their belongings are dispersed, those who remember them lose the familiar, home, places in which they habitually met. They had set up unconscious habits and previous times – the chair, the arrangement of table settings, the ashtray and vase on the mantelpiece that would be reminders of the ordinary times together have now gone. An ordinary death and an ordinary disposal of belongings destroys a great many prompts that might recall habitual conduct. This chapter is concerned with such loss, but on an extraordinary and a shared scale. It is also concerned with the other end of life, when attachments to maternal and paternal figures and domestic things have their greatest scope and significance – the immensity of corners and the potency of repeated, familiar things. What if that is lost, not just beyond recall as a mysterious hint, but denied by some destructive force? What does the survivor do to fill in that absence?

So, this chapter is concerned with loss of the props of memory that prompt recall. What stirs recall is an internal soliloquy or dialogue, or an external conversation, a story or a thing, a text, an image, a place or a person. Some things are there just to stir, such as a memorial. All these, including the last, compound what is remembered by the new memory of its recall, and so on. So recall must be distinguished from memory.[1] But it is not always possible to use the word 'recall'. My discussion will be concerned with and will refer to, 'props of memory', which stir a chain of recalling attached to an original memory trace. They are the materials for the transmission of recall. And they are constantly being changed or lost. I want to ask what is the relationship between an internal and an interpersonal transmission of such a loss on the one hand, and the conventions and institutions that commemorate loss on the other. I will argue that the relationship is one of recognition. I will first set out the conceptual parameters of my argument. The case studies that follow both concern the so-called Holocaust or Shoah. One case exemplifies the use of the Holocaust as a paradigm for recognition of catastrophic loss: the case of Binjamin Wilkomirski's childhood. The other indicates how that historical loss impinged on one person's conventional, orthodox Jewish mourning: the case of Leon Wieseltier.

Recognition of loss of recall

Loss of a prop of memory is incurred by the loss of any object of attachment. But this can be compounded. Freud includes among lost objects the loss of country and not just loss of loved and hated persons.[2] We can add removal, by forced dislocation or by destruction, of persons and of things that were themselves the props of memory: the familiar suppliers and prompters of anecdote, peoples and places, indoors and outdoors.

In such cases, grief and mourning are more likely to remain unfinished. Loss demands confirmation. A death ritual confirms and recognises whatever is the loss that mourners sense, and it does this by means of a convention and eschatology of departure and continuity. (By 'eschatology' I mean a more or less well-defined apprehension of what is beyond departure and loss of life). It can help to complete mourning without further need for recognition; but it may not be enough. Interpersonal or internal dialogue transmitting the sense of loss may demand further recognition, which can be an extension or a greater version of the first death ritual in another form of commemoration. Cases of devastating loss on a greater scale than can be recognised in death rituals have been unfortunately common; what is important here is that they have demanded other rituals than conventional mourning and ways of honouring the departed, other forms of commemoration and compensation, to give them authoritative recognition. The recognition of a loss that is the destruction or removal of most of the persons and extensions of memory for survivors must pose special problems for mourning and authority. When people also lose contact with their children, or are killed before they can transmit a sense of loss to their children, the child survivors suffer a loss even greater than the props of memory themselves. So orphaned child survivors, without their memory, must be the most acute case of loss (which can nevertheless be transmitted because of the mere fact of survival).

The demand for acknowledgement of such grievous loss and the assigning of a responsibility for it – from the grievance of the slave transports to the more recent dislocations and deportations that so many populations have suffered – is often a grievance described and treated in terms very like that of debt, something which needs redemption. Redemption here implies recovery by means of what is often a new status, that of acknowledged victim (which may also be religiously justified as deserved or fated). The victim gains through recognition a certain dignity; the ideal closure would be that now by due recognition the status of victim can itself be given up. But this ideal is frequently a cover for a defended grievance, a treasuring of the status of victim. Nostalgia for the irrecoverable and demand for its recognition create sites for the transmission of grievance, further demands for redemption and for a place in the world where what had been forgotten can be recreated.

Plainly there are two agencies involved in any relation of recognition. One is the agency of the seeker for recognition, using one or more modes and institutions for the transmission of loss. The other is a realiser of that demand, within the mode or institution in which the authority of recognition and its transmission

77

are vested. The authority of recognition includes a judgement that there has indeed been a loss that is worthy of recognition. There may be several such authorities, including objects and events (stories, myths, images) that have already been created and established to mark loss. They serve as screens for other senses of loss. Each has its own conditions of existence as an ordering practice, a kind of communication, or a way of entering into and being 'heard' (or 'seen') in a public space. Such objects or events screen a personal sense of loss. They prompt it but they transmit it in a standardised form. They make possible projection, transmission and recognition. But they have their own character and force that directs whatever is projected into them.[3]

This is even more true of those rituals or other procedures of recognition that contain a more explicit element of judgement. The authority of judgement of grievance can be either what is recorded and created as history, or what is treated as an eternal truth. It may be a supreme God, or it may be a cosmological process, a universal law, a natural law or simply a tradition of how things are. In any case it is policed by institutions with procedures of validation and verification. Recognition is a mirror-structure in which the griever and the personal grievance are magnified and focused by authority. But note that this is truly a mirror structure because it also works in the other direction, from authority to potential grief petitioner. That which authorises and recognises, itself demands recognition.

To put this in terms of the internal psychic processes that must be at play within the external conventions and institutions of recognition, there is a projection upon (and realisation of the projection in) an authorising institution or procedure and its symbolic objects. At the same time, there is an introjection of the desire of the object clothed in authority for its authority to be confirmed. Activation of the recognising institution realises this specular fantasy. Authority is characteristically singular and surrounded by ritual even if secular. The personal loss of the seeker for recognition is equally singular. But from the point of the authorising institution it is replicable and multiple. Singular authority is claimed for the grievous loss as a case of a shared condition, and then, as such, it too becomes singular and sacred.

This creates a drama. The demand to be authoritatively recognised is exacerbated by the threat of betrayal, by dilution or replication of the singularity of the great, shared loss. In this same drama, the recognising authority itself demands recognition and is also threatened by replication and betrayal. For instance, the Creator imperiously demands recognition by His creature, the Sovereign by his subject, the celestial by the human. In less monotheistic terms, the responsiveness of a deity is also a demand for respectful offerings and loyalty. In mundane institutions, recourse to the authority of law has its counterpart in the demand of the law to be remembered and the implied dread that it be ignored or mistaken. My point here is that the demand for authority is never securely located. This recognition structure, linking loss to judgement, will be explored in the two studies that follow.

The Holocaust as an historical icon of recognition: the case of Bruno Grosjean/Binjamin Wilkomirski and the tribunals of fact and fiction

Two kinds of loss exert an insistent pressure for recognition. One is a memory against which the subject defends itself, such as the shame of torture and debasement. The other is the confusion that results from the destruction of the props of memory. Often the two are suffered together. In the late 1990s, a curious drama involving the Holocaust and both these kinds of loss occupied pages of newspapers and magazines, and hours of television. What was at stake in this drama was the idea of the Holocaust both as a unique loss and as an icon of loss for the world, a template event by which loss can be recognised.

The case was that of the son of Yvonne Grosjean, a poor working woman in war-time, neutral Switzerland. She became pregnant after a transient affair. During pregnancy she was involved in a motor accident, which disfigured her face. She gave birth by caesarean to a boy whom she named Bruno, but she immediately put him into the care of the authority of the town of Biel and returned to work in a watch factory. Perhaps she was repeating her own history: she had been what was called an 'earning child', sold as child labour. In any case, what she did was to transmit something unbearable to her into a loss suffered by her son.

Four years later the boy was fostered, and twelve years after that he was legally adopted by foster parents, called Dössekker. The four years in care are undocumented, but they and the early years of fostering haunt the man. After a series of re-inventions of himself[4] he would say that, after liberation from a concentration camp, he was taken to a Jewish orphanage of child survivors in Krakow, and from there was taken to Switzerland by a Frau Grosz (note the shared syllable with Grosjean). He insists that he is Binjamin Wilkomirski, not Bruno Grosjean. Binjamin claims that Bruno is two years younger than him, another child adopted by the Dössekkers from the same orphanage in the town of Biel, switched soon after to other foster parents, who then emigrated to the United States.

These are the bare essentials of the disputable life story of a man who is celebrated because of the extraordinary book he began to write in 1984. That book, *Fragments*, was published in 1995.[5] It was widely acclaimed; it won the Jewish Book Council's prize for a 'memoir', and *The Jewish Quarterly* in 1997 awarded the book its prize for non-fiction. But by the late 1990s doubts were spreading. Gary Mokotoff, a member of the Council, wrote to the Council three days after the award expressing doubts about its authenticity, but his letter was ignored. As he later summarised his doubts, 'The facts did not add up. As a Jewish genealogist and student of the Holocaust, I knew that the book was historical fiction.'[6]

And Mokotoff was not the only one to doubt the historical veracity of Binjamin Wilkomirski's *Fragments*. In 1998 Daniel Ganzfried, another Swiss author, published a book of Holocaust fiction (*The Dispatcher*) and a Swiss cultural magazine commissioned him to write a long portrait of Wilkomirski. As he

pursued his research the portrait became an exposé, not suitable for the magazine, which had wanted something on the creative process of a man who bridged
writing and music (Wilkomirski is a clarinet maker). Instead it was published in a
weekly newspaper in August 1998. What Ganzfried exposed, through documentation from the town of Biel and elsewhere, was the strong likelihood that
Binjamin Wilkomirski is Bruno Grosjean. Although Yvonne Grosjean had died,
her brother was still alive. A DNA test could decide whether there was any relationship; when this was suggested to Bruno/Binjamin he refused. The following
year, 1999, the man who had had the fleeting affair with Bruno's mother Yvonne
emerged, to be filmed for a BBC1 television programme (*Inside Story*, 3 Nov.
1999). Photographs of himself and Bruno/Binjamin at about the same age show
remarkable similarities. Bruno/Binjamin again refused a DNA test to see
whether this man is indeed his father. He treats scientific attestations in the same
way as, in the 'Afterword' to *Fragments*, he looked upon documents: 'Legally
accredited truth is one thing – the truth of a life another' (p. 154).

The bare bones of Bruno/Binjamin's life as I have sketched them here are
drawn from two subsequent investigations which built on Ganzfried's. One was
carried out by Elena Lappin, editor of *The Jewish Quarterly*, and the other by the
investigative journalist Philip Gourevitch, editor of *Forward*, a Jewish New York
weekly, and regular writer for *The New Yorker*.[7] These investigations included
extensive interviews – not only with Bruno/Binjamin himself, but also with his
musician friends of former years, his ex-wives, his present partner, his close
friends and supporters. They act as tribunals of fact, trying to settle for themselves and their readers two questions. One is whether or not *Fragments* is
verifiable, to which they both answer 'no'. The other question is what makes
Wilkomirski so convinced and so convincing in person.

Elena Lappin, even after reading Ganzfried's exposé, writes that:

> Whenever he talked about the camps, I believed him. His anguish was
> so genuine. It was impossible that someone could fabricate such
> suffering simply to justify the claim of a book. I returned to my hotel
> [from a day talking to him and his partner in his home] exhausted and
> convinced that I had been in the presence of a witness to some of the
> worst horrors of this century's history.
>
> (p. 20)

But she nonetheless concludes that he had constructed an identity for himself,
starting at the age of 18 or before, with an accumulation of details from film
documentaries and a growing personal library and archive on the Holocaust.

Philip Gourevitch notes how Bruno/Binjamin tries to accommodate every
challenge. For instance, he responded immediately to Ganzfried's findings by
telling a Swiss reporter that 'It was always the free choice of the reader to read
my book as literature or to take it as a personal document. Nobody has to believe
me.' But like many others, Gourevitch is concerned that what claims to be testi-

80

mony should be verifiable fact. If it is not, it casts doubt on the testimonies of survivors, and can be used against the documented truth of the Holocaust painstakingly built up by lifelong archival authenticators. It dilutes the authority of the historical recognition of their loss. In other words, his concern with the veracity of *Fragments* is part of a larger concern with the empirical truth of the Holocaust itself.

The issue of verifiable fact, including the facts of Bruno/Binjamin's body and its DNA, is inescapable. It nags beyond the truths of rhetoric and genre that any narrative also tells. We have here two narratives. On the one hand, the Swiss musician who wrote *Fragments* finds in 'the Holocaust' a recognisable past out of which he can write the years of his early childhood, in which he experienced something undisclosable.[8] The Holocaust is his authentification. On the other hand, Ganzfried, the first of those who exposed *Fragments* as fake, published a book in the same year as fiction even though it is based on what he had recorded for many hours: his father's memories of surviving Auschwitz.

Every book is an externalisation – a product bound to its writer, but outside and twice removed. In it and in its reception by others the author can recognise a self construed as its maker. That much is as true of a fiction as it is of a non-fiction. The author's self is more or less attached to the product according to whether it bears the same name as that by which he or she is identified in everyday life, and according to the extent to which he or she has produced it as a self-portrait. For Bruno/Binjamin it is a named self-portrait, since he calls himself Binjamin Wilkomirski in everyday life. His attachment to the name is authenticated by the extent to which the book as an independent object is recognised by others as the author's life as well as his creation, all the more so when it is non-fiction. As for fiction, the reader appreciates the work, reads it as a potential author or puts herself into its stories, or does both, and appraises it accordingly. For each reader it is a singular and moving account. For the writer each such reader is multiplied into a singular Public of her creation. Wilkomirski's book is about a child with that name who passes through scarcely experienced and barely understood horrors. Whether it be fact or fiction, a reader is invited to imagine how must it have been to go through such experiences, block them away and, much later, be enabled to recall them, and to ask how well this writing conveys a small child's view.[9]

A reader brings to a book empathy, with the named subject of the book or with the creative skill and imagination of the author; both are mobilised in the play of recognition. Elena Lappin draws attention to what such empathy is to the man who names himself Wilkomirski, to his need for a truth whatever the documents, to his lack of circumcision and to his refusal to take DNA tests, and suggests that the acceptance of *Fragments* for publication was for Wilkomirski a proof of his identity (p. 60).[10] Documentation and empirical verifiability are necessary for the reconstruction of this truth; yet for Wilkomirski they are incidental. As with religious faith and theological truth, times and locations are incidental, even while the facticity of incident is necessary to them.

The subject is in a mortal time and space which is also the location and occasion of other people's truth, and therefore contestable. Its adjudication is the profession of historians and of investigative journalists such as Ganzfried, Lappin and Gourevitch. Wilkomirski preserves the recognition he seeks by admitting it could be fallible, by professing a higher and more experiential truth, yet he also re-remembers every adaptive detail of circumstantial information he must absorb to sustain it. The Holocaust is a sacred truth, authenticated by circumstantial fact, both for him and for his detractors. It provides Bruno/Binjamin with something he would otherwise deeply miss, recognition of loss and devastation, even if it is not identical with the loss his memoir depicts.

In the opposite direction of recognition, others are prepared to overlook the boundary between fiction and non-fiction and feel recognised by what he has written. Israel Gutman, for example, was an historian at the Yad Vashem in Jerusalem, consulted by Lappin. Like other Jewish historians of the Holocaust, he is committed never to allow it to be forgotten, constantly to battle against its trivialisation, making it something recalled beyond the Jewish world. Gutman is a survivor of the Warsaw ghetto, a setting of childhood that Wilkomirski later rejected. He is also a survivor of the death camps Majdanek and Auschwitz, both of which Wilkomirski had identified as the camps he had survived (though Gutman was older, in his late teens, and so capable of remembering more circumstantial information). Gutman's comment on *Fragments* was:

> It has to be checked very thoroughly but – I don't think it's that important. Wilkomirski has written a story which he has experienced deeply, that's for sure. So that, even if he is not Jewish, the fact that he was so deeply affected by the Holocaust is of huge importance.[11]

Gutman, in short, is gratified by so intense a recognition of the truth of the Holocaust through which he lived, although he doubts the veracity of Wilkomirski's memoir.[12] *Fragments* is for him a welcome additional recognition of his own loss and wounds. So here we have another side to this play of recognition and authentification: a deeply empathic fiction for the survivor.

Gourevitch is surely right that in this time of remaining witnesses, Wilkomirski's book lent a voice to the predicament of those who survived as children, the great majority without a clear identity (p. 55). But despite the obvious importance of empathy to the lost and their survivors, and Wilkomirski's own care about the facts of the Holocaust, for Gourevitch Wilkomirski has usurped its sanctity: 'Instead of persuading others of his memories, Wilkomirski was now allowing himself to be persuaded by others' (p. 66). I agree that Wilkomirski has invited survivors and those who suffered catastrophic loss to adopt him and 'allowed' them to make him one of them. But I would qualify the condemnation. For Bruno/Binjamin the Holocaust is an icon of his unremembered childhood, in which he can recognise himself and be recognised. He is not the only one. The use of the Holocaust as an icon of loss has become a widespread phenomenon through the very efforts of its historians, and their determination never to let anyone forget or deny this abominable catastrophe.

Survivors object to this dilution of the singularity of their experience. They have reason for refusing to accept Wilkomirski's book even when published as fiction, since some have chosen to publish their own testimonies, or as in Ganzfried's case the testimony of his father, in the same category. How could they accept Wilkomirski's fiction when for them 'fiction' has itself become something which can be claimed to be authentic or not? Ann Charney wrote to *The New Yorker* (19 July 1999) after reading Gourevitch's article about Wilkomirski. She had decided to place *Dobryd*, her account of her survival as a child in Nazi-occupied Poland, in the category of fiction. Her German publisher – also the publisher of the original *Fragments* (*Bruchstücke*) – had pointed out that her book would sell much better as non-fiction, but she had conscientiously not accepted the suggestion because she 'did not trust the factual accuracy of my recollections'. Furious, she writes that 'Wilkomirski's success in impersonating a Holocaust survivor confirms my suspicions about the increasingly rapacious nature of the Holocaust industry.' She ends her letter with an attack that hints at the devaluation of her own memories: 'Wilkomirski may have invented a new genre, which could attract other practitioners: impersonators more real than the real thing, who thrive as devoted fetishists of suffering.' For her, the investigations of Gourevitch are important. They make verifiable fact a critical issue, for both fact and fiction. What is at stake for her and other child survivors is adequate recognition of the powerful but forgotten or obscurely recalled memories of surviving catastrophe, a catastrophe that destroyed almost all the props of memory, most importantly the parents and close family upon whom children rely for memories of themselves. But then, that is also what Bruno Grosjean lost.

What determines the decision of someone like Ann Charney to write fiction while at the same time making sure it is known she is a survivor? One determining factor must be the props of memory available to the writer, by which she or he has been able to identify a childhood, a subsequent self in one direction and its prehistory in the other. In either case, for each the writing is an externalisation that reflects back, more or less personally, more or less as a general context within which they or their losses and memories are recognised by others. Publication in an impersonal mode of transmission presents recognition of truth back to them. The empathy of others (unlikely to be victims of the same trauma) is the recognising authority of the loss transmitted.

The man who now insists he is Benjamin Wilkomirski has brought a past out of the empty years of his earliest childhood in which he can recognise himself. But the ghost named Bruno Grosjean haunts those years. Factual investigations, which save the historical recognition of victims and survivors, bring the ghost back to his life. Wilkomirski's own agent has had to commission an investigation, the result of which is to show that Wilkomirski's book is an uncannily empathic fiction.[13]

The work of tracing the authenticity of Holocaust writing will not end. It will be checked and doubted and checked. The authenticity of fiction is a challenge both to the imagination and to the tribunal of evidential fact.[14] It has the potential to stand as a work of reminder, like a modern myth – itself an icon by which others can share a horror and a loss, beyond the circumstantial detail. But circumstantial detail and historical authenticity are nevertheless necessary to the authority of modern myth.

Mourning and justice: the kaddish of Leon Wieseltier

Like myth, death and death rituals invariably bring to mind a time and its rhythm beyond the span and chronology of a life, against which to relate events. It is a time inhabited by an imagery of angels, monsters or demons, ghosts or shades, and supreme gods who are figures of ultimate justice and universal recognition; a time in which the righteous are freed and sinners are imprisoned. Death is the moment of access not only to the bliss of the deserving and the punishment of wrong-doers, but also of intercession for something beyond justice: mercy, which is the supplement of justice, where angels of passion and mediation take over from logic and rule.

In *Kaddish*, his journal of reading and reflection on the rite of the mourning kaddish he performed daily for the year of grieving the death of his father, Leon Wieseltier makes the very interesting (for my purposes) observation that the mourner's kaddish is still a kaddish, which is simply a song in praise of God and divine justice.[15] Its praise of the Creator, the Ancient of Days, is a justification of the creation of both good and evil. Praise is offered as atonement for disobedience. It brings a blessing on the dead but it does not refer to them, let alone name the one who is mourned.

There is an intriguing interplay between the eternity of justice and the necessity of history in the justification of evil. Nahmanides, an inspiration for Wieseltier, who refers to him as the thirteenth-century genius of Spanish Jewry, wrote that 'man in the absence of the evil impulse would not build a house and take a wife and sire sons and daughters' (p. 13). In other words, the creation of evil is the creation of the possibility of being in the world, in its shade and so also in its light. By praising evil as well as good in Creation we learn to accept what happens to us as justice. In this religion sin is not to live in the service and praise of the Creator. In the projected eyes of the eternal, sin is why we live in a secular history, cast out from but hoping to re-enter eternity. But this is not all. Between history and eternity, a third time is instituted, the messianic time of ultimate judgement and redemption of the loss of bliss and timelessness. In Judaic and other religions this third, historic time is conceived in the grandest terms, of aeons and kalpas, and in the contrasts of utopian hope and dystopian realism.

Every death individuates messianic time in speculation upon a soul's passage through torture or limbo between history and eternity. In this third time the Creator can be persuaded to show mercy to sinners by angels expounding to him the meaning of the law of his word. The earliest authority Wieseltier finds for this is an eighth-century work of exegesis of the letters of the Hebrew alphabet, attributed to Rabbi Akiva. As Wieseltier informs us, in Isaiah it is written 'Open ye the gates, that the righteous nation which keepeth the truth may enter in.' 'Truth' in Hebrew is a pun, whose other meaning is 'amens', and amens are another praise of the Lord. Now one of the righteous listening to God in the Garden of Eden sings so resoundingly that the wicked in the darkness of limbo on the other side of its gates hear and respond to the exhortations to say amen. Thus they punctuate the kaddish. They also sing out the passage from Isaiah. God hears them and the angels by his side persuade Him that the pun allows Him to hear what has become a plea and to release them for a time on the Sabbath (pp. 13–14 and 36–9). By learned Talmudic argument, mercy overrides justice within strict time limits. Singular authority is replicated and counter-manded by the very word of authority.[16]

Other religions contain other, more definite and elaborate images of heaven and hell, of merciful intercession for sinners and for their release from hell and justice. But the spread of images of justice and mercy, the two kinds of all-seeing all-hearing recognition, is amazing. They are to be found in the death rituals of Buddhism, Daoism, and Christianity, as well as Judaism and Islam. Messianic time in them all is both a return and a future, an ultimate historic event of apocalypse and judgement leading to a return to bliss. At the level of the individual soul, however, it is pictured as a passage through judgement to paradise or hell.

For mourners, death rituals contain memories of the dead, and of further and more catastrophic scales of loss, which are historical events. How do the two registers, of eternal justice and of historical event and personal loss, interact? Do they fuse in the third time of law and apocalypse? Wieseltier keeps an engagement to give a speech at the Washington Holocaust Museum. His father's childhood home was destroyed in the Nazi onslaught. He wants to honour the engagement but also not to waver in his duty to say the kaddish for his father every day, three times. Friends arrange a prayer forum to gather in the museum's atrium in the evening, before his speech. The words of praise 'fly past the glass on which the name of his burned birthplace in Poland is carved, and drift into the halls that show the pictures of what was done to his world; and the syllables of my father's kaddish cling to those images like spit' (pp. 16–17). The two regis-ters of the kaddish and the museum concatenate, but they do not merge. The museum is a historical recognition of evil; the kaddish is an act of personal and collective recognition of duty and authority in the image of a just God. Without asking him, it is not possible to say how Leon Wieseltier related the two. But it is apparent from his book that the museum was incidental. Shul (his preferred designation for what others call synagogue) and the ritual of the mourner's kaddish were the cherished and sufficient authorities for mourning the loss of his father. Yet the intense reading he undertakes in his researches about the mourner's kaddish places the eternal in a historical context. He learns that this liturgical custom only started after the Crusades. 'This cannot have been a coin-cidence' he writes. 'The Crusades provoked the first major attempt to exterminate an entire Jewry in Europe. It failed but it left many, many mourners in its wake' (p. 81).

Eternity in turn registers and recognises history. Liturgy and rite carry the aura of tradition and therefore of temporal indeterminacy. In this case the aura can be found in the third time of ultimate judgement and mercy. Medieval European Jewish liturgy absorbed history, each event being a repetition of what was and an anticipation of what will be, awaiting deliverance. A pogrom in Poland in 1648 was commemorated with the penitential prayer composed for a twelfth-century slaughter of Jews in France. In the words of the Polish rabbinic leader: 'what has occurred now is similar to the persecutions of old, and all that happened to the forefathers has happened to their descendants'.[17]

Liturgical and historical recognition are different and often opposed things. Nevertheless, the historiography of loss, the recordings and writings of witnesses of desecration, museums of Judaic ritual instruments, clothing and other remnants of the life of destroyed Jewish communities, are vital registers and recognitions of loss even for the most religious of Jews. The two registers do not fuse, but they do supplement each other. Eternity absorbs history as Law. History absorbs eternity as memorial and the justice of verification.

Promises of closure

Funerals of the veterans of catastrophes of loss demand an addition to the usual rites, a marking of the more general loss and membership of that common loss. Such markers are added to the liturgy, either in the mode of eternal judgement, as in the case of the kaddish, or in a mode of commemoration as in Holocaust memorials, or war memorials. Death rituals and historic commemoration both contain a sanctified imagery of justice and truth, each compensating for the other's inadequacy: the inadequacy of eternal justice to historic atrocity, the inadequacy of historical knowledge to prevent enormities of injustice and to recognise personal loss.

The search for recognition of irrecoverable loss is all of three things: evidential, symbolic, and a search for justice, if only the justice of being recognised as a victim. Further, it seems that justice for victims is a setting of the world to rights. It can be by revenge, the switching of humiliation into victorious pride, or it can be by an angelic mediation.

Like fictional or biographical narrative, legal judgement too attempts closure after the event, while liturgy turns that narrative into an eternal truth. Fiction, biography, history, legal judgement and liturgy turn chance into story, good and evil into design. They create figures by which loss, confusion and the unacceptable intrusion and contradiction of chance are recognised as destiny. Destiny is also the recognition, or validation, of the triumphant victim. But the interventions of evidential authentication, in establishing the verisimilitude of a fiction and the truth of a history, are like the procedures of a legal court, regulated and determinate. As procedures and devices of proof, their objectivity stands in contrast to the passions of the desire for recognition and judgement that shine through them. The closure of a performance of recognition for the professionals of the institutions of recognition (audiences, actors, priests, lawyers, judges, journalists, historians and publishers) more often than not blurs into many similar performances. But for the moved and mobilising operator (whether reader or writer, performer or audience) for whom it is an act of recognition, it becomes a vivid memory. It encapsulates but at the same time heightens what required recognition, so that it becomes a significant object of a past for the schema of the world held in mind. Closure enlivens recall. Yet at the same time it threatens, makes it vulnerable to challenges of fact and reinterpretation, which are its duplicates in other operators of the same or a similar icon of recognition. Even more so when that loss is massive and therefore shared.

When the icon of recognition is an event it is vulnerable to factual revision and reinterpretation, threatening its sanctity as a container, enclosing countless recognitions of loss. When it is an eternal singularity (God, an immortal hero, a saint, a totem) there are tribunals of belonging and faith that police the containers of recognition and say who can enter its light. But they can and do multiply into sectarian rivals. Each promise of closure bears the threat of betrayal. But that is the chance of further mediation by some more inclusive, external authority. And so it goes on.

Notes

1 Maurice Bloch, *How We Think They Think: Anthropological Approaches to Cognition, Memory, and Literacy*, Boulder, CO: Westview Press, 1998, pp. 118–19.

2 Sigmund Freud, 'Mourning and Melancholia', trans. Ernest Jones, Standard Edition, vol. 14, London: The Hogarth Press and the Institute of Psycho-Analysis, 1957.

3 Alfred Gell argues that created objects work as agents by prompting a cognitive operation that implies agency – they are understood both as the outcome and as an instrument of social agency. Their form and style, their differentiation from other objects, channel the inference of agency and the way they command a response. The mental operation involved does not have a narrative structure. It is a schema into which any one object is placed in relation to other objects and persons. One of his examples is the exchange of valuables in the Kula ring, whose operators:

> must be able to comprehend the manifold and inordinately complex field of exchanges and evaluate their outcomes .... His mind, in other words, must work as a simulation device – and this indeed is what all minds do, more or less – presenting a synoptic view of the totality of Kula transactions [or of any other totality], past, present and to come.... his mind has become coextensive with that world. He has internalized its causal texture as part of his being as a person and as an independent agent ... and – not to put too fine a point on it – something like godhead is achievable. This (relative) divinization through the fusing together of an expanded, objectified agency, and the myriad causal texture of the real world seems to me to be the ultimate objective of the Kula.
>
> (*Art and Agency: An Anthropological Theory*, Oxford: Clarendon Press, 1998, p. 231)

4 By the time he was eighteen years old he was telling a girl friend, a fellow musician with whom he had taken Christian confirmation lessons, that he was a child of the

Holocaust from the Baltic states. In one of the television interviews broadcast in the 1990s, she says that when she confronted him, telling him that he was just showing off and looking for attention, he admitted it was a lie. But he persisted. He complained to close friends that his cold adopting parents wanted him as a medical experiment, that they were neo-Nazis fascinated with having at their disposal a child who had been experimented upon by the famous Dr Mengele in Auschwitz. A few years later he was claiming to be a Jew with the family name of Wilkomirski, who was saved from the Nazis by a Swiss nanny, and that he had been in the Warsaw ghetto. He also claimed to have been an agent of Mossad, the Israeli secret service.

5 Binjamin Wilkomirski, *Fragments: Memories of a Childhood 1939–1948*, New York: Schocken, 1996, London: Picador, 1997.

6 Elena Lappin, 'The Man with Two Heads', *Granta*, 66, 1999, p. 49.

7 Philip Gourevitch, 'The Memory Thief', *The New Yorker* 14 June 1999, pp. 48–68.

8 Bruno Grosjean's father speculates about the effect of his womb experience when his mother was in the car accident. René Aeberhard, the older adopted son of the foster parents of Bruno Grosjean, wonders about the terrible fits of rage by his foster-mother which led to René successfully begging the authorities to take Bruno away from her (BBC1, *Inside Story*, 3 November 1999).

9 I, among hundreds of thousands of readers, imagined *Fragments* to be a revelation of a child's perspective on being the accidental and bewildered survivor of deprivation and lethal brutality. We read it as experiential testimony. But if we had not thought it was testimony, if we thought it was fiction, would we have asked questions about reconstruction more sharply? Ganzfried and others who did suspect it was fiction comment on the unlikelihood of episodes such as Wilkomirski's having been able to survive the cracking open of his head, when flung against a wall by a guard. More tellingly, he notes how the sharpness of what Wilkomirski claims to be his photographic memory is like a cinematic screenplay, supplying ghoulish details of extreme violence and horror, quite unlike survivor testimonies which leave such things unspoken because to bring up the memory would be intolerable (BBC1, *Inside Story*, 3 November 1999). As strangers to the experience, when we read what purports to be testimony are we not over-willing to suspend disbelief, even to indulge the ghoulish? On the other hand, the closest textual analysis finds that he has reproduced features of how child survivors recount severe trauma so accurately that they could simply be the transposition of an actual experience of another trauma on to 'the Holocaust'. I am most grateful to Sue Vice of Sheffield University, for showing me a draft of her own close textual analysis that makes this point.

10 To the accolades he has received because of his book must be added recognition by an old Israeli rabbi that Binjamin is the son he had lost in the Holocaust, despite a DNA test that proved this was impossible. All this has allowed Wilkomirski to be persuaded into the identity that he has desired with such dedication and faith. The physiognomic changes his head and face have undergone in the process are equally remarkable, from a wavy haired and sporting young man looking straight out of photographs he acknowledges to be of himself, to his older curly hair and downcast look.

11 Lappin, op. cit., p. 46.

12 Wilkomirski (Chapter 14) claims to have been in Auschwitz but hidden by women. In Israel Gutman's account:

> everybody had to be counted at roll call. If the roll call wasn't exact, you could stand all night in the cold, until they found the person somewhere in the barrack, or someone fell. But it was also forbidden to have one extra. The problem is not just how he survived or managed day to day – the problem is: how did he breathe?
>
> (Lappin, op. cit., p. 47)

13 *The Guardian, G2*, 15 October 1999, pp. 2–3.

14 Consider this other example, the reverse of *Fragments*. *Yosl Rakover Talks to God* started as a Yiddish story, a construction of an address to God written and hidden as his last act by one of the fighters in the ruins of the Warsaw ghetto. It was soon accepted as fact. More, its meditative profundity merited inclusion in US Jewish prayer books. When Zvi Kolitz claimed he was its author and that it was a fiction, he, not it, was denounced as a fraud. Then, in the 1990s its authenticity was questioned, its author traced, and the story of the story published alongside a new translation of the original (Zvi Kolitz, *Yosl Rakover Talks to God*, London: Jonathan Cape 1999).

15 Leon Wieseltier, *Kaddish*, New York: Knopf, London: Picador, 1999.

16 Wieseltier also finds the extraordinary story of a first-century dispute between two rabbis. One of them received the miracle of the Divine Voice, placing authority on his decision. But Divine authority was withdrawn when the other rabbi asserted 'Since the Torah [the written law] has already been given at Mountain Sinai, we pay no heed to a Divine Voice.' Hearing this 'God smiled and said: "my sons have defeated Me, my sons have defeated Me"' (Wieseltier, op. cit., p. 107).

17 Yosef Yerushalmi, *Zakhor: Jewish History and Jewish Memory*, Seattle and London: University of Washington Press, 1996, p. 50.

Part III

WHAT MEMORY FORGETS: MODELS OF THE MIND

Introduction

Susannah Radstone and Katharine Hodgkin

The chapters in this section are both psychoanalytic in perspective, and focus on the rise to dominance of particular understandings of memory within psychology and the social sciences. Both argue that the influence of these understandings of memory has prompted important but unwelcome moves away from the psychoanalytic theories that they each seek to defend. For Antze and Papoulias, psychoanalysis reveals that the core of the mind – its 'centre of gravity', to use Paul Antze's phrase – lies outside consciousness. For both, this idea of an 'otherness' within – an otherness inassimilable to consciousness – is the radical insight of psychoanalysis. Both contributors suggest that this radical and enriching psychoanalytic idea is domesticated by the particular configurations of mind and memory that they each seek to challenge.

Paul Antze's essay discusses the centrality of the idea of learnt, procedural, non-representational memory to a field of psychology known as neuro-cognitivism and explains why this foregrounding of procedural memory is finding favour within certain strands of contemporary psychoanalysis. Tina Papoulias focuses on developments within the social sciences, where a strong tendency now views memory as material social practice rather than as mental faculty. Both these chapters focus on a turn from seeing memory as primarily individual and private, to seeing it as produced *through* intersubjective relations.

Both Antze and Papoulias mount defences of Freudian or post-Freudian psychoanalysis and offer critiques of (related) theoretical turns, on the basis that the understandings of psychic life that they produce offer more reductive and less radical accounts than those of the theories that they revise. Paul Antze contrasts neuro-cognitivism's approach to memory with Freud's own writings on memory, while Constantina Papoulias contrasts approaches to memory as social

practice within the social sciences with the work of the post-Freudian psychoanalyst Jean Laplanche, whose writings also discuss the social dimensions of
psychic life.

One response to the recent loss of faith in psychoanalysis has been the attempt
to anchor psychoanalytic theory more firmly in science. Thus a new branch of
psychoanalytic theory has developed: neuro-psychoanalysis. The psychological
ideas that inform this new theory, explains Antze, are mainly concerned with
memory, but, he goes on to argue, the account of memory that they offer is
incompatible with what he sees as the most valuable insights offered by Freud.
According to neuro-cognitivism, the psychological theory that informs neuro-
psychoanalysis, memory operates in two registers: declarative and procedural
memory. Whereas declarative memory is concerned with the remembrance of
specific events, people and the like, procedural memory refers to the learning of
skills and habits, such as walking or bike-riding, for instance. Antze foregrounds
the crucial difference between these two types of memory. For neuro-cognitivists,
only declarative memory has recourse to symbols and representation; procedural
memory is encoded directly into neural programmes, by-passing symbolic or
representational mental systems. And, importantly, they classify emotional
patterns as procedural. Neuro-cognitivists believe that, like walking or riding a
bike, the emotional habits and patterns of the child's earliest social relations are
also encoded directly into neural systems. Neuro-psychoanalysis seeks to find
ways, then, of re-coding these neural systems so that new and less pathological
relational habits may be learned.

Antze's central argument is that, in making procedural memory central to an
understanding of psychic life, neuro-psychoanalysis abandons psychoanalysis's
crucial understanding of the place of systems of representation and symbolisa-
tion within psychical life. This leaves neuro-psychoanalysis unable to address the
question of the mechanisms involved in 'translating' early learned habits into
adult contexts. The theory of neural encoding cannot explain, argues Antze,
how it is that a person might behave towards their boss, for instance, *as though* he
were their father. It is only by means of symbolic relations that this transference
between one context and another can be grasped. 'While proceduralists seem to
miss the implicit role of symbols in mediating different settings', concludes
Antze, 'this was absolutely central to Freud' (p. 100).

Antze continues by arguing that, although memory and forgetting occupy
pivotal positions in Freud's writings, on closer inspection, analysis turns out to
seek not actual memories of the past, but a set of 'scenes' which shape dreams
and the sense that is made of waking life. These 'scenes' constitute that inherent
'otherness' of the self emphasised, Antze reminds us, in the psychoanalyst Jean
Laplanche's revision of Freud. Though these 'scenes' are related to infantile life,
they are not memories as such, indeed their relation to memory may be highly
mediated. The force of these 'scenes' derives, in fact, from the *desire* that they
represent. In analysis, argues Antze, the patient is encouraged to trace the
metaphorical associations between dreams, for instance, and these formative

'scenes'. The relationship between these 'scenes' and the dreams and apprehensions of the present are best understood, then, as *metaphorical*.

For Antze these 'scenes', loaded with desire, are metaphorical structures which can be apprehended through the careful analysis of the ways in which dreams transform daily life. These scenes, which may have only the most tenuous relation to actual memories, are both alien to the self and yet form the core of that self. For Antze, psychoanalysis delivers this radical insight that at the core of the self are these metaphorical structures, these 'scenes', which make their presence felt through condensations and displacements but which cannot be directly apprehended. New developments in psychoanalysis would have it that memories are simply encoded into neural systems, by-passing systems of representation. Antze argues that, by taking this turn, this 'new' psychoanalysis forgets what psychoanalysis has previously offered: a rich and complex view of a self driven by desire, a self whose centre of gravity lies 'elsewhere', only traceable through the labyrinths of metaphor and symbol.

Paul Antze's critique of neuro-psychoanalysis deploys a depth model of the psyche. Unlike neuro-cognitivism, which stresses the encoding of memories into neural systems, Antze's reading of Freudian psychoanalysis delivers a model of the mind in which buried 'scenes' – 'scenes' from elsewhere – make their hidden presence felt. As Tony Bennett argues in this volume, this 'depth' model of the mind had its origins in those nineteenth-century regimes of memory which *also* delivered the model of 'organicist' memory to which contemporary theories of neural encoding are related. Antze's chapter can be read, then, as a call to revise rather than abandon this earlier regime of memory.

As the general introduction to this volume showed, the figure of the buried city was central to Freud's attempt to model an 'elsewhere' of the mind. Although Freud talked of this 'elsewhere' in terms of preserved memory-traces, Paul Antze suggests that this 'elsewhere' or 'otherness' of the self is better thought of as a set of scenes – scenes that are inextricably bound up with desire and that constitute a driving force within the self. Like Antze, Constantina Papoulias also refers back to Freud's metaphor of the buried city, and seeks to remind us of psychoanalysis's radical emphasis on the mind's otherness to itself. Like Antze, Papoulias suggests that current understandings of memory domesticate this radical idea. Unlike Antze, however, for whom Laplanchian psychoanalytic theory constitutes a mere staging-post on a journey back to Freud himself, Laplanchian psychoanalysis lies at the centre of Papoulias's argument.

Papoulias takes as her starting point theories of social, collective or cultural memory that are currently being deployed in cultural studies, sociology and political science. As Papoulias explains, these new theories of social memory are part of the 'turn to practice' in the social sciences – a turn which seeks to replace the fixity and reification of structures with the fluidity, provisionality and contingency of practices. At the heart of these new approaches to memory lies an overturning of the idea of memory as mental faculty by the idea that memory is constituted through material social practices that are passed between subjects.

Borrowing from Geertz, then, Papoulias argues that in these new theories of intersubjective practice, the guiding metaphor becomes not Freud's (buried) city of the individual unconscious, but the market-place of intersubjective exchange.

Papoulias's central argument is that these theories of memory as material social practice *appear* to destabilise the sovereignty of the possessive individual. Yet Papoulias argues that this de-stabilisation is, in her terms, 'more imaginary than real', since theories of memory as social practice approach the question of individual memory as the sedimentations of material social practices while forgetting that radical psychoanalytic insight concerning the 'estrangement' of the self from itself that is the theme of Paul Antze's chapter. Papoulias then goes on to argue that Freudian psychoanalysis's emphasis on the fixed structures of Oedipus and castration render it inassimilable to social theory's 'turn to practice'. However, she points out that a wish to move beyond psychoanalytic 'structuralism' and towards an understanding of the intersubjective and histori-cally specific dimensions of psychical life lies at the heart of the work of the French psychoanalyst Jean Laplanche. The core of Papoulias's chapter, then, turns on the central incompatibility between the psychoanalytic theories of Jean Laplanche and psychological theories of memory as intersubjective practice.

Papoulias reminds us that in the 'turn to practice', the unconscious becomes aligned with memory as the sedimentation of daily gestures, habits, practices. Yet as Papoulias goes on to explain, for Jean Laplanche, the unconscious *is not* memory. For Laplanche, rather, the unconscious is formed from the detritus, or waste-products of social exchange – those enigmatic messages that cling to everyday gestures due to their being suffused by untranslatable, incomprehen-sible desire. The combination of the theoretical turns both to memory and to practice delivers a view of the psyche as an effect of the social practices of memory. But the 'untranslatable' elements, which come from the other, line all social exchange, argues Papoulias, and render any account of the psyche as an effect of social memory utterly inadequate.

For both Papoulias and Antze, then, the focus falls on the over-centrality of memory to current theorisations of intersubjective relations and to understand-ings of the inner world. They both argue that the current centrality accorded to memory in contemporary understandings of the self and of social relations excises an understanding of the subject's inherent otherness to itself. For Papoulias and for Antze, the key insight of psychoanalysis is that the subject is not sovereign, is not 'self-determining' in any straightforward sense. Rather, the subject's core and drive remains other to itself. Whether this otherness is under-stood in terms of unconscious 'scenes' that shape the inner world's transformations of daily life, or of the untranslatable waste-products of social exchange, this otherness is both inaccessible to ordinary consciousness and is inextricably associated with desire.

Taken together, Antze and Papoulias offer a far-reaching critique of those regimes of memory that are currently being embraced within the social sciences. Understandings of memory that foreground its intersubjectivity and its sociality and that shift from a structuralist to a practice-oriented perspective are currently being heralded as radical in their de-stabilisation of sovereign subjectivity. Yet Antze and Papoulias both suggest that this de-stabilisation is illusory and remind us of the radical yet currently marginalised psychoanalytic insight concerning the inherent otherness of the subject to itself. In the general introduction, we discussed the history of the relation between regimes of memory and regimes of subjectivity. Regimes of memory have foundered, we argued, on the rocks of the individual/social relation. The new perspectives discussed here by Antze and Papoulias constitute a wholesale swing towards locating memory *within* social relations. Yet this swing leaves us with a question concerning the politics of these regimes of memory: why might it be that these apparently radical regimes of memory turn their backs on unruliness, on desire, on an otherness within? And how might these domesticating turns be contextualised and understood?

5

THE OTHER INSIDE

Memory as metaphor in psychoanalysis

Paul Antze

Psychoanalysis is often credited with giving us a new understanding of memory. For most of us, however, this understanding is less a clear doctrine than a halo of loosely connected ideas, all identified with Freud: memory traces never leave the mind. Painful memories can be put out of consciousness or repressed. Repressed memories, rooted in the traumas and sexual conflicts of early infancy, remain active forces in adulthood, shaping our personalities and returning sometimes to inflict neurotic suffering. Analytic therapy can relieve this suffering by getting to the truth of what was repressed, freeing us to lead happier and more productive lives. These notions are all so familiar that it is easy to lose sight of their strangeness. As Ian Hacking has noted, they reflect an assumption that is 'dazzling in its implausibility: the idea that what has been forgotten is what forms our character, our personality, our soul'.[1] And yet it would be fair to say that these notions or something like them have been elements in an unspoken faith shared by educated Westerners through much of the twentieth century.

Today, at least in the English-speaking world, that faith is in full retreat. Over the past thirty years, psychoanalysis has moved from the centre to the margins of medical psychiatry, edged out by tightly focused 'brief therapies' and a new generation of mood-altering drugs.[2] This same period has seen a wide-ranging intellectual attack on the methods and assumptions of analysis that may be even more damaging in the long run. On the one hand philosophers and academic psychologists have made a new and more forceful case for some of the best-known objections to analysis – that its treatment remains unproven, that its elaborate metapsychology is more mythology than science, that its supposed discoveries are often untestable or palpably false.[3] On the other hand, revisionist historians have raised serious doubts about Freud's own credibility as a researcher. They point out, for example, that he was not averse to claiming cures where none had occurred and to substituting his own speculations about patients for what they actually told him.[4]

Much of this recent critical work bears directly on psychoanalytic teachings about memory. At the most general level, critics have pointed out that empirical research on memory does not begin to support Freud's postulated storehouse of permanent 'mental traces'. On the contrary, what emerges from this work is an understanding of memory as something more like a faculty for imaginative reconstruction, one that relies heavily on contextual cues as it patches together an untidy collection of scenes.[5] They also argue that evidence for repressed memories of any kind is at best weak and equivocal, and that research on traumatic memories has shown that they are far more likely to return intrusively than to quietly slip away.[6] At the same time, a sizeable literature has emerged on the powerful role played by persuasion and expectations in all forms of therapy, raising serious doubts about free association as a way of getting at some unknown prior truth lodged in the patient's memory.[7] Finally, as the philosopher Adolf Grunbaum has tirelessly argued, analysts have as yet produced no evidence that their interpretations succeed by bringing previously unconscious memories into consciousness or by accurately reconstructing earlier events or attitudes in their patients' lives.[8]

Analysts troubled by these developments have responded in two very different ways. One group has turned away from Freud's scientific claims to embrace a wide-ranging reformulation of analytic understanding in narrative or hermeneutic terms.[9] Its advocates argue that since psychoanalysis deals in meanings rather than causes, it has a closer kinship to disciplines like history and literary criticism than it does to physics or biology. The key difference is that, while practitioners of these academic crafts interpret public materials with many different ends in mind, the analyst does his or her interpretive work in the context of a private dialogue that is meant to help a patient. Thus the mark of a good or 'sound' interpretation is not simply its cogency or fidelity to the known facts, but its effect on the patient – its power to move or change him in a beneficial way. As Donald Spence points out, achieving this effect depends so much on rhetoric, timing and aesthetic form that the success of an interpretation (its 'narrative truth') need have no particular bearing on the actual events (or 'historical truth') behind a patient's suffering. Roy Schafer has argued for a similar view in even more radical form, noting that the very idea of 'insight' or 'therapeutic benefit' depends on the story that the analyst has come to believe or to fashion about the patient, and that in any given case there are many possible stories.[10]

The second response is the one that really interests me here. Over the past decade a growing number of analysts have turned in the opposite direction in an effort to re-establish their work on solid scientific ground. They agree that many of Freud's assumptions about memory and biology are no longer credible. At the same time, they say, narrative or hermeneutic versions of analysis have proved sterile because they sever the all-important link between therapy and theory, reducing the former to a practical art and the latter to a mere philosophy of mind.[11] They argue that psychoanalysis can move forward only by returning to its early promise as 'a complete science of the mind', and that the best way to achieve this is by joining forces with the emerging field of cognitive neuroscience.

For many analysts, especially those with academic positions in psychology or psychiatry, the prospect of such an alliance has become a source of great excitement. Beyond restoring analytic ideas to scientific respectability, they see it as a way of infusing the whole movement with a new intellectual energy.[12] There are some indications that this is already happening. At recent meetings of the American Psychoanalytic Association sessions with papers on neuroscience have drawn large and interested crowds. Journal articles are multiplying rapidly,[13] and there is now at least one popular book.[14] As I write this, the 'First International Neuro-Psychoanalysis Conference' is under way in London, sponsored by the Anna Freud Centre. The event is billed as the founding meeting of a new 'International Neuro-Psychoanalysis Society', which will have its own journal.

How will this 'neuro-psychoanalysis' differ from its various Freudian progenitors? It is still too early to say. Current writing on the subject includes a good deal of programmatic rhetoric, and so cynics might be excused for regarding the changes as purely cosmetic. However, the rhetoric does rest on a core of substantive ideas. These have been the real source of the excitement, I think, and as it happens they are mainly about memory.

In what follows I want to examine this new view of memory and to consider its implications for psychoanalysis. My aim here is not so much to decide whether this approach is 'correct' or well-founded as to ask just how it might change the whole analytic enterprise. Neuro-cognitivists make an eloquent case for the gains that psychoanalysis would make by embracing their ideas. Would it also have something to lose?

We cannot begin to answer this question without moving beyond the halo of popular Freudian ideas mentioned earlier to a more careful scrutiny of Freud's own understanding of memory. My aim in doing this, however, will not be to encapsulate what Freud 'actually said' about memory – which is in any case an impossible task. Freud was a master of ambiguity, and it is as easy to find a proto-science in his words as a proto-poetics or hermeneutics. What I hope to do, rather, is to assess a fundamental difference between his own interpretive use of memory and the one informing the neuro-cognitive model. As I shall try to show, the contrast between these two very different ways of invoking memory raises some interesting questions about the value of psychoanalysis, not just as a science or a clinical art, but as an expressive idiom and a model of human personhood.

The neuro-psychoanalytic approach to memory takes its departure from the work of cognitive scientists studying patients with amnesia caused by brain damage. Research conducted over several decades[15] has shown convincingly that patients who have completely lost the capacity for direct recall and verbalisation often still retain an ability to develop skills through practice. For example, amnesiac subjects presented with the same puzzle on different occasions may insist repeatedly that they have never seen it before, and yet they become increasingly skilful in solving it. These findings have led to the hypothesis – now widely accepted – that there are two distinct kinds of memory, laid down in different ways and differently inscribed in the brain. *Declarative memory* is the memory of specific events, facts, scenes or experiences that can be recalled or represented, either in language or sensory images. *Procedural memory*, on the other hand, refers to the vast array of skills and habits that inform everyday behaviour, like talking, walking or driving a car, but which defy direct recall.[16] Advocates such as Robert Clyman explain the neurological reason for this difference as follows: while declarative memories are symbolic and referential, 'procedures are encoded directly in the neural program which underlies the skill; procedurally encoded information does not stand for anything else'. As a result, procedural memory cannot be conscious, although sometimes 'the procedural program can be translated into declarative knowledge'. Thus, to cite a key formula, '[d]eclarative knowledge can be remembered; procedural knowledge can only be enacted'.[17]

For psychoanalysts, the distinction between these two types of memory takes on more interest when coupled with an additional widely accepted claim, namely that they belong to a developmental sequence. A number of studies suggest that we store procedural knowledge almost as soon as we are born, while the capacity to form declarative memories doesn't start until late infancy and isn't fully functional until about the age of five.[18] Psychoanalysts who have taken up this theory then emphasise a further crucial point: among the procedures we learn in early infancy are those involving patterns of emotional response. Here again, most of the learning is automatic, since 'young children can decipher the rules by which their families operate and develop strategies for meeting their [own] needs ... without any intermediate declarative steps'.[19] Because emotional procedures of this kind take place outside declarative memory, they are unaffected by repression or childhood amnesia and are thus extremely tenacious. Later in life these procedures may become 'sub-optimal' for all sorts of reasons. Yet because they lie outside of awareness, they are extremely difficult to revise.

Armed with these principles, analysts like Robert Clyman, Matthew Erdelyi and Daniel Stern have proposed a wide-reaching reformulation of psychoanalytic theory. Seen from this new standpoint, the neurotic symptoms that bring patients to analysts are not the result of repression or unconscious conflict, but of maladaptive emotional procedures. The repetition compulsion, which Freud ascribed to the death instinct, turns out to have a much more prosaic basis in the conservative nature of procedural learning. Clyman illustrates this point with the analogy of a man who has kept his socks in the top drawer of his dresser for years and then moves them to the second drawer: 'The "driven" quality of the repetition compulsion in part reflects the automatic nature of the procedure,' he says, 'just as our hypothetical man feels "driven" to reach in the wrong drawer for his socks.'[20] By the same token, transference is simply the enactment of early emotional procedures in the analytic setting. The task of the analyst is to help the patient to change what is maladaptive in these procedures. Sometimes this involves giving explicit, declarative form to the rules behind a procedure so that they can be modified and a new procedure practised (this is the role of 'insight'). At other times the analytic situation itself may provide the corrective experiences needed to learn new emotional procedures.

Clearly there is much to be said for this theory. The distinction between declarative and procedural memory is a compelling one, and it seems highly plausible that many people's problems have some basis in emotional procedures learned early in life. There is also ample reason to believe that many forms of therapy, psychoanalysis included, involve a kind of emotional relearning that may take place outside of awareness.[21] Actually a very similar claim was advanced more than forty years ago by partisans of behaviourism, who explained neurosis as a result of maladaptive learning and depicted therapy as a process of teaching new and more effective responses.[22] Being averse to all things mental, however, the behaviourists said very little about memory. By contrast, the new theory of 'emotional procedures' is explicitly a theory about memory.

How does this view of memory differ from Freud's? Certainly there are affinities – the procedural theory treats our desires as essentially conservative, accords a formative role to early experience and takes psychopathology to be a kind of re-enactment, just as Freud did. The obvious difference is that Freud advanced – or presupposed – a conception of memory that was symbolic and representational, whereas the procedural theory does not. Neuro-cognitivists would add that this is precisely the advantage of their theory. In a single stroke it avoids the most dubious aspects of the standard Freudian view – the storehouse of mental traces and the whole implausible scenario involving repressed events from childhood that are recovered accurately in analysis to effect a cure.

These merits notwithstanding, the theory of emotional procedures does elide an important question. It is easy enough to see how procedures learned in early childhood might explain broad adult personality traits like shyness or impulsiveness. However, psychodynamic therapies normally grapple with much more complex and idiosyncratic patterns arising in human relationships. If these patterns are really procedural residues from early family life, then re-enacting them means applying them to completely new settings, so that, for example, I now resent my boss as I used to resent my father. It is hard to see how this leap could be made without some recourse to symbolic memory. After all, my boss is not my father, and I don't harbour the same resentment for everyone. In order to react the same way, I need to see my boss *as* my father, or I need some third category (such as 'father-figure') to which they both belong. In either case the problem is the same: I resent my boss not for who he is but for what he represents to me. In order to generalise any complex emotional procedure, in other words, I have to deploy some form of representational memory, though of course it needn't be a conscious, declarative memory of any specific event. While proceduralists seem to miss the implicit role of symbols in mediating between different settings, this was absolutely central to Freud.

This brings us to a second and more complicated point. As a matter of historical fact, psychoanalysis has always been something more than a clinical technique or a mental science. It is also a set of interpretive practices. In this latter guise its theories take on a different kind of importance; they are no longer simply models *of* reality but models *for* understanding – by therapists and patients to be sure, but by the rest of us as well, as we try to make sense of our lives and of what it means to be human. To look at an interpretive theory from this standpoint is to ask a different set of questions: What are its expressive possibilities? What does it allow us to see and to say? How does it invite us to live? Assessing a new version of psychoanalysis in these terms is hardly a straightforward task. To even make a beginning, however, we must look more closely at the way Freud himself understood memory as a force in illness and treatment.

Freud said many things about memory and spoke in many voices. Some of his comments hardly fit the textbook stereotypes. In his 1899 paper on screen memories, for example, he wrote of 'the tendentious nature of our remembering and forgetting' and ended by doubting 'whether we have any memories *from* our childhood; memories *relating* to our childhood may be all we possess'.[23] His 1909 paper on Leonardo compared our memories of early childhood to the self-serving legends that successful nations conjure up about their humbler beginnings. Even his early theory of trauma included the concept of *nachträglichkeit*, which gave later events, even in puberty, the power to confer new traumatic meanings on previously innocuous childhood experiences.

These sceptical comments about actual, individual memories appear amid passages that strike a very different tone and in which memory assumes a different aspect. Here it is no longer a banal string of doubtful recollections but a mysterious force at work in the mind – substantial but elusive, intimate and yet wholly foreign. Freud seems unable to approach memory in this second sense without invoking analogies from medicine, geology, archaeology, political history, classical mythology or romantic literature. These figures need to be taken seriously, in part because they convey nuances missing from Freud's drier expository accounts but also because – for all their diversity – they show an interesting convergence.

Historically speaking, psychoanalysis begins with the book *Studies on Hysteria* and its famous claim that 'hysterics suffer mainly from reminiscences'. To describe the enduring power of traumatic memory, Freud and Breuer liken it to 'a *foreign body* which long after its entry must continue to be regarded as an agent that is still at work'.[24] The simile conveys several ideas at once: that pathogenic memory is distinct from (indeed *foreign to*) the rest of mental life, that it is harmful because it is hidden, and that cure is a matter of extracting or releasing it somehow. Later in the book Freud points out that the foreign body image is misleading to the extent that it implies a tightly bounded object. In its place he offers another medical figure, the 'infiltrate' – still foreign, still harmful, but not so easily separable from the rest of mental life.

As Freud's thinking matured, he moved further in this direction, away from an interest in specific traumas and toward a much broader study of infantile experience and its relation to adult life. In doing so he seized on a different metaphor, one that remained central to all his later accounts of analytic research. In this figure the memories to be uncovered were no longer foreign bodies but fragments of a lost world or buried city, and the analyst was a kind of archaeologist. Freud elaborated this idea in several ways. First there was his cherished comparison of the analytic task to an archaeological excavation: both required slow, patient work, a sifting away of debris to reveal incomplete objects that could be understood only indirectly, through painstaking comparisons and reconstructive conjectures.[25] Then there was the idea that repressed memories are buried in layers, that some lie deeper than others, that burial is what preserves them, and that they only begin to change once they are exposed to the light of day. From here it was a small step to the idea that infancy is something like a lost civilisation, that we return to this archaic world in our dreams, and that deciphering its language is something like reading hieroglyphics.[26]

A third constellation of metaphors running through much of Freud's work presents memory not simply as foreign or buried, but as an active – though hidden – force in our daily lives. The implicit premise here is that all desire is laden with memory, that buried memories are also buried desires, and that these can force themselves upon us in unexpected ways. In the final chapter of the *Interpretation of Dreams* Freud compares unconscious wishes to 'the legendary Titans, weighed down since primeval ages by the massive bulk of the mountains which were once hurled upon them by the victorious gods and which are still shaken from time to time by the convulsion of their limbs'.[27] They are also like ghosts in the underworld of the Odyssey 'which awoke to new life as soon as they tasted blood'.[28] A few pages later, still on the same theme, he quotes a line from Virgil which also serves as the book's epigraph: '*Flectere si nequeo superos, Acheronta movebo*' ('If I cannot bend the gods above, I will move the infernal regions.') These figures all point to what Freud would later call 'the return of the repressed', which he came to align, at least in some cases, with the Death Instinct and the experience of 'being pursued by a malignant fate or possessed by some "daemonic" power'.[29] Freud drew on the same idea to explain the experience of 'the uncanny'. Sometimes, he said, what was abandoned or overcome in infancy can force its way back into consciousness and 'become a thing of terror, just as, after the collapse of their religion, the gods turned into demons'.[30]

Looking back now at these different figures – the foreign body, the buried city, the underworld denizens struggling to break out – it is easy to see that they all converge on the idea of an otherness inside ourselves, as though there were something inherently alien in our own make-up. They are all reminders that, as Freud put it, 'the ego is not master even in his own house'.[31] However there is something more here as well. Except in the case of the foreign-body simile (which Freud soon abandoned), the figures imply an otherness not so easily segregated from the rest of our lives. Learning about it is no simple matter of remembering, but of patient sifting, conjecture, working backwards from effects. We get at it through *interpretation*.

In an important recent book Jean Laplanche[32] has coined the term *étrangèreté* (literally 'strangerness') to capture this dimension of Freud's thought. He equates it with what he takes to be truly revolutionary in psychoanalysis, the 'Copernican' idea of a subject whose centre of gravity lies elsewhere, outside consciousness. As Laplanche points out, this theme appears in many forms over the course of Freud's work, ranging from his early seduction theory to his late mythology of Eros and Thanatos. However it vies for ascendancy with another, equally pervasive, but opposing current of thought. This is the current one sees in the theory of narcissism, projection and paranoia, for example, but also in the late ego psychology. It is most obvious in statements like this one, which Freud addresses to an imaginary patient: 'Nothing has entered into you from without; a part of the activity of your own mind has been withdrawn from your knowledge and the command of your own will.'[33] Laplanche depicts this latter, 'Ptolemaic' tendency as a retreat to more conventional thinking, as though Freud periodically lost the courage of his convictions. He argues that the struggle between these two tendencies created a fundamental tension in Freud's thought:

> 'Internal foreign body', 'reminiscence': the unconscious as an alien inside me and even one put inside me by an alien. At his most prophetic, Freud does not hesitate over formulations which go back to the idea of possession.... But on the other side of these Copernican advances ... the dominant tendency is always to relativise the discovery and to re-assimilate and re-integrate the alien, so to speak.[34]

Laplanche shows that this tension accounts for a certain incoherence in some of Freud's central concepts, since they were born of two conflicting impulses: on the one hand, the bold and troubling perception of *étrangèreté*, on the other, the need to domesticate it. This is especially evident in the case of memory. The familiar doctrine of 'repressed memories' that comes down to us in popular versions of Freud is largely a product of this second, domesticating impulse: in response to conflict or trauma we have split certain memories away from consciousness, thereby giving them the power to make us ill; therapy is then a simple matter of undoing the repressions, filling in the gaps, restoring what was originally ours. This is more or less what happens in *Studies on Hysteria*, where Freud's cases all look something like detective stories. However, as Laplanche points out, Freud turned away from this simplistic notion when he rejected the seduction theory.[35] From that point onward both his theoretical writings and case histories show clearly that he was groping toward something else.

This 'something else' can be seen throughout Freud's mature work, but it appears most vividly in his 'Wolf Man' essay,[36] which is justly celebrated as the richest and most 'historical' of his clinical cases. Certainly it extends the interpretive reach of adult analysis more deeply into the events of childhood than any other. It also tells an extremely complex story, full of strange turnings, reversals and unexpected revelations. This has made it into something of a paradigm case for all those who view psychoanalysis as a narrative art.

When examined closely, however, the case takes on a slightly different complexion. Freud tells a complicated story (actually several stories serving a variety of ends, including a polemic against Adler and Jung)[37] concerning a small number of *scenes*. As the connections between these scenes become apparent, they begin to look less like stages or steps in a linear plot and more like nodal points in a dream. What are these scenes? To be sure, some of them – for example the Wolf Man's seduction by his sister at the age of four – can claim to be taken as memories in the ordinary sense of the word. Others – for example the early encounter with Grusha the maid – are interpretive elaborations, worked up from the barest of memory fragments. The most important memory reported by the patient (and the pivotal event in his story) is actually a dream. Finally, of course, there is the scene that explains it all, the famous 'primal scene' of parental coitus *a tergo*, which the patient never remembered and which, as Freud cheerfully admits, may simply never have happened.

Clearly this is not a biography or a history of events in the ordinary sense of the word. To Freud's critics, in fact, it is simply another instance of the liberties he took in fictionalising patient's lives. However, according to Laplanche, Freud was aiming at a history not of events, but of repression, 'a history with discontinuities … in which the subterranean currents are described in as much … if not more detail than the manifest character traits'.[38] This is a history of repressed or estranged memory, a history of scenes. He explains the relation between its elements by pointing to Freud's famous simile of the 'Eternal City' – ancient Rome with its numerous monuments still intact, sharing their space with a series of later structures including those standing today – in *Civilisation and Its Discontents*.[39] Laplanche argues that this passage, with its deliberate focus on individual buildings, was never meant to convey the idea of the psyche as 'a complete hologram of everything experienced'. What it presents is rather 'a succession and superimposition of fixed images, independent of each other' like contrary impulses in the unconscious. 'The imperceptible stages, the moments of transition, are abolished here in favour of a succession of fixed archetypes, each forming a whole.'[40] While Freud does describe these changeless objects as memories, Laplanche warns against confusing them with 'a trivial memorisation':

> The unconscious, if the reader is prepared to follow us, is *not* memory; repression is not a particular modality of memorising. Repression – cataclysm and burial in the unconscious – is as different from memorisation as the engulfment of Pompeii is from Joinville's Chronicle of the Seventh Crusade of Louis IX, perhaps even more different.[41]

If Laplanche is right, then psychoanalysis as Freud understood it was not a mere search for repressed memories but an enquiry directed to something entirely different – a series of affectively powerful scenes situated in the field of early childhood, scenes at once deeply alien and intimately connected to our adult lives. Viewed as a set of interpretive practices, psychoanalysis may be said to *read these scenes into* our everyday experience and into the fabric of our culture.

What does it mean to do this? And if these scenes are not memories as such, what are they? Do they have some basis in reality? Laplanche responds to these questions by offering a conjecture of his own about the enduring effects of ambiguous sexual messages on children.[42] However it is not quite clear what he means, and in any case his hypothesis does nothing to advance our understanding of psychoanalysis from an interpretive standpoint. For that we must turn back to Freud himself, and to the account of analytic treatment given in some of his papers on technique.

Freud's 1914 essay, 'Recollection, Repetition and Working Through',[43] offers the clearest articulation of his thesis that neurotic patterns in adults are repetitions or re-enactments of something from infancy. This, of course, is just what the advocates of procedural memory suggest, with the difference that proceduralists see them as repetitions pure and simple, whereas for Freud they were substitutes for repressed memories. Freud went further, in fact, to insist that it was precisely the condition of being repressed that gave them the 'uncanny' power to intrude on the lives of patients. Treatment was thus a matter of turning the repetition back into a recollection, or as Freud put it, 'translating it back again into the terms of the past'. This last, familiar formula would draw objections not only from the proceduralists (who would say there is nothing to recall), but also from Laplanche, who might easily take it as an instance of the domesticating, conventionalising impulse in Freud.

When we look more closely at what Freud actually meant by recollection, however, a more complex picture emerges. He begins the 1914 essay by contrasting his early use of hypnosis to retrieve lost memories with 'our present-day technique', which concentrates on interpreting the patient's resistances: '[t]he physician discovers the resistances which are unknown to the patient; when these are removed the patient often relates the forgotten situations and connections without any difficulty'.[44] When analysis is carried out in this way, however, it turns out that very little has been forgotten: 'The forgetting of impressions, scenes, events nearly always reduces itself to "dissociation" of them. When the patient talks about these "forgotten" matters he seldom fails to add: "In a way I have always known that, only I never thought of it".'[45] Regarding memories of purely internal processes (fantasies, impulses, feelings, connections), the case is even stronger: 'With these processes it particularly often happens that something is "remembered" which never could have been "forgotten" because it was never at any time noticed, never was conscious.... The conviction which a patient obtains in the course of analysis is quite independent of remembering it in that way.'[46] Finally, Freud says, there is 'one special kind of highly important experience' that can never be remembered: 'these are experiences which took place in very early childhood, before they could be comprehended, but which were *subsequently* interpreted and understood. One gains a knowledge of them from dreams and is compelled to believe in them on irresistible evidence in the structure of the neurosis....'[47]

What Freud appears to be saying very forcefully here is that the kind of recollection that matters in successful analysis has very little to do with recovering 'declarative memories' as cognitive psychologists understand that word. Rather, it seems to be a matter of 're-collecting' them – joining them together differently, so that they take on new meanings and connections and thus come to depict previously unsuspected situations and relationships. Seeing these connections vividly for the first time can of course feel to the patient something like a new memory. However, Freud hardly saw this as a necessity. As he put it in his late essay, 'Constructions in Analysis',[48] 'Quite often we do not succeed in bringing the patient to recollect what has been repressed. Instead of that, if the analysis has been carried out correctly, we produce in him an assured conviction of the truth of the construction which achieves the same therapeutic result as a recaptured memory.'[49]

Freud says that this kind of recollection occurs only after the resistances have been removed – another familiar formula. What does he mean? Here again there is a contrast between the early view of resistance (the patient rejects valid interpretations, fails to free-associate) and Freud's later and more complex understanding of this term. By 1912 he had come to see the resistances as embodied mainly in the phenomenon of transference, the patient's intense but ambivalent relationship to the analyst during treatment. He also came to believe that while transference serves the cause of resistance, it also provides the analyst with an essential tool, since it 'render[s] the invaluable service of making the patient's buried and forgotten love-emotions actual and manifest'.[50] Thus Freud counselled analysts to accept both the erotic and hostile versions of transference, admitting them to the analytic situation 'as if to a playground'. The point was that transference embodied, vividly and overtly, the same repetitions, the same re-enactments driving the neurosis:

> For instance, the patient does not say that he remembers how defiant and critical he used to be in regard to the authority of his parents, but he behaves in that way towards the physician…. He does not remember that he was intensely ashamed of certain sexual activities, but he makes it clear that he is ashamed of the treatment to which he has submitted himself, and does his utmost to keep it a secret; and so on.[51]

As a result of this shift in viewpoint, Freud came to see analytic treatment, not as a search for repressed memories to be abreacted, but as a slow process of interpreting, 'working through' and ultimately resolving the transference relationship. But transference, like neurosis, is a form of repetition, and resolving it is a matter of 'translating it back again into terms of the past'. So we face the same question again. Granting that many formative infantile scenes are not memories and not recollectable even in principle, what are they? And what is their relation to transference or neurosis?

The concept of transference itself offers an important clue to the answer. Beyond using it to describe the patient's relation to the analyst, Freud gave the word a second, broader meaning central to the whole dynamic metapsychology that he developed in the *Interpretation of Dreams*. His central argument there was that dreams draw their energy, their animating force, not from the relatively feeble wishes of everyday life, but from the repressed wishes of early childhood – those 'Legendary Titans' mentioned earlier. Being repressed, these early wishes were barred from direct expression, but were able to elude the censor by cloaking themselves in relatively innocuous recent memories. Freud came to believe that all adult dreams were made in this way. Thus he arrived at his famous definition of the dream as *'a substitute for an infantile scene modified by being transferred onto a recent experience'*.[52] The important point was that the dream produced by this kind of transference was always a compromise-formation, one that served to disguise infantile wishes but that also distorted the materials of recent life as well.

From an interpretive standpoint, the task of analysis was to recognise these distortions and thus to arrive at the infantile scenes or wishes behind them. This meant placing the manifest dream in the context of the patient's recent experience, following out the associative pathways to the latent dream thoughts and then observing the way these thoughts had been revised by the dream-work and its underlying aim of wish-fulfilment. The revision involved a complex series of symbolic processes (condensation, displacement, reaction-formation, etc.), but once they were decoded, the result was always the same: the dream treated the persons and situations of adult life *as if* they were figures and scenes from early childhood. Thus, for example, Freud interpreted dreams of being naked in a familiar public situation (at work, at a party, etc.) as a hearkening back to the unfettered exhibitionism enjoyed by young children. Or again, he found that patients dreaming of rivals in love or in work often gave them traits borrowed from a sibling envied long ago. Of course in most dreams the relationship between infantile and adult components was far more complex, involving multiple conflicting wishes and several layers of increasingly archaic early scenes. But even in these cases the effect of the dreamwork was the same: to refashion adult experience by merging it with one or more infantile scenes. The ultimate point of interpretation was to infer these scenes from the subtle changes, the distinctive coloration they imparted to the materials of the dreamer's recent life.[53]

These considerations suggest an interesting possibility. Linguistic structures that present one thing as if it were another are examples of *metaphor*. Dreams are not linguistic structures, but, as understood by Freud, they assume a similar function: the relationship they present between infantile and adult life is at bottom a metaphorical one. The 'transference' of an infantile scene onto a recent experience is the same kind of transference as that achieved by metaphor – namely to convey meanings from one semantic domain into another. It is interesting, in fact, that Freud used the German word *übertragung* to denote this process. Like its equivalent in English – transference – this word comes from a verb that means 'to carry over'. The word 'metaphor', which exists in both English and German, is derived from the Greek verb *metapherein*, which has exactly the same meaning.

Freud characterised dreams as 'another kind of remembering, although one that is subject to the conditions that rule at night and to the laws of dream-formation'.[54] If my surmise about them is correct, then the task of discovering just what it is that dreams 'remember' comes down to a search for the implicit metaphorical structures underlying the transformation of the day's residues by the dreamwork. Those structures *are* the infantile scenes. According to Freud, moreover, the transferential process guiding the dream-work was fundamentally the same as that seen in neuroses and in the analytic situation. Though subject to 'the conditions that rule at night', it reflected the same infantile scenes and mediated the same conflicts. Thus there are good grounds for regarding the relationship between infantile scenes and the behaviour of neurotics (or analysands) as a metaphorical one as well.

Earlier I suggested that psychoanalysis could be viewed as an interpretive practice that reads a certain class of putative memories into our lives and our cultural productions. Because of ambiguities in Freud's language and conflicts in his own thinking, however, it was hard to be sure what such a reading entailed. The above discussion now points the way to a more definite hypothesis: while Freud often spoke of recovering repressed memories, his mature interpretive practice involved something quite different: a gradual weaving together of connections between existing memories and other materials (dreams, symptoms, free associations, transferential behaviour) in an effort to arrive at a coherent pattern uniting all these elements in the patient's life. Freud thought of this pattern as originating in one or more infantile scenes, but acknowledged that these could be known only indirectly, through the traces they left on various aspects of the patient's symbolic productions. We can now add that, from the standpoint of Freud's interpretive practice with patients, it did not matter whether these scenes had any basis in historical reality, since their relation to the raw materials of analysis was never historical or causal, but metaphorical. In constructing them Freud was of course guided by his own theoretical assumptions, but he also needed to instil that 'sense of conviction' which he saw as the therapeutic equivalent of actual recollection. Doing this meant finding scenes with the figurative power to capture something central about the patient's life that had previously been obscure. In this respect, the interpretations that 'worked' for Freud's patients were still grounded in a kind of reality; however, that grounding was poetic rather than historical.

Having come this far with Freud, we may now go a little further. Let us suppose that the sceptics are right, and that the scenes 'recollected' in therapy have no real basis in the patient's early history. What then of the whole drama of infantile sexuality that is so central to psychoanalytic theory? Is it merely fiction? If the view I have been proposing is correct, then the answer would appear to be yes, although 'merely' is not quite the right word. Viewed strictly as an interpretive practice, psychoanalysis can be seen as shuttling between two poles. The first consists of the patient's symbolic productions – his dreams, recollections, associations, symptoms. The second pole is situated in the space of early childhood memory and consists of a small cluster of ambiguous but emotionally potent figures, all drawn from the master trope of infantile sexual life: the breast, the phallus, the three erogenous zones, the primal scene, the Oedipus complex, castration, and so on. The work of interpretation is then the slow process of both reading these figures into the patient's life and symbolic productions, and fleshing out the figures themselves, until an arrangement is found that seems to capture the truth of the patient's current predicament. Seen in this light the 'repressed memories' of infancy so important to psychoanalysis take on a new meaning. They operate here, not as a series of determining events or even as a set of blindly learned emotional procedures, but as a metaphorical resource. They open an imaginative space where something other than me, something I am not, can be used to re-imagine what I am.

Thinking about psychoanalysis in this way leads quickly to a series of critical questions about the metaphors themselves. Why these metaphors? What makes them apt? What is the source of their authority? What do they exclude? What are the implications of situating them in the field of early childhood? How might they be imagined differently? These are important issues, some of them at the focus of current debates in the arts and humanities.[55] They remind us that psychoanalysis as an interpretive practice is an ongoing project, one that belongs at least as much to the politics and ethics of culture as it does to medicine. Thus the figures it invokes are – and should be – matters for critique and revision.

The theory of procedural memories has the advantage of avoiding such questions, but it does so at a price – not the price of neglecting declarative memories (as we have seen, Freud did not give them great weight) – but of dispensing with the whole metaphorical apparatus at the centre of psychoanalysis. Why does this matter? One answer lies partly in the generative and unpredictable character of all rich metaphorical systems, but also in the challenging 'otherness' built into the particular metaphors that Freud chose. Situated at the foundational – but inaccessible – site of early childhood memory, these figures support a view of persons as inherently open-ended, complicated and incomplete. Certainly classical analytic therapy, whatever its healing powers, offers patients an extended initiation into this kind of personal complexity. By contrast, the new 'neuro-psychoanalysis', with its focus on procedural memories, reduces suffering to a series of bad habits and therapy to a kind of emotional retraining. In doing so it affirms a flatter, more tightly bounded, more mechanical conception of what it means to be a person.

The difference at stake here is nicely captured in a question that Jonathan Lear posed recently to Freud's critics: 'Are we to see humans as having depth – as complex psychological organisms who generate layers of meaning which lie beneath the surface of their own understanding? Or are we to take ourselves as transparent to ourselves?'[56] If we accept the latter view, then the proceduralists are right regarding healing as a straightforward instrumental task with unproblematic goals. If we accept the former, on the other hand, we come back to the more ambitious and uncertain enquiry pioneered by Freud, and to his underlying premise that, as Lear puts it, 'the human soul is too deep for there to be an easy answer to the question of how to live'.[57]

PAUL ANTZE

Notes

1 Ian Hacking, 'Memory Sciences, Memory Politics', in P. Antze and M. Lambek (eds) *Tense Past: Cultural Essays in Trauma and Memory*, New York: Routledge, 1996, p. 70.
2 See Nathan Hale, *The Rise and Crisis of Psychoanalysis in the United States*, New York: Oxford University Press, 1996, and T.M. Luhrmann, *Of Two Minds: The Growing Disorder in American Psychiatry*, New York: Random House, 2000. Meanwhile, at the level of popular culture, attacks by feminists have aligned Freud's name with the denigration of women and an indifference to the reality of child abuse. Here the effect has been not only to drive away potential clients, but to foster the rise of a narrower and more literal view of trauma among some analysts. See the literature reviewed in Elizabeth K. Wolf and Judith Alpert, 'Psychoanalysis and Sexual Abuse: A Review of the Post-Freudian Literature', *Psychoanalytic Psychology* 8, 1991, pp. 305–27 and the more recent critique in Frederick Crews, *The Memory Wars: Freud's Legacy in Dispute*, New York: New York Review of Books, 1995.
3 See Adolf Grunbaum, *The Foundations of Psychoanalysis*, Berkeley, CA: University of California Press, 1984, and Malcolm MacMillan, *Freud Evaluated: The Completed Arc*, New York: North-Holland, 1991.
4 See Allen Esterson, *Seductive Mirage: An Exploration of the Work of Sigmund Freud*, Chicago: Open Court, 1993, and Mikkel Borch-Jacobsen,'How a Fabrication Differs from a Lie', *London Review of Books* 13 April 2000, pp. 3–7.
5 Daniel Schachter, *Searching for Memory: The Brain, the Mind and the Past*, New York: Basic Books, 1996.
6 Elizabeth Loftus and Katherine Ketcham, *The Myth of Repressed Memory: False Memories and Allegations of Sexual Abuse*, New York: St Martin's Press, 1994.
7 Jerome Frank and Julia Frank, *Persuasion and Healing*, Baltimore, MD: Johns Hopkins University Press, 1991.
8 Adolf Grunbaum, *The Foundations of Psychoanalysis*, Berkeley, CA: University of California Press, 1984.
9 Paul Ricoeur, *Freud and Philosophy: An Essay on Interpretation*, New Haven, CT: Yale University Press, 1970; Donald Spence, *Narrative Truth and Historical Truth*, New York: Norton, 1982; Roy Schafer, *Retelling a Life*, New York: Basic Books, 1992.
10 Spence, op. cit. and Schafer, op. cit.
11 Eric R. Kandel, 'Biology and the Future of Psychoanalysis: A New Intellectual Framework for Psychiatry Revisited', *American Journal of Psychiatry* 156(4), 1999, pp. 505–24.
12 Ibid., p. 506.
13 See, for example, Robert B. Clyman, 'The Procedural Organization of Emotions: A Contribution from Cognitive Science to the Psychoanalytic Theory of Therapeutic Action', in T. Shapiro and R. Emde (eds) *Affect: Psychoanalytic Perspectives*, Madison, CT: International Universities Press, 1992; D. Olds and A.M. Cooper, 'Dialogues with Other Sciences: Opportunities for Mutual Gain', *International Journal of Psychoanalysis* 78, 1997, pp. 219–25; K. Lyons-Ruth, 'Implicit Relational Knowing: Its Role in Development and Psychoanalytic Treatment', *Infant Mental Health Journal* 19, 1998, pp. 282–9; Mark Solms, 'Preliminaries for an Integration of Psychoanalysis and Neuroscience', *British Psychoanalytic Society Bulletin* 34, 1998, pp. 23–37; Daniel Stern, 'The Process of Therapeutic Change Involving Implicit Knowledge: Some Implications of Developmental Observations for Adult Psychotherapy', *Infant Mental Health Journal* 19, 1998, pp. 300–8); and Kandel, op. cit.
14 Susan C. Vaughan, *The Talking Cure: The Science Behind Psychotherapy*, New York: G.P. Putnam's Sons, 1997. The author, a medically trained therapist, explains psychodynamic therapy as a form of 'neural micro-surgery'.

15 W.B. Scoville and B. Milner, 'Loss of Recent Memory after Bilateral Hippocampal Lesions', *Journal of Neurology and Neuro-Surgical Psychiatry* 20, 1957, pp. 11–21; N.J. Cohen *et al.*, 'Different Memory Systems Underlying Acquisition of Procedural and Declarative Knowledge', *Annals of the New York Academy of Science* 444, 1985, pp. 54–71.

16 Ibid.

17 Clyman, op. cit., p. 352.

18 D.B. Pillemer and S.H. White, 'Childhood Events Recalled by Children and Adults', *Advances in Child Development and Behavior* 21, 1989, pp. 297–340.

19 Clyman, op. cit., p. 360.

20 Ibid., p. 369.

21 See the studies collected in Shapiro and Emde, op. cit.

22 J.Wolpe, *Psychotherapy by Reciprocal Inhibition*, Stanford, CA: Stanford University Press, 1958.

23 Sigmund Freud, 'Screen Memories', in *The Standard Edition of the Complete Psychological Works of Sigmund Freud*, Vol. 3, ed. J. Strachey, London: Hogarth Press, 1981 [1899], p. 322.

24 Sigmund Freud and Joseph Breuer, *Studies on Hysteria*, London: Penguin Books, 1974 [1895], p. 57.

25 Here are two examples, separated by more than thirty years:

> In the face of the incompleteness of my analytic results, I had no choice but to follow the example of those discoverers whose good fortune it is to bring to the light of day after their long burial the priceless though mutilated relics of antiquity. I have restored what is missing, taking the best models known to me from other analyses; but like a conscientious archaeologist, I have not omitted in each case to mention where the authentic parts end and my constructions begin.
>
> ('Fragment of an Analysis of a Case of Hysteria ["Dora"]', in A. Richards [ed.] *Sigmund Freud: Case Histories I, 'Dora' and 'Little Hans'*, London: Penguin Books, 1977 [1905], p. 41)

> [The analyst's] work of construction, or if it is preferred, of reconstruction, resembles to a great extent an archaeologist's excavation of some dwelling-place that has been destroyed and buried or of some ancient edifice. The two processes are in fact identical, except that the analyst works under better conditions and has more material at his command to assist him.... Both of them have an undisputed right to reconstruct by means of supplementing and combining the surviving remains. Both of them, moreover, are subject to many of the same difficulties and sources of error.
>
> ('Constructions in Analysis', in P. Reiff [ed.] *Freud: Therapy and Technique*, New York: Collier Books, 1963 [1937], pp. 275–6)

26 It is clear that Freud took this side of his metaphor quite literally at times, especially in his speculations about phylogenetic memory. On such occasions he came close to presenting psychoanalysis and archaeology as complementary approaches to a common human prehistory whose vestiges were buried equally beneath the soil and under the surface of consciousness. See especially 'Totem and Taboo', in A. Richards (ed.) *Freud: The Origins of Religion*, London: Penguin Books, 1984 [1912–13] and 'Leonardo Da Vinci and a Memory of His Childhood', in A. Richards (ed.) *Freud: Art and Literature*, London: Penguin Books, 1985 [1910].

27 Sigmund Freud, *The Interpretation of Dreams*, ed. J. Strachey, New York: Avon, 1965 [1900], p. 592.

28 Ibid., p. 592 n.

29 Sigmund Freud, 'Beyond the Pleasure Principle', in A. Richards (ed.) *On Metapsychology: The Theory of Psychoanalysis*, London: Penguin Books, 1984[1920], p. 292.

30 Sigmund Freud, 'The Uncanny,' in Richards (ed.) *Sigmund Freud: Art and Literature*, op. cit., p. 358.
31 Sigmund Freud, *Introductory Lectures on Psychoanalysis*, J. Strachey and A. Richards (eds) London: Penguin Books, 1973 [1915–17], p. 326.
32 Jean Laplanche, *Essays on Otherness*, New York: Routledge, 1999.
33 Quoted in ibid., p. 66.
34 Ibid., p. 65.
35 As Laplanche points out, what troubled Freud about this early theory was not simply its unconvincing mechanical link between seduction and hysteria, but the naïve optimism it implied about therapy. If the unconscious was simply a repository for missing memories, then it would be possible, at least in principle, to make it disappear. As Laplanche puts it, 'once the memory because of which you fell ill has been re-assimilated, you will be ill no longer ... and you will have an unconscious no more' (ibid., p. 70). Having rejected this notion, Freud's problem was then to reconcile his doctrine of repression with the inexhaustibility of the unconscious.
36 Sigmund Freud, 'From the History of an Infantile Neurosis ("The Wolf Man")', in A. Richards (ed.) *Sigmund Freud: Case Histories II*, London, Penguin, 1979 [1918].
37 As a number of commentators have noted, Freud's account weaves together at least three different storylines: the patient's development from infancy; his progress in therapy; and the progress of Freud's understanding of the case.
38 Laplanche, op. cit., p. 148.
39 Sigmund Freud, *Civilization and its Discontents*. New York: W.W. Norton & Co., 1962 [1930].
40 Laplanche, op. cit., p. 151.
41 Ibid., p. 152.
42 Laplanche does not regard the infantile scenes in analysis as actual memories, but he seems to regard them as screens or substitutes for sexually charged communications between children and parents that occur before children are able to understand them. These remain buried in the unconscious, although, strictly speaking, Laplanche says, they were never forgotten and are not part of memory.
43 Sigmund Freud, 'Recollection, Repetition and Working Through', in Reiff (ed.), op. cit.
44 Ibid., p. 158.
45 Ibid., p. 159.
46 Ibid.
47 Ibid. Freud was alluding here to 'primal scenes' such as the witnessing of parental intercourse in the Wolf Man case.
48 Sigmund Freud, 'Constructions in Analysis', in Reiff (ed.) op. cit.
49 Ibid., p. 282.
50 Sigmund Freud, 'The Dynamics of the Transference', in Reiff (ed.), op. cit., p. 111.
51 Freud, 'Recollection ... ', op. cit., p. 160.
52 Freud, *Interpretation* ..., op. cit., p. 585.
53 Freud readily acknowledged that this was not a simple or direct task, since the clues to the infantile wishes or scenes behind a dream lay not in the dream itself, but in the relation between the 'manifest dream' and the 'dream thoughts' linked to it by way of the patient's free associations. Moreover, the relationship was typically disguised by the need to elude censorship. Thus, in many cases, as Freud said, 'only some small peculiarity in the dream's configuration will serve as a finger-post to put us on the track of the powerful ally from the unconscious' (ibid., p. 592).
54 Sigmund Freud, 'From the History of an Infantile Neurosis', op. cit., p. 285.
55 The literature on this subject is now immense, to say the least. For representative examples from feminist, postcolonial and queer theory respectively, see Jacqueline Rose, *Sexuality in the Field of Vision*, London: Verso, 1996; Ann Pellegrini, *Performance*

Anxieties: Staging Psychoanalysis, Staging Race, New York: Routledge, 1996; and Judith
    Butler, *Gender Trouble: Feminism and the Subversion of Identity*, New York: Routledge, 1990.
56 Jonathan Lear, 'The Shrink Is In', *The New Republic*, 25 December 1995, pp. 18–25.
57 Ibid.

6

FROM THE AGORA TO THE JUNKYARD

Social memory and psychic materialities

Constantina Papoulias

[H]uman thought is basically both social and public ... its natural habitat is the house yard, the market place and the town square. Thinking consists not of happenings in the head (though happenings there and elsewhere are necessary for it to occur) but of trafficking in ... significant symbols – words for the most part but also gestures, drawings, musical sounds, mechanical devices.

(Clifford Geertz, *The Interpretation of Cultures*)[1]

What is the relation of repression to memory such as it is generally studied in psychology? The path I deliberately took consists in considering the unconscious element or trace *not as a stored memory or representation, but as a sort of waste-product of certain processes of memorisation.*

(Jean Laplanche, 'A Short Treatise on the Unconscious', italics in original)[2]

What happens when the market place and the town square replace the head as the spatiality through which memory is imagined – as they do in the above passage from Clifford Geertz's *The Interpretation of Cultures*? In other words, what can the tropes through which social memory is currently being invoked tell us about the kinds of assumptions that have contributed to its study? The current investment in memory in cultural studies, political science and social theory is most frequently entwined with an appeal to its materiality as a social practice. This new memory studied by literary scholars, anthropologists and cultural historians can no longer simply be deemed synonymous with a mental faculty, the hallmark of the individual's private realm. For the scholars of social, collective or cultural memory, the concept of the 'mental faculty' has been replaced with the processes of 'trafficking in symbols': the production and circulation of experience across cultural pathways of meaning. In this sense, social memory does not simply refer to a set of explicit recollections concerning a personal or collective past. In addition to such acts of recollection, memory has now come to name the very texture of cultural specificity, reconceived as a multiplicity of corporeal performances: a layering of ritualised behaviours, belief systems and forces of habit that constitutes the everyday experience of a cultural space.[3] Memory thus begins to resemble the 'practical schemes' that for Pierre Bourdieu make up a social 'habitus': an inventory of bodily practices through which shared beliefs and habits are carried on into the present.[4] This use of memory, then, defines the 'inner world' as the sedimentation of social knowledges through skills, dispositions and patterns of action in the world.

Geertz's oft-cited relocation of human thought from the individual to the public realm provides us with an epigrammatic rendering of this shift in the study of subjectivity. However, it is my claim here that such a shift may be more imaginary than real, in that it ends up reasserting the very terms that it was set up to displace: namely, the subject's autonomy, separateness and impregnability in the face of the social field. In the terms of Clifford Geertz's definition, 'the market place' may have replaced the 'head' as the privileged spatiality through which memory is imagined, but this substitution has done little to challenge the particular spatial logics underlying the psychological models of memory as 'happenings in the head'. Rather, I will claim, 'the market place' figures the expansion of these spatial logics into an imagined spatiality of public exchanges.

As I will go on to suggest, this substitution of the social for the mental sidesteps the more radical psychoanalytic accounts of subjectivity and its location: that is, Freud's positing of the unconscious as a kind of spatial disturbance, an irreducible rift that both constitutes the subject and divides it from itself. That side-stepping occurs, I will claim, because the unconscious *cannot* be translated as a social spatiality because, as Jean Laplanche reminds us, it is a '*sort of waste-product of certain processes of memorisation*' (original italics).[5] The purpose of this chapter is to interrogate the epistemological and political logics that have coalesced into a particular understanding of social memory as a term suppressing and neutralising the psychoanalytic insights into subjectivity: neutralising, in other words, the 'trouble' that psychic reality and desire may represent for an analysis of social formations. In other words, I want to consider the unconscious as a site of waste subtending the din of memory and of Geertz's market place. In effect, I will argue that the currently emerging orthodoxy on the social production of memory eschews the orthodox psychological understanding of memory, only to substitute for it the imagined reciprocity of the well-governed city.

Memory as social practice

Geertz's relocation of memory to the market place is emblematic of memory studies' de-psychologisation of memory and its re-definition as a *social* process. It is emblematic, in other words, of the resurrection of the sociological legacy of Maurice Halbwachs.[6] For the American historians of memory studies, Halbwachs' work became a useful reference point because of its definition of memory as a set of social representations and, therefore, as a tool for grasping the symbolic realities and continuities of a particular social group. For Halbwachs, memory was not an individual faculty but rather a technique of framing experience, generated through the group. The personal, private aspect of an individual's memory was thus not to be understood through reference to a world of inner thought. Rather, in Halbwachs' definition, the personalised aspect of memory, the sense that my memory is unique and different from yours, was derived from the social fact that each individual is positioned not in one but in several social groups – for example in relation to class, gender, kinship and so on. In this sense, what appears as an individual's unique inner world of memory is in fact nothing other than the uniqueness of the layering of social memories. Thus the particularity of memory is an effect of the coming together of several social vocabularies of experience within each individual. For Halbwachs, then, such uniqueness is not an illusion: what is illusory is its association with a psychological world that is separate from the social.

Intersubjectivity as the site of agency

This redefinition of memory as social practice could be said to occupy the epistemological terrain of social reproduction.[7] This succession, however, becomes a significant displacement: with the emphasis on memory, the passing on of shared habits and behaviours implied in the term 'reproduction' is not made equivalent to a passive internalisation of something like 'the collective will'[8] from one generation to the next. As Susannah Radstone has recently observed, the use of the term 'social memory' testifies not to a simple internalisation of ideological norms but rather to a more nuanced understanding of how the very processes by which such norms become embodied and transmitted necessitate their transformation.[9] Indeed the 'turn to memory' may be thus said to rely on an understanding of subjectivity as such a site of transformation. Scholars use memory not in the broad sense of representation or ideology but in the restricted sense of a local inflection of a shared story. In so doing, they translate the malleability of memory into the condition and location of agency: memory here points to the process by which people make sense of and transform their past.[10] It is in this latter sense that memory (as marginal stories) is usually opposed to History (as publicly legitimated narratives). In this context, Geertz's market place does not simply figure the social nature of memory and symbolic activity. In addition, it figures their production *through and as* a certain form of negotiation. What the image of the market place suggests, in other words, is that the sociality of memory consists in the fact that memory *cannot* simply be apprehended as a reproduction or a re-enactment of ideological forms through corporeal habits; instead, memory is said to be social to the extent that it functions as the site of transformation of such norms.

'Memory' thus begins to shape itself as one of the current incarnations of what anthropologist Sherry Ortner hailed in 1984 as 'the turn to practice' in the social sciences. Briefly, Ortner's argument was that, since the mid-1970s at least, a sizeable part of the social sciences had moved away from their institutional clustering around structuralist and Marxist frameworks. In that earlier clustering, cultural practices could be approached through a reference to an underlying system (whether symbolic or economic) that they were said to represent and reproduce. More recent scholarship in the social sciences claimed, by contrast, that the specificity of 'what people do' and with it the very agency of cultural actors is lost in a methodology that privileges the underlying system generating social actions. Instead, more recent scholarship has proposed that social practices should be studied not as simple enactments of a pre-existing system but as variable performances in which a cultural world comes provisionally alive.[11]

Likewise, for the scholars of memory studies, memory needs to be apprehended on the level of 'what people do' – that is, as a socially embedded action. In other words, the social aspect of memory tends to be inflected towards a practice of local re-inscription rather than a structure of regulation. Furthermore, cultural historians have proposed that memory be further extended as the very *process* holding groups together: as the constant re-negotiation and circulation of such collective stories and practices that produces and maintains community.[12] In this context, 'the social' figures in two distinct incarnations in memory studies. On the one hand, 'the social' stands for a public memory which is de-individualised in so far as it is produced through social institutions. On the other, 'the social' also stands for an arena of exchange: it becomes equivalent to the conversations through which memory is shaped. As cultural historians insist, what makes memory social is *talk*. Indeed, for some cultural historians, memory is a process of self-making: it names 'the ways in which people shape and transform' not only their past but crucially 'each other through collectively authored stories'.[13] In its latter sense, memory becomes the conductor of what one historian has called 'a hitherto unsuspected form of sociability',[14] in other words, of the very social bond through which the exchange of stories, conversations and other social acts becomes possible in the first place. Thus defined, memory becomes equivalent to an inventory of bodily practices through which certain aspects of a past are continued into the present, as well as to the relational or intersubjective space of exchange through which such aspects are constituted and maintained. In this sense, memory works as the privileged instantiation of a space in-between. It is a space neither individual nor collective, but one that emerges as a site of intersubjectivity:

> Memory cannot be strictly individual, inasmuch as it is symbolic and hence intersubjective. Nor can it be literally collective, since it is not superorganic but embodied.[15]

The market place may then be said to figure this space in-between as a site of exchange.

Since memory studies works with embodiment, affective and relational experience, and the intimacies of conversation, it manifests a proximity to the categories of experience with which psychoanalysis has also concerned itself. Accounts of the dynamics of social memory refer to the unconscious, to trauma and mourning, and generally make use of what may appear as a psychoanalytic vocabulary in their analysis of the transmission of the past in the present. This investment in psychoanalysis, is, however, characterised by a curious eclecticism. As historian Kerwin Lee Klein aptly observed in a recent essay on how memory is conceptualised in the academy, 'we do not hear much about Oedipus or the primal scene'.[16] Instead, Klein suggested that the preferred terms for those invoking psychoanalytic terminology are those – like trauma, mourning and working through – which signal Freud at 'his most redemptive' by foregrounding the therapeutic aspirations of the psychoanalytic enterprise. While it is difficult to disagree with Klein's assessment that certain areas of memory studies read narratives of remembrance therapeutically, I would like to suggest a further interpretation of this forgetting of Oedipus.

Perhaps Oedipus is incompatible with the strategies of a cultural analysis that uses 'memory' as the sign of a socially constructed psyche. That is because Oedipus stands outside the world of historical contingency that is the world of memory studies. Oedipus, as the law of desire, signposts the *systemic* determinations of the Freudian psyche. It represents the universalising thrust in Freud's work, and commands us to turn away from historical contingency and the specificity of experience, towards another kind of order through which to interpret the workings of fantasy. While Freud's writings emphasise the memorial operations of the psyche, they also render such operations captive to the laws of fantasy. In Freud's psyche, both social relations and the events of the individual's affective life are made subordinate to these laws: the shapes of memory are ultimately determined by unconscious fantasmatic scenarios, by indelible sexual templates, to which all of an individual's variable experience and social interaction must return. In short, Oedipus is to memory studies as structuralism is to the 'turn to practice'.[17]

If the current investment in social memory excises the structural aspects of psychoanalysis from an understanding of subjectivity, how might this excision enable a rethinking of the psyche? What might it mean to articulate a relational, experientially produced self? In what follows, I will be looking at how current reinventions of the psyche as an effect of social contingencies deploy the *intersubjective relation* in the place of the Freudian unconscious (that field subtending and determining the shapes of memory). To this end, I will concentrate on one such site of reinvention: the work of contextualist psychologists. Contextualist psychology, like the cultural analysis of memory, is also wedded to an exploration of intersubjectivity. This is in part because both projects define themselves within the same epistemic upheaval that I have highlighted here in shorthand as 'the turn to practice'.[18] In the latter part of this chapter, I will juxtapose the work of French philosopher and psychoanalyst Jean Laplanche to the contextualist project. My aim here is to show that while Laplanche, too, proposes a rethinking of the psyche through the specificities of intersubjective relations, he does not render the psyche commensurable with the memorialising effects of such relations. Rather, he insists on prioritising desire and sexuality as an extra-memorial dimension of the psyche, which – while emerging in the spatial encounters between subjects – is *not* equivalent to memory or to the vagaries of intersubjective relations. It is this particular formulation of the unconscious as the site of desire which, by contrast, disappears from contextualist accounts and the cultural analysis of memory alike.

Contextualist psychology locates itself against classical psychology insofar as it imagines memory through a language of communicative interaction and a cultural repertory of rituals and gestures. It does so, I will argue, through an appeal to the intersubjective relation as an originary configuration through which both thought and memory will proceed. It is this relation that is incorporated by the young child – the cultural apprentice – who will gradually carve out an internal world of memory and self-reflection. The recasting of Freud's work proposed by French philosopher and analyst Jean Laplanche insists, by contrast, that we turn to desire as a necessary aspect of intersubjectivity, an aspect, furthermore, that is *irreducible* to memory. Laplanche's re-reading of Freud thus aims to re-think the psychoanalytic notion of the unconscious as a radical priority of otherness within the self. For Laplanche, this is not the otherness of the other *person*, a simple relativising of the self produced in relations with others (as the provisional, negotiated space between me and you). Rather, it is the otherness of another *thing*: of desire as a residue of communication, of an impossible spatiality that disrupts the space of communication. In this sense, Laplanche reads psychoanalysis as fundamentally unsettling: that is, as unsettling to itself as it is to any other discourse that purports to partake of it. For Laplanche, it is not the intersubjective relation as such that produces the unconscious but rather desire – desire as a marginal effect and necessary offshoot of this intersubjective relation.

Memory in accounts of social development: scaffolding, intersubjectivity and embodiment

Accounts of the turn to social context in psychology discuss the change of emphasis as an epochal transformation, as a paradigm shift that is often figured as nothing less than the overdue emancipation of the mind sciences from the sterile and mechanistic narratives of cognitivism. We are thus told that '[the new perspective brought] … the mind out from behind closed doors and into social spaces where meanings can be shared and constructed'.[19] As social psychologist Kenneth Gergen put it, this younger, contextualist perspective succeeded in overcoming psychology's epistemic dilemmas concerning the relationship between the mind and the world by challenging 'the concept of knowledge as mental representation … something people possess somewhere in their heads'. Instead, contextualism begins with the claim that knowledge is 'something people do together'.[20] Research projects in contextualist psychology that make use of the contextualist epistemology of knowledge systems and the new anthropology of material culture abandon the examination of mental

119

structures to 'focus on the way our words are imbedded in our life practices'.[21] Consequently, such research also abandons the laboratory for a more 'naturalistic' study of social spaces.

Such narratives of a radical break with cognitive psychology underplay, however, a more basic continuity of assumptions concerning the nature of memory and its place in the psyche: namely that, for cognitivism and contextualism alike, memory continues to function as the placeholder of subjective experience, insofar as subjective experience is founded on a notion of self-reflexivity and self-possession. Certainly, contextualists move away from earlier cognitive models' juxtapositions between an active mind and a series of environmental stimuli, to concentrate instead on the relations between social beings. Nevertheless, the psyche of the contextualists can still only be theorised as that which *transforms* incoming stimuli. What psychologist Jerome Bruner has epigrammatically defined as the crux of cognitive psychology, that is to say the human ability to 'go beyond the information given',[22] continues to function as the central assumption within contextualist perspectives as well. Here memory becomes the defining capacity of the mind insofar as it is the ability to abstract and organise incoming stimuli and interactions into meaningful and mutable patterns. In this sense, the psyche in cognitive and contextualist psychology alike remains identifiable as *a process of organisation of a particular space*. What changes within contextualist perspectives is that this space now becomes the space of the social rather than that of an isolated mind and, furthermore, that the principle of organisation extends to include behavioural patterns and a whole range of extra-verbal and non-cognitive activity such as emotional experience.

One of the clearest ways to glimpse this undeclared continuity between cognitive psychology and the more recent, contextualist models of memory, is by turning to current accounts of social development and the studies of infant behaviour that support them. In these studies, I will claim, infant behaviour is described as the origin and prototype of adult mnemic activity, insofar as this behaviour is said to regulate a particular kind of spacing between adult and child in which memory and representation can emerge. Briefly, contextualist approaches modify orthodox psychological accounts – accounts hailing from the legacy of Jean Piaget – according to which the young child is an information-gathering unit who gradually constructs a world through repeated trial and error. Contextualists claim instead that 'culture' is the determining force of child development, by which they mean that the child constructs a world through joint actions with its carers and in the context of culturally constrained communicative sequences.[23] This contextualist reading thus parallels Bourdieu's well-known recapitulation of cognition as enculturation:

> Between the child and the world the whole group intervenes not just with the warnings that inculcate a fear of supernatural dangers, but with a whole universe of ritual practices and utterances which people it

with meanings structured in accordance with the principles of the corresponding habitus.[24]

In this reading, memory is thus cultural from the start: what appears as 'the most private and personal experience' is in reality an effect of 'conventionalisation and acculturation'.[25] Here, contextualists explicitly adopt the culturalist line of Soviet psychologist Lev Vygotsky, for whom:

> every function in the child's cultural development appears twice: ... first between people (*interpsychological*) and then *inside* the child (*intrapsychological*).... All the higher functions originate as actual relations between human individuals.[26]

On Vygotsky's account, remembering is thus a *skill*, gradually mastered through the measured assistance of a social network. Like other skills, memory develops within a web of 'actual relations': in this case through conversations as well as non-verbal exchanges accruing between children and adults. Such exchanges construct the narrative framework through which the flickering and furtive impressions of the first years of life eventually come into focus as meaningful experiences that will lend themselves to description and recollection. The young child's ability to remember past events is thus an effect of her 'learning the narrative structure of recall'.[27] Through such narrative enrichments, the child learns to position her floating impressions as particular details within a structured story about the past. This process of assisted memory production, commonly referred to as scaffolding,[28] describes language and self-memory acquisition as a process of expansion, whereby the social other enriches and reshapes the toddler's competencies. Thus, what the adult transmits to the child through scaffolding is not the *content* of a past but a series of cultural *framing devices* through which the child will make sense of present and past alike.

Through the repeated rehearsal of such framing devices, the child assimilates the set of narratives, story grammars or scripts that render the past intelligible and the future anticipated.[29] In this sense, contextualist psychologists' claims that the ability to remember is socially mediated are illustrated through an exemplary vignette: that of an adult inciting evocative recollection by punctuating a child's fleeting and unstructured impressions in culturally constrained ways: 'children's parts in the interactions are determined for them.... Adults provide directions for the activities, and often even supply the lines.'[30] However, this vignette also invites a very different reading, which moves against the grain of contextualist accounts: it resurrects the spectre of social engineering with the suggestion that the child, rather than being active and competent from the start, is simply a vessel for the directions provided by the adults and the wider cultural knowledges they represent. In order to disavow that possibility of psyche-making as the implantation of consciousness within a passive and malleable infant, contextualist approaches to memory development propose that the child is always-already an interactive partner in the process of transmission:

> Although adults direct the action and set the goals, they do not neces-sarily provide direct tuition for the child; rather they provide conditions under which the child fills in the expected role activity.... The knowl-edge that results from the child's participatory interaction may be quite different from the structure of the event as viewed by the adult.[31]

In other words, the child is not directly presented with the skills through which to produce a mnemic output: the process is, rather, one of 'implicit instruction' where skills of recollection emerge as 'a natural by-product of involvement in tasks with adults or more competent peers'.[32] It is this emphasis on the *implicit* nature of instruction, I would suggest, that distinguishes the contextualist account of memory and self-emergence from a model of social engineering. If instruction is implicit, the child cannot be said to learn mechanically: indeed, it is understood to do more than simply reproduce a number of lines provided by the carers. The carers may be responsible for providing the activities through which the child will – as it were – learn to remember, but within this picture there is an important disjunction between what is provided by the adult and what is remem-bered by the child. This disjunction suggests that the young child is already in possession of a repertory of procedural rules which enable it to assimilate creatively aspects of maternal communication even before it comprehends language:

> What the mothers say does not tutor infants. Because infants already perceive speech, they are able to assimilate baby talk as a carrier of maternal subjectivity ... taking [it] into their own patterns of commu-nicative expression and deriving organisation from what the mothers do. They take what they require and let the rest go by.[33]

It is here that the hypothesis of primary intersubjectivity comes into play in contextualist accounts. The child is able to internalise-with-a-difference only to the extent that installed within her is a space of negotiation: a proto-agora as it were, a priming for relational life. This proto-space is theorised as the infant's 'preadaptive capacities for human interaction ... for recognising recurrent patterns',[34] in short, as an innate predisposition to affiliate with others.[35] This predisposition is said to be visible by dint of the infant's early movements and cries, the positioning of its body and face and its use of sound in relation to its carers. In this reading, care-taking movements and rituals will assist in the making of a relational space out of such predispositions. Carer–child interac-tions henceforth testify to the generation of a space of relationality and communication, in which communication is produced through and as a proto-social bond. For some, this relational space is an extension of what is considered to be essentially a physiological attunement. Thus the psychiatrist Emde implies that a biological fittedness exists between infant and carer:

> Infant affective expressions are used to guide caregiving. The mother hears a cry and acts to relieve the presumed cause of distress. She sees a smile and hears cooing and cannot resist maintaining a playful interaction.[36]

For other researchers, attunement is not innate but an early and provisional achievement that emerges gradually through a series of mutual adjustments between the behaviours of the infant and those of the mother. Thus, for example, while the mother adapts her breast-feeding rhythms to the infant's breathing reflexes, so the infant responds by transforming his reflexes into rhythmic patterns.[37] Whether or not the infant already demonstrates intention is a moot point: what is imagined here is a subtle call-and-response ritual, in which an approximate and dynamic *mutuality* is negotiated through a series of micro-adjustments:

> The infant needs a partner but knows the principle of the dance well enough, and is not just a puppet to be animated by a miming mother who 'pretends' her baby knows better.[38]

Early infant movements, be they gurgling or hand grasping, provoke translation by the adult and therefore initiate a choreography of interactions. What is posited as the child's openness to interaction, its hard-wired predisposition to sociality, enables it to learn turn-taking through the rehearsals of this dance, and to internalise the function of 'reciprocal roles in discourse'.[39] In this way, joint actions establish 'states of intersubjectivity',[40] that is to say, spaces of interaction in which 'the sharing of emotional states … and a shared focus on external events' become possible.[41] In such an account, interaction leads to the emergence of 'dialogue' – in the sense of rules *organising* and constructing a joint activity. From these interactions, the child will gradually abstract a set of 'generative procedural rules' – for example, it will learn that the act of pointing is something separate from the particular toy pointed at and can therefore be used to get the adult to bring over other toys, food and so on. Acts, in other words, can be detached from their present coordinates to serve as regulating frameworks for new experiences.[42]

It is the assimilation of those rules that forms the basis of memory as the patterning and transformation of experience. In this sense, those rules of turn-taking work as the basic constraints through which more specific cultural frameworks will later be erected. Thus, while the adult is clearly in possession of cultural codes unknown to the infant, the infant is from the beginning a partner in the communication process and henceforth co-regulates social stimulation. 'Primary intersubjectivity' thus provides the foundation for the later development of explicit recollection by opening up a proto-social space in which stimulation can be transformed into meaningful experience.[43]

This, then, is how the transition from *inter*-mental to *intra*-mental is narrated in contextualist accounts. The early establishment of a communicative space enables the child to recognise the basic rules of exchange. Thus, even when the child is unable to understand the meaning of the adult behaviour, she is nevertheless equipped to tune into the framework within which this behaviour occurs *and appropriate it as her own*. The appropriated framework will then provide the regulation and internal scaffolding for the child's own memories, creating in this way her sense of self. In this model, the child's embodied memory consists in the creative reinterpretation of the adult's behaviour as this behaviour had unfolded in the space of interaction with the child. The child's embodiment thus both repeats and transforms the cultural frameworks of meaning constituting the familial habitus.

The model of memory adumbrated in contextualist psychology is thus a fully social memory, not only because it is constituted through socially constrained framings of experience but, more importantly, because it is produced within 'states of intersubjectivity' that are quite literally spacings of sociality. This memory is rooted in the body, but this is a body configured as a 'matrix of communication'[44] that is characterised by its openness to the other.[45]

Memory disrupted: Laplanche on intersubjectivity

For the contextualists, then, the infant's memory schemata reshape themselves around the rhythm of others' communications, thereby building memory out of them. As against this reading of the foundations of the psychic world through a dialogic space which is then appropriated by the child, Laplanche's reading of Freud insists that the Freudian unconscious cannot be reduced to a memory founded upon intersubjective exchange. Rather, Laplanche claims that Freud's unconscious must be understood as a heterogeneous eruption that is produced by the web of communication and yet is irreducible to its memorialising effects. In other words, for Laplanche the unconscious arises as a disturbance in memorial – subjective space – as the latter is conceived in both social theory and psychology.

Laplanche, considering the exchanges orchestrated between the carer and the infant, suggests that the asymmetrical nature of those exchanges cannot be fully accounted for by psychologists' models of 'implicit learning'. What is missing from the contextualists' discussion of the scene of exchange, Laplanche suggests, is the sexuality of the carer's messages. In other words, what is not accounted for is the fact that there is an aspect to the proto-dialogue that can only be communicable as excitation and bodily arousal. That is because the choreography between adult and child, the gestures of 'everyday practice', are inevitably imbued with sexual significance, either because they echo an earlier sexual exchange of the carer (touches, sounds and movements which have already functioned in the carer's sexual history, and which now reappear in the context of care) or because they accidentally stimulate the infant (gestures of care which may accidentally become physically exciting for the infant, etc.). If, for the contextualists, the infantile body is a communicational grid, for Laplanche, this body is primarily defined by a boundary which is always precarious, always open to the possibility of an exciting caress. In Laplanche's reading, this caress, this sexual dimension of the message, is neither assimilated as an organising framework nor simply goes by unnoticed. Rather, it penetrates and marks the subject. Its unreadability is not simply an effect of the child's innocence: it is not that the child is simply too young or too immature to comprehend the sexual message. Rather, the unreadability of the message is radical for *both* parties in its transmission: 'the adults themselves do not have the code'.[46] As such, this aspect of the exchange persists as a disturbance in the spatiality of exchange, as an excitation that – insofar as it can be neither memorialised nor ignored – overwhelms the infant.[47] It is this sexual excess of communication, this constitutive disturbance in intersubjective space that, for Laplanche, generates the unconscious. In this sense, the unconscious is not *another* spatiality but *other to* spatiality. This unconscious is neither a by-product nor a foundation of exchange: it is rather its residue. For psychoanalysis, the psyche is not coterminous with a memorial space, whether that is conceived as mental function or as social practice. Rather, the unconscious can only be perceived in its proper sexual dimension if it is firmly positioned as a disturbance in spatiality, and as the detritus of social relations. In this sense, memory, as narrative or embodied experience, is but one aspect of psychic life.

Laplanche, then, reads the psychoanalytic unconscious as the dimension of seduction that cuts across the communicative encounter: the unconscious is the effect of the other's desire and of its surfacing in the act of communication as the question 'What does the other want of me?' For Laplanche, it is this insistence on the priority of the other's desire that constitutes the psychoanalytic project. That priority survives as an alien aspect, or residue, within all interhuman communication. Crucially, desire here is not simply hostage to the Oedipal scenario: it does not follow a universal language. Indeed, Laplanche suggests that it is constituted 'at the core of intersubjective structures [predating] its emergence in the individual'.[48] In this account, desire is irreducible insofar as it arises through the specificity of relations with others, through the brushing of skin in communication. In Laplanche's reading, desire emerges as both an effect of social relations *and* as an aspect of the psyche that is irreducible to memory (both conscious and unconscious):

> The thing-like presentations which form the kernel of the unconscious are to be conceived as that which eludes the child's first attempts to construct for itself an interhuman world, and so translate into a more or less coherent view the messages coming from adults.[49]

In other words, desire is a kind of social residue lining the relations to social others, in a way which is in itself traumatic in that it both conditions *and* disturbs relationality. Indeed, in Laplanche's Freud, desire is a particular kind of human reality that is equally irreducible to either the world or the mind – to the social world and to the world of lived experience – but which nevertheless conditions and disturbs the exchanges between the two. In this insistence on the centrality of desire for the formation of psychic reality, Laplanche proposes a different reading of intersubjectivity from that favoured in contextual psychology and memory studies alike. Here, the intersubjective relation oscillates between the production of a space of memory and the interruption of this space through the vicissitudes of desire.

While Laplanche's reading of unconscious materialities diverges from current work on social memory, the methodological and epistemological stakes of this reading remain closely related to such work. If memory studies, as I contend, is an exemplary instantiation of the turn from structure to practice, then Laplanche's Freud can similarly be positioned as an attempt to rethink the psyche in terms of the contingency of experience and the forces of intersubjective fields. As such, Laplanche's reading is explicitly set up as a polemic against the French structuralist readings of Freud as well as the structuralising impulses evident in American psychoanalysis and cognitive psychology. Indeed, Laplanche's sustained critique of Lacanian structuralism parallels Pierre Bourdieu's case against structural anthropology. While Bourdieu famously departed from structuralism insofar as the latter made of language a reified abstraction, a concept with 'the power to act in history',[50] Laplanche similarly criticised Lacanian psychoanalysis for 'creating abstract entities and attributing to them their own efficacy'.[51] While Laplanche praises Lacan for emphasising the distinction between 'the subject' according to psychoanalysis and the subject of the psychologists, he nevertheless claims that Lacan's structuralism ends up disembedding the unconscious from any historical specificity, to 'open [it] into all the winds of language'.[52]

Laplanche's project, then, partakes in the turn away from a structural logic insofar as it attempts to locate the psyche as an effect of historical specificity. Crucially, however, Laplanche does not turn instead to the provisional embodiments of such a system, that is to say, he does not find the psyche in the gestures of everyday life where Bourdieu finds the 'logic of practice'. Rather, he finds it in the margins of such gestures, as 'a *third domain of reality*, which is *neither* the pure materiality of the gesture … *nor* the pure psychology of the protagonist(s)' (italics in original).[53] The unconscious in this sense is a third reality, which is neither individual nor cultural but which nevertheless arises as a marginal product of intersubjective exchanges and negotiations. For Laplanche, the materialities of the psyche cannot become equivalent to a socially and intersubjectively produced memory: rather, these materialities are precisely what such memory cannot translate and contain. Laplanche's writings urge us to recognise that the understanding of memory as a social practice must pass through the detritus, just as descriptions of market places must always remember that junkyards are never far away.

As I write this, I come across yet another invocation of social memory as bodily communication, in an essay by American cultural historian Jonathan Boyarin. He writes:

> Perhaps the most obvious link between memory and the body is through mnemonic marking. Intriguingly, nonstate collectives seem most often to mark individual bodies as a sign of inclusion, whereas states most often mark bodies precisely to exclude them.... In the case of torture or terrorism, the bodily practice marks both the boundary between violator and victim and, less obviously, the link that binds them in their reciprocal imaginings.... When the marks of torture on the bodies of its victims are displayed – for example, by international human rights organizations – what was intended to terrorize the memory of the individual victim is transformed into a sign by which 'the world' is made to remember the wrongs done that victim.[54]

This vignette is intended to illustrate the redemptive lability of social memory. It suggests that even the most brutal and dehumanising inscription – a torturer's destruction of his victim's body – can, insofar as it is a mnemonic device, be recontextualised into a memorial of resistance and of solidarity. Leaving aside for the moment Boyarin's brusque change of perspective – for whom is the memory recontextualised? – such a reading of this vignette excludes what Laplanche would identify as the excessive aspect of all communication. Its excess lies in this case in the fact that bound within this redemptive translation of the scar as a mnemic sign (the world feels outrage for the perpetrator and solidarity with the victim) is a certain enjoyment derived from the consumption of this spectacle (the audience may be thrilled and appalled, i.e. excited by the victim's plight). While the possibility of this enjoyment does not diminish the accountability of the torturers or the seriousness of the offence, it nevertheless complicates it considerably. It complicates it insofar as it suggests that the same message which incites the call for justice may also incite a certain desire which does not know justice. In this sense, such a possibility marks the translation between first meaning and second meaning (from mark of degradation, to call to solidarity) with a sexual remainder, as its literal waste-matter. That is to say, there is an unredeemable aspect of the communication that cannot simply be transformed and returned to circulation: no coin of the realm, no manifestation of solidarity, finally, no mnemonic reconstruction, can either redeem or erase it.

Notes

1 C. Geertz, *The Interpretation of Cultures*, New York: Basic Books, 1973, p. 45.
2 J. Laplanche, 'A Short Treatise on the Unconscious', in *Essays on Otherness*, London: Routledge, 1999 (essay originally published in French in 1993), p. 89.
3 For example, N.C. Seremetakis, *Perception and Memory as Material Culture in Modernity*, Boulder, CO: Westview Press, 1994; J. Shotter, 'The Social Construction of

Remembering and Forgetting', in D. Middleton and D. Edwards (eds) *Collective Remembering*, London: Sage, 1990; and N. Wachtel, 'Introduction' (to special issue on Memory and History), *History and Anthropology* 2, 1986, pp. 207–24.

4 P. Bourdieu, *The Logic of Practice*, trans. R. Nice, Stanford, CA: Stanford University Press, 1990, p. 68.

5 Laplanche, op. cit., p. 89.

6 For example, J. Fentress and C. Wickham, *Social Memory*, Oxford: Blackwell, 1992; N. Gedi and Y. Elam, 'Collective Memory – What Is It?', *History and Memory* 8, 1996, pp. 30–50; P.H. Hutton, 'Sigmund Freud and Maurice Halbwachs: The Problem of Memory in Historical Psychology', *Historical Reflections* 19, 1993, pp. 1–16; Middleton and Edwards (eds), op. cit.; J. Olick and J. Robbins, 'Social Memory Studies: From "Collective Memory" to the Historical Sociology of Mnemonic Practices', *Annual Review of Sociology* 22, 1998, pp. 105–40. For Halbwachs' seminal work on memory see M. Halbwachs, *On Collective Memory*, ed. and trans. L. Coser, Chicago: University of Chicago Press, 1992 (originally published in French in 1941 and 1952).

7 For example see Olick and Robbins, op. cit., p. 122.

8 Fentress and Wickham, op. cit., p. ix.

9 S. Radstone, 'Working with Memory: An Introduction', in S. Radstone (ed.) *Memory and Methodology*, Oxford: Berg, 2000.

10 See D. Thelen, 'Introduction: Memory and American History', in D. Thelen (ed.) *Memory and American History*, Bloomington, IN: Indiana University Press, 1989, p. xiii. This understanding of memory is greatly indebted to British readings of social history and cultural formations, and in particular to the formulation of the concept of 'popular memory' by researchers associated with the Birmingham Centre for Contemporary Cultural Studies (see Popular Memory Group, 'Popular Memory: Theory, Politics, Method', in R. Johnson *et al.* (eds) *Making Histories: Studies in History, Writing and Politics*, London: Hutchinson, 1982; S. Radstone (ed.) *Memory and Methodology*, op. cit.

11 S. Ortner, 'Theory in Anthropology Since the Sixties', *Comparative Studies in Society and History* 26, 1984, p. 148.

12 I. Irwin-Zarecka, *Frames of Remembrance: The Dynamics of Collective Memory*, New Brunswick, NJ: Transaction Publishers, 1994.

13 G. Lipsitz, *Time Passages: Collective Memory and American Popular Culture*, Minneapolis, MN: University of Minnesota Press, 1990, p. 220.

14 Wachtel, op. cit., p. 220.

15 J. Boyarin, 'Space, Time and the Politics of Memory', in J. Boyarin (ed.) *Remapping Memory: The Politics of TimeSpace*, Minneapolis, MN: University of Minnesota Press, 1994, p. 26.

16 K.L. Klein, 'On the Emergence of *Memory* in Historical Discourse', *Representations* 69, 2000, p. 141.

17 There is of course an intense preoccupation with Oedipal configurations and with fantasy in the work of several feminist historians. However, what I am focusing on here is the more recent tendency in memory studies to either sidestep Freud or – under the auspices of 'trauma theory' – to declare allegiance to concepts of 'trauma' and 'working through' that have little to do with psychoanalysis (on this point, see S. Radstone, 'Trauma and Screen Studies: Opening the Debate', *Screen* 42.2, 2001, pp. 188–93).

18 This claim challenges the assumption that disciplines construct their objects differently because they have distinct institutional histories and are bound by different methodological traditions. Let me be clear: I do not wish to deny that different methodological paradigms give rise to different objects. Rather, I want to explore the history of such paradigms in order to identify the cross-disciplinary traffic that may have played a constitutive role in their emergence and legitimation.

19 D. Gillespie, *The Mind's We: Contextualistism in Cognitive Psychology*, Carbondale: Southern Illinois University Press, 1992, p. 47.

20 K.J. Gergen, 'The Social Contextualist Movement in Modern Psychology', *American Psychologist* March 1985, p. 270.

21 K.J. Gergen, 'Social Psychology and the Wrong Revolution', *European Journal of Social Psychology* 19, 1989, p. 472. The references usually drawn upon here are: P. Berger and T. Luckmann, *The Social Construction of Reality*, New York: Anchor Books, 1967; Geertz, op. cit.; and M. Sahlins, *Culture and Practical Reason*, Chicago: University of Chicago Press, 1977.

22 J. Bruner, 'Going Beyond the Information Given', in J. Bruner (ed.) *Contemporary Approaches to Cognition*, Cambridge, MA: Harvard University Press, 1957.

23 M. Cole, 'The Zone of Proximal Development: Where Culture and Cognition Create Each Other', in J.V. Wertsch (ed.) *Culture, Communication and Cognition: Vygotskian Perspectives*, Cambridge: Cambridge University Press, 1985.

24 Bourdieu, op. cit., p. 82.

25 M. Tessler and K. Nelson, 'Making Memories: The Influence of Joint Encoding on Later Recall by Young Children', *Consciousness and Cognition* 3, 1994, p. 309.

26 L.S. Vygotsky, *Mind in Society: The Development of Higher Psychological Processes*, ed. M. Cole, V. John-Steiner, S. Scribner and E. Souberman, Cambridge, MA: Harvard University Press, 1978, p. 57.

27 R. Fivush, 'The Social Construction of Personal Narratives', *Merrill-Palmer Quarterly* 37, 1991, p. 75.

28 J. Bruner, 'From Communication to Language: A Psychological Perspective', *Cognition* 3, 1974, pp. 255–87.

29 The terms are associated respectively with J. Bruner, 'The Narrative Construction of Reality', *Critical Inquiry* 18, 1991, pp. 1–21; J.M. Mandler, 'A Code in the Node: The Use of a Story Schema in Retrieval', *Discourse Processes* 1, 1987, pp. 14–35; and R.C. Schank and R.P. Abelson, *Scripts, Plans, Goals and Understanding*, Hillsdale, NJ: Lawrence Erlbaum, 1977.

30 K. Nelson, 'Social Cognition in a Script Framework', in J. Flavell and L. Ross (eds) *Social Cognitive Development*, Cambridge: Cambridge University Press, 1981, p. 106.

31 Ibid., pp. 106–7.

32 P.H. Miller, *Theories of Developmental Psychology*, 3rd edn, New York: Freeman, 1993, p. 382.

33 C. Trevarthen, 'Communication and Cooperation in Early Infancy: A Description of Primary Intersubjectivity', in M. Bullowa (ed.) *Before Speech: The Beginning of Interpersonal Communication*, New York: Cambridge University Press, 1979, p. 340.

34 V.E. Demos, 'The Early Organization of the Psyche', in J.W. Baron, M.N. Eagle and D.L. Wolitzky (eds) *The Interface of Psychoanalysis and Psychology*, Washington, DC: American Psychological Association, 1992, p. 213.

35 Accounts of an innate predisposition to sociality are provided in T.G.R. Bower, *Human Development*, San Francisco: Freeman, 1979; M. Bullowa (ed.), op. cit.; and J. Kagan, 'Overview: Perspectives on Human Infancy', in J.D. Osofsky (ed.) *The Handbook on Infant Development*, New York: Wiley, 1979. Perspectives on hard-wired sociality are summarised in R.D. Parke, 'Social Development in Infancy: A 25-year Perspective', in D.M. Reese (ed.) *Advances in Child Development and Behavior*, vol. 21, Orlando, FL: Academic Press, 1989.

36 R. Emde, 'The Prerepresentational Self and its Affective Core', *Psychoanalytic Study of the Child* 38, 1980, p. 173.

37 See J.D. Call, 'Some Prelinguistic Aspects of Language Development', *Journal of the American Psychoanalytic Association* 28, 1980, p. 268.

38 Trevarthen, op. cit., p. 347.

39 Ibid., p. 347.

40 The term is used in R. Rommetviet, 'Language Acquisition as Increasing Linguistic Structuring of Experience and Symbolic Behaviour Control', in J. Wertsch (ed.), op. cit.

41 B. Rogoff, *Apprenticeship in Thinking*, New York: Oxford University Press, 1990, p. 82.

42 See Bruner, op. cit., p. 269.

43 The term 'primary intersubjectivity' is coined by Trevarthen, who explicitly borrows the concept of intersubjectivity from Habermas; see Trevarthen, op. cit., p. 347, n. 1.

44 Call, op. cit., p. 260.

45 Some psychologists go so far as to render the metaphor of internalisation redundant, suggesting instead that children simply appropriate whichever practices they are engaged in (see Rogoff, op. cit., p. 195).

46 J. Laplanche, 'The Drive and its Source-object', in Laplanche, *Essays on Otherness*, op. cit., p. 127.

47 *À propos* of the excessive nature of the gestures of maternal care, Laplanche cites a telling mistranslation of Freud: in a passage from Freud's early work, his editors corrected his word for the maternal response to the infant's cries from *Nahrungseinfuhr* (insertion of food) to *Nahrungszufuhr* (delivery, proffering of food). Thus Freud's reference to an excessive response in which food is stuffed into the infant turns into a measured and regulated exchange: the mother now offers food to the infant. We have moved from the excessive stimulation of sexuality, to something resembling Emde's account in which the mother's response to infantile needs installs a proto-dialogue. According to Freud's editors, this is, after all, what Freud must have meant (Laplanche, 'The Unfinished Copernican Revolution', in *Essays on Otherness*, op. cit., p. 75, n. 49).

48 J. Laplanche and J.-B. Pontalis, *The Language of Psycho-Analysis*, trans. D. Nicholson-Smith, London: Karnac, 1988 (first published 1973), p. 421.

49 Laplanche, 'A Short Treatise on the Unconscious', op. cit., p. 93.

50 Bourdieu, op. cit., p. 37.

51 Laplanche, 'A Short Treatise on the Unconscious', op. cit., p. 115.

52 Laplanche, 'Transference: Its Provocation by the Analyst', in *Essays on Otherness*, op. cit., p. 225.

53 Laplanche, 'Seduction, Persecution, Revelation', in *Essays on Otherness*, op. cit., p. 169.

54 Boyarin, 'Space, Time and the Politics of Memory', op. cit., p. 22.

Part IV

WHAT HISTORY FORGETS: MEMORY AND TIME

Introduction

Susannah Radstone and Katharine Hodgkin

The two chapters that comprise this section set up a conversation about the relationship between history, memory and time – a conversation in which the conscious intentions of historians are set against the unconscious forces that subtend the historical enterprise. Bill Schwarz's chapter proposes that history might expand its *consciousness* by embracing, in its historiographies, a conception of temporality that includes the times of memory. Karl Figlio's chapter suggests, on the other hand, that *at an unconscious level* history is always and inextricably caught up with memory. Thus these two chapters are concerned with both the conscious and unconscious relations between history and memory. Yet Figlio's chapter does not constitute a reply to Schwarz's argument, for to be unconsciously caught up with memory is by no means the equivalent of a conscious attempt, by historians, to understand memory as the subjective dimension of history.

As both Schwarz and Figlio show, the question of memory's relation to history is bound up with questions of temporality. For, notwithstanding their different projects, what both these essays undertake is a critique of historical time as it is currently understood and deployed by historians. Schwarz suggests that, even at their most advanced and sophisticated, accounts of historical temporality retreat from the complexities of memory's times. Figlio proposes, on the other hand, that the linear time that structures every aspect of Western, secular culture, including historical understandings of temporality, is the very conduit for the phantasies that he associates with remembering – phantasies which in his account subtend all Western, secular historical enquiry.

There are good reasons for Schwarz's proposal that historical consciousness might attune itself to the times of memory. If history is, as Schwarz suggests, the study of historical time – of relations between the past and the present – and if the concept of historical time first emerged 'as a means to think about the scope of specifically human action' (p. 136), then it follows that the full complexity of that specificity cannot be grasped without taking on board the subjective dimension of historical time, i.e. memory. Schwarz's chapter points to certain texts in which a historical grasping of the times of memory has been initiated. This is to be found, he suggests, in modernist interventions into the question of historical time, in the works, for instance, of the historian Fernand Braudel, but also in the writings of the Marxist theorist Louis Althusser and in the literary modernism of the author Virgina Woolf. Schwarz begins by discussing Fernand Braudel's proposal that history moves at different speeds. Braudel identified three overarching historical times: geographical, social and individual times – of which he regarded the last, individual time, as the least interesting for history. Schwarz suggests that, although Braudel himself stepped back from the complexities of individual time, historians ought no longer to step away from this crucial dimension of history. Instead, history might begin to develop its understanding of individual time by focusing more specifically on memory's *relation* to historical time. Staying with Braudel's three dimensions of historical time, Schwarz suggests that memory either 'undermines and complicates the Braudelian concept of individual time … or … represents a fourth, discrete dimension of historical time' (p. 139). Yet, as Schwarz goes on to suggest, the embracing of this 'fourth dimension' by historians is by no means straightforward. As he reminds us, memory has been considered by some historians as an anathema to history. If historical time is conceived of as external and objective, then memory, understood as interior and subjective time, appears pre- or anti-rational and thus, by definition, must be excluded from historical consciousness. But Schwarz's chapter insists that it would be a mistake to follow through on this line of argument. If history is to 'grasp the irreducibly human dimensions of historical reality' (p. 146), then it is to the transactions between external and internal times – the times of memory and of history – that it must attend. In conclusion, then, and in keeping with his focus throughout on modernist theories of historical time, Schwarz proposes that historiography might have more than a little to learn from the modernist literary experiments of Virginia Woolf, whose lifetime quest was for a mode of literary writing that could represent precisely those transactions between inner and the outer worlds, the times of history and of memory, from which history might learn.

Schwarz's chapter focuses on the necessary complications or re-thinkings of the objectivity and externality of historical time demanded by an attention to memory. Karl Figlio's chapter suggests, however, that the qualities of objectivity and externality commonly associated with the linear time of history are more apparent than real. Figlio's central argument is founded on a particular psychoanalytic understanding of memory: '(i)n object-relational terms', he explains, 'remembering is a form of phantasying, primarily working over the disturbing aspects of internal objects' (p. 155). From an object-relations perspective, the inner world is constituted by relations towards whole and part objects. Though these objects are formed in relation to real people – primarily parents – they should not be confused with them, since inner objects are shaped by *phantasy*.

From this psychoanalytic viewpoint, Figlio specifies, the most important question about object relations is the attitude towards those internal objects. Figlio's central thesis is that from this perspective, Western, secular historical enquiry is inextricably bound up with this kind of remembering. The rational quest to understand the past, that is, is driven by phantasies concerning the objects of the inner world. Figlio's argument is framed by a psychoanalytic reading of historical time. In this account, the linearity of Western, secular historical time suggests that all that separates the past from the present is distance – a distance that might be overcome by travelling back in time. What this view of historical time screens, he goes on to suggest, is the *difference* between then and now, between the past and the present, between ourselves and our parents. For Figlio this evasion of difference is highly significant, for it underwrites a series of infantile narcissistic phantasies bound up with a primary desire to 'be there at the beginning'. The phantasy of being there at the beginning is a primal phantasy – a phantasy of witnessing or even taking some part in one's own conception. Figlio explains that this phantasy involves a number of omnipotent, narcissistic moves, each of which denies difference. The primal phantasy depends, for instance, on denying the differences between the generations, and it denies the necessity of two different sexes in order to make a child. Variations upon this primal phantasy, suggests Figlio, are woven through history's rational enquiries into the past.

The phantasy of being there at the beginning is given 'uncanny concrete reality', he argues, by the linear historical time of secular culture. It is this understanding of time that makes possible the phantasy of moving back along the line: if all that separates the present from the past is distance, then that distance can be phantasised as traversable.

Figlio argues, then, that in historical 'consciousness' the wish to know – to get back to the past – is always driven, in part, by processes of remembrance/phantasy in which omnipotence is key and in which what is central are desirous, reparative and revengeful fantasies towards parental figures. In answer to the question 'How does history come into it?', Figlio responds:

> the historical mentality reconstructs the past. We are invited to 'remember' it, but remembering is filtered through unconscious processes, through phantasies of parenthood and childhood … a historical consciousness … establishes the past in its own right, but it also calls up the phantasy that the past lives in us and we live in the past.
>
> (p. 159)

Taken together, Schwarz and Figlio's chapters offer two complementary responses to the question of history's 'forgetting' of memory. Schwarz's discussion suggests that, until now, history has resisted any full engagement with the temporality of memory. Yet historical consciousness will only truly begin to grasp the human dimension of history, suggests Schwarz, if it can overcome this resistance. Karl Figlio's chapter suggests that historical consciousness is already caught up with memory. Remembering, understood here as phantasies around inner objects, subtends all historical consciousness, where historical time is conceived of as linear. These chapters leave us with an abundance of questions: to what extent are history's rational aims impeded by historical phantasy, and could a revised understanding of historical temporality mitigate the less helpful aspects of these phantasies? What might be the effects on the hidden phantasies of history of an attention to transactions between the times of history and of memory? What seems certain is that neither historical consciousness, nor the unconscious of history, can any longer be discussed without reference to the times of memory.

7

'ALREADY THE PAST'

Memory and historical time

Bill Schwarz

> With her foot on the threshold she waited a moment longer in a
> scene which was vanishing even as she looked, and then, as she
> moved and took Minta's arm and left the room, it changed, it
> shaped itself differently; it had become, she knew, giving one last
> look at it over her shoulder, already the past.
>
> (Virginia Woolf, *To the Lighthouse*)

When late in life the magisterial French historian, Fernand Braudel, was asked to
reflect on his contribution to historical thought he simply had this to say: 'My
great problem, the only problem I had to resolve, was to show that time moves at
different speeds.'[1] This is a gratifyingly philosophical, though for this reason
perhaps an unexpected, statement for a historian to propose.

For all the theoretical difficulties this idea bequeaths, it serves to focus our
minds on an important, if neglected, moment in the development of historical
thought. I like to think of Braudel's conception of the differing speeds of historical time as a discovery, in the received or popular sense of discovery, proximate to
those other scientific discoveries of the early twentieth century, which – in Eric
Hobsbawm's words – snapped the link between the world of the intellect (or what
could be imagined theoretically) and the everyday world of sense-experience.[2]
Admittedly, to elevate Braudel as a lone intellectual pioneer is a rather old-fash-
ioned way of seeing things: the insight was not his alone; his discoveries largely
codified what was already known, or half-known, as opposed to a discovery which
– in a flash of insight – alighted upon a hitherto unseen particle of knowledge;
and so on. But discovery suggests drama, and Braudel's impact has been
dramatic. To imagine history to be composed of multiple historical times is to
locate historiography directly in those 'relativist' paradigms which recast the
natural sciences at the same period in the early decades of the twentieth century.
If relativity unhinged positivist conceptions of time and space in the Newtonian
redoubt of physics then, we might assume from Braudel's reasoning, similar
developments might prove to be possible in historiography.

If one were to follow this argument further, it might also provide a means for
opening lines of connection between conventional historiographies and that

aesthetic ferment of the early twentieth century which we know by the name of modernism. That is my suspicion, at any rate, and I'll offer one or two observations on this question, not so much to clinch the argument but, hopefully, to open up further reflection.

It is perhaps not surprising that a Braudelian conception of differentiated historical time exists at a meta-level of historical thought, the equivalent to one of those elegant algebraic abstractions in mathematics which announces a potential new finding but which brings with it manifold concrete difficulties. Until quite recently historians, certainly in the anglophone world, have gone about their business without worrying too much about meta-theories of historical time. In so doing, wilfully or not, they have tended to find themselves underwriting a conception of historical time which, theoretically, precedes Braudel. (This is a tangled story, with many interesting crosscurrents. I think it could be demonstrated, in the British case, by exploring the intellectual tradition that takes us from G.M. Trevelyan in the early part of the twentieth century to Simon Schama in the latter part. But to tell that story requires a different occasion.) Insofar as historians of late have heeded questions about the complexities of historical time and, crucially, about the appropriate narrative structures which follow, most frequently these debates have been described in catch-all terms as engagements with post-structuralism or postmodernism. My own view is that much of what has passed as debate about postmodernism in the historical journals is more properly understood as a belated confrontation with the fall-out from high modernism, and indeed, from Braudelian-type insights which we have yet to catch up with. A measure of epistemological relativism; open-ended narratives; the transactions between the psychic realities of the inner life and the external world; the semiotic ordering of the real; the anarchic relations between signifier and signified – all of these had a prior life, in more practical form, in the imaginative products of high modernism at the start of the twentieth century and (as modernist theorists came to see) in carnivalesque low-life for very much longer. There may be a case for historians to think more carefully about modernism, and to take a break from yet another excitable, abstract encounter with postmodernism. And tacitly I'm suggesting that most of the current experiments in cultural history – the kind of histories which, I should say, have the capacity to move me – owe more to these supposedly remote antecedents than they do to current notions of post-structuralism.

It is perhaps self-evident that what historians study, as their particular object of knowledge, is historical time. So far as we can say, that's what history is: the study of the relations between the past and the present. There is still much that is persuasive in the idea that the concept of historical time first appears as a means to think about the scope of specifically human action, cast in opposition to a perception of the world ordained by the whims of the deities. Subsequently, what has been conceived as human action has progressively if unevenly broadened, to include not only the rulers but the ruled, not only men but women, and so on. But this broadening in our understanding of historical agency has not always brought with it a broadening of our understanding of historical time.[3] So long as the underlying dynamic of history was theorised as singular – civilisation, reason, the spirit of the nation, climate, the people, class – then historical time was necessarily singular too. I think it's probably only in the twentieth century that we can properly begin to identify the emergence of a contrary, plural conception of historical time. And this is precisely the innovation which, at the end of his intellectual life, Braudel looked back to and remembered as a kind of revolution in his discipline.

Braudel's own specific resolution to this problem has been well rehearsed. In his most famous book, *The Mediterranean and the Mediterranean World at the Time of Philip II*, written over half a century ago, he identified three overarching historical times: geographical or environmental time, which moved at glacial speed; the time of social structures – of economic systems, states, societies and civilisations; and the time of events, which he believed to be often the most exciting but in which he, as a historian, was least interested.[4] These he summarised as geographical, social and individual times, recognising that his hopes for rendering a total history depended upon understanding the superimposition of these variant movements of time. The remainder of his long professional life was devoted to the attempt to refine a historiography that could encompass the interconnections of these different historical times.

Braudel was sufficiently self-conscious, theoretically, to appreciate that these distinctions (geographical, social, individual) derived from a point of view which was largely descriptive rather than conceptual.[5] He experimented with many different formulations, which can be seen both in his attempts to coin abstract principles and in his concrete historical writing. He swung back and forth in his commitments to structuralism. For a while he toyed with the idea of importing into historiography models drawn from a discipline he described as social mathematics.[6] But throughout, the core problem remained constant: the need to identify and think together the full conjunctural complexities of competing historical times.[7]

It seems as if many French historians of *annaliste* temperament shared these concerns. He himself mentions a 'manifesto' on the theme having been presented to a congress of historians in Rome in 1955.[8] It is paradoxical, perhaps, that a variant of structuralism (not known for its sympathies for a historical mode of thinking) supplied an appropriate theoretical idiom in which these matters of temporality could be addressed. However, the enthusiasm for structural thought displayed by some of the leading *annalistes* should not be conflated with the Saussurian structuralism introduced into French intellectual life at the end of the 1950s, with many fanfares, by Roland Barthes and Claude Lévi-Strauss – though Braudel was always an admiring and respectful reader of Lévi-Strauss. In the concluding pages to the last edition of the second volume of his history of the Mediterranean, he emphasised that his commitments lay with a 'historian's "structuralism"' which 'does not tend toward the mathematical abstraction of relations expressed as functions, but instead towards the very sources of life in its most concrete, everyday, inde-structible and anonymously human expression'.[9] Yet even if we take these contrasts into account, it is striking how the language of structures provided the means first fully to theorise the dynamics of historical time. It is evident in Braudel's 'historian's structuralism'. And, most dramatically, it is evident in the rather different version of structuralism adumbrated by Louis Althusser in the early 1960s. In Althusser's two defining collections of this period – *For Marx* and *Reading Capital* – the issue of historical time lay at the very centre of his bid to reclaim the fundamentals of historical materialism.[10] Historians reared in the *Annales* traditions may have had their difficulties with Althusser, and many admitted that they remained unpersuaded by his attempted philosophical resuscitation of Marxism. But in one respect they shared a common belief: that, faced with the multiplicity of historical time, it was incumbent upon historians to imagine new ways of writing history.[11]

The impetus for my argument derives from Braudel; I'll comment on Althusser in a moment. It may be valuable, however, simply to indicate just one other strand of theoretical influence in these reconceptualisations of temporality. Behind the historiographical debates within French intellectual life lay the larger presence of Marxism – sometimes explicit, sometimes implicit – in which many of the key formulations concerning temporality had first come to life.[12] Of particular significance were forms of Marxism which, in retrospect, we judge to be resoundingly orthodox. I'm thinking especially of the upheaval in Marxist theory brought about by the revolution in Russia. Early twentieth-century Marxism was endlessly disputatious; every arena of social life became an appro-priate matter for investigation. Pre-eminent was the question of Russia itself. The peculiarities of the Russian formation and its dislocation from the historical times of the core capitalist nations of Europe became a matter of theoretical and political urgency. Over a number of years discussion gave rise to a theoret-ical-cum-agitational literature which introduced (or gave new prominence to) a vibrant set of ideas concerning uneven development and the combination of different modes of production. In turn, spilling out from the irrepressible imagi-nation of Leon Trotsky, this led to the elegant theoretical proposition of 'combined and uneven development'. Faced with the historical realities of Russia it was readily apparent that inherited schemas – most of all that to be found in the classic *Communist Manifesto* – were in themselves too weak in explanatory power to be of practical political service. In a series of intriguing interventions, attention shifted to the internal properties of historical time itself, as realised in all its bewildering complexities within Russia.[13] I'm not suggesting there were always direct lines of connection between these older Marxist debates, shaped at every turn by contingent political imperatives, and the philosophising of a later generation of French intellectuals. (It is unimaginable, for example, that Althusser, a militant in the French Communist Party, was reading Trotsky at the end of the 1950s.) But, given the political proclivities of the intellectual culture in France from the Popular Front of the 1930s to the events of 1968, these disputes about the specificities of Russian historical development, and the broad conceptual terms in which these debates had been couched, would have been known to historians and philosophers alike. The *orthodoxy* of these founding theorisations was, I think, to have interesting consequences.

I'll come back to these points. What, though, of memory? How do these seemingly arcane notions of historical time, locked into pasts which by all accounts have now vanished, connect with our own anxious, contemporary investigations into the mechanisms of memory?

My own sense is that the recent arrival of memory as an object for study can, in this context, be understood in two alternative ways. One could either suggest that it undermines and complicates the Braudelian concept of individual historical time. Or, to follow the drama of Braudel's own initial breakthroughs, one could raise the stakes and – working from the tripartite division he espoused – propose that memory represents a fourth, discrete dimension of historical time: a conception of time of the inner life, of the mnemonic itself.

This may be unduly polemical. But it's apparent that Braudel himself was unsettled by the fact that, in his categorisation of individual time, he was unable to resolve what he perceived as the shifts between the conscious and the unconscious aspects of human action. Indeed, his prose suggests that he found something peculiarly troubling about this entire dimension of historical time. His acceptance of the Marxisant or structuralist premise – that men and women make history but not in circumstances of their own making – blurred the boundaries of a historical time deemed specifically 'individual'. In his earliest formulations he implied that true or authentic historical time was to be found enveloped in the Earth's social ecologies, whose movement day by day remains imperceptible: 'a history of constant repetition'.[14] The historical time of events, on the other hand, he believed, represented little more than a 'surface disturbance' – 'a dangerous world', as he put it, for the historian to consider, a world swept up in all manner of 'spells and enchantments'. Indeed, the historian, he declared, needed to 'exorcise' these troubling features of individual historical time by paying due attention to the quieter, more profound and ultimately more meaningful rhythms of the long duration.[15] This is a strict, early rendition of his interpretation of historical time, and one that was to be modified thereafter. But, modifications notwithstanding, similar anxieties always seemed to reappear. In a later essay, for example, he described this domain of time as 'the most capricious', and as 'deceptive', and emphasised the salience of a 'social unconsciousness lying some way away from us'. He observed the need to distinguish between what he enigmatically called 'the clear surface and the dark depths' and between 'noise and silence'.[16] This metaphorical, even poetic, vocabulary is not one that is usually associated with Braudel. Yet far from clarifying things it evokes only further, barely comprehended complexities.

For all his sophistication Braudel could never, at least to his own satisfaction, arrive at an appropriate theorisation of individual historical time. Or, to use his own vocabulary, he never discovered the means by which he could exorcise the caprice, spells, enchantments, deceptions and noise of a historical temporality that refused to work by the same rules as those of the long durations of environmental or geographical history. We need to ponder why he felt compelled to cast the historian in this role of exorcist.

The answer turns, in part, on the question of memory. At some point, any theory of temporality has to confront memory, as the subjective dimension of time itself. Memory confounds many preconceptions of how time works. In this sense it is, in tendency at least, a refractory object of study. As we know from contemporary debates among historians, memory continues to provoke and unsettle, and it can still be perceived to threaten all that history – as the objective study of social time – stands for. Memory, for those who follow this view, is not the ally of history, but its contrary. Its fallibility is the reason why historiography is required. Memory, though patently a component of temporal life, cannot (so the argument continues) qualify as a component of *historical* time. A powerful expression of such a view – perhaps the most powerful – can be found in the recent essays of Eric Hobsbawm.[17] Braudel's worries represent, I believe, an early manifestation of this same unease.[18] One can see why he (and those who hold to this position) are perplexed or even wary, and it would be foolish to underestimate the conceptual and ethical difficulties which follow the commitment to understand memory as a dimension of historical time.

Braudel's apprehensions about his capacity to reconcile the conscious and the unconscious were not misguided, for the problem remains with us, unresolved as ever, and assumes ever greater centrality as the question of memory looms larger. However much we might wish historiographical protocols to be stretched, or turned inside out, elemental requirements of historical practice – fidelity to evidence and all its consequences – remain unnegotiable. Many problems arise. It is not clear, for example, whether the time of memory moves with excessive speed or with excessive sloth, although I imagine Braudel would have argued for the former.[19] Questions like these, and their many correlates, pose serious difficulties. Historians are not wrong in seeing the enormity of the impact of memory on historiography. When Braudel proposed that the historical time of events represents a 'surface disturbance' it would – by extension – make sense to see the historical time of subjective memory as a disturbance of a disturbance, or maybe even a *deep* rather than a surface disturbance. None of these issues offers a situation that is comfortable for historians to inhabit, for historians are reared in an intellectual culture organised to encourage more rectilinear modes of thought. Disruptions (precisely) interrupt narrative cohesion, and neat narratives are what historians, among others, are trained to like.

Yet we can track the conceptual dynamic which underpins the movement in Braudel's thought. On the one hand is his commitment to a rational, scientific historiography, driven by an uncompromisingly secular theoretical language. On the other is what he regarded as the spells, enchantments and so forth which, he claimed, needed to be brought within the orbit of historiography, organised by a properly secular, critical conceptual system. That this was never fully achieved is

140

apparent from his recurrent returns to his troubled encounters with the domain of individual time. Yet I don't think that this difficulty was Braudel's alone. It has a more general provenance. Subjective time, memory included, cannot be accommodated within a theory of historical time that is based only on a conceptualisation of time as external and objective. An overly rationalist temporal theory can only recognise the mechanics of interior time as pre- or anti-rational, as falling outside the realm of reason itself, and thereby conclude that the exercise of reason must strive for greater vigilance.

Thus (from a Braudelian perspective) interior time could become the object of history, in much the same way as, say, witchcraft or shamanism has become a staple of historical study. But the temporal logics inscribed in interior time could never, from within this perspective, contribute to historiographical *analysis* – to our understanding of the historical world – because interior time defies the temporal regime of objective social time, reaping confusion where the historian must impose order. The logic of interior time can become the object of history, but never the means by which history itself is explained. It was here, I think, that Braudel found himself turning back from his own discoveries, caught in a double symmetry in which social time was hermetically divided from interior time, just as reason was divided from unreason. Those of us who learn from Braudel, who remain in his debt, are not required to repeat this retreat. Historiography and memory are not *the same*. That much is true. But nor are they always, necessarily mortal enemies – as Braudel suspected and as Hobsbawm claims out loud. Indeed, we have some extraordinary examples in which the analytical interaction between history and memory produces what can only be described as new knowledge, expanding the possibilities of what the historical imagination, with all its givens, can do.[20] These texts, and others like them, do not work to dissolve social time, reducing all temporalities to a vague moment of human consciousness.[21] They do, however, vividly demonstrate the fact that any theory of composite historical time is the more powerful for incorporating not only objective or social temporalities, but its lived, phenomenological forms as well.

Or, to make the same argument in another way: it is at this moment – when we encounter the complexities of interior time – that we come up against the limitations of Braudel's 'historian's "structuralism" '. Memory, subjective and interior times, the lived forms of external histories: all incessantly intrude on objective time, and work to make more labile, or more fluid, the suppositions of the structuralists. This signals the 'deep' disturbance which memory brings to traditional or structural theories of temporality.

This encounter with interior time entails, too, a revision of the terms of Braudel's founding concepts. To claim that time moves at different speeds implies that time remains essentially forward-moving: that although history travels at different rates, it works toward a common destination. Maybe one can detect a residual evolutionism in Braudel in which history becomes the vehicle by which modernity arrives. Memory, undoubtedly, disrupts any uni-directional movement from past to present to future. In memory, past and present are compressed, such that the past itself remains peculiarly resistant to transcendence in the present. This requires us to think in terms not only of speed, but of direction – or better, in terms of the realms or locations of memory. These spatial metaphors (which were prominent in the modernist re-theorisations of memory at the start of the twentieth century) invoke too that difficult moment in thought when time and space converge.

These are problems which fall within the terrain of historiography, and they need to be resolved within historiography. However, it is important to note, if only in passing, that there exists a philosophical counterpoint to these historiographical contentions. If in the post-war world various modes of structuralism enabled the theorisation of historical time, they did so at the cost of suppressing a rich phenomenological tradition that had addressed the question of interior time. Alongside Freud, Bergson and Proust, as the great modernist re-inventors of memory, one should place Husserl.[22] In 1904–5 Husserl delivered a series of lectures at Göttingen on 'Internal time-consciousness', exploring precisely those issues of the lived relations of temporality and subjective time which Braudel, among others, found so intractable. His declared purpose – one can imagine the grief this would have brought the *annalistes* – was to conduct a study which called for 'the complete exclusion of every assumption, stipulation, or conviction concerning Objective time'.[23] These lectures were subsequently edited (by Heidegger), and the resulting work inaugurated a continuing body of analysis devoted to the phenomenology of time, which at various moments drew in Heidegger, Ricoeur and, arguably, Derrida as well.[24] As we know, translating philosophical enquiry, especially philosophical enquiry pitched at this level of abstraction, into usable concepts for historiographical thinking is not easily achieved; it is a practice which does much to test the patience of historians, whose principal concerns are formed by quite different temperaments and intellectual requirements. But so long as the relations between memory and historical time remain contentious – as they surely will – at some juncture, just as historians have found themselves engaging with psychoanalysis, so they will, I believe, find themselves having to explore this tradition of phenomenological thought.

I say this parenthetically, not as a prelude to a frenzy of proclamations, edicts and manifestos. But it touches directly on the question of Althusser's determination to re-think historical time. It was largely against this phenomenological tradition that Althusser developed his own theoretical positions, and in so doing presented his findings as a reassertion of a Marxist orthodoxy – though even he was under no illusions that this was an orthodoxy with many heterodox elements thrown in.[25] In 'Contradiction and Overdetermination', his most convincing – wonderful – discussion of temporality, he drew directly on Lenin, Marx and Engels in order to devise what he considered to be a specifically materialist understanding of historical transformation. But just as with Braudel's resolutely objective or scientific conception of time, so too with Althusser's. Quite contrary preoccupations intrude.

In order to theorise the composite structure of historical time Althusser (with a helping hand from Lacan) introduced the concept of overdetermination.[26] This had its origins in psychoanalysis, particularly in *The Interpretation of Dreams*, where it is linked to the generic concepts of displacement and condensation. The term had been employed by Freud to think through the connections between the manifest and latent in dream-work, and also informed his understanding of memory. In Althusser's audacious transposition, it turned into a Braudelian endeavour to uncover the subterranean, unseen dimensions of historical time.[27] Yet overdetermination also carried with it, in Althusser's rendition, an extraordinarily subtle appreciation of the dynamics of historical movement quite foreign to the usual formalism of structural thought.

This comprises what is a subordinate argument in his essay. Its greater purpose was more strictly philosophical. Althusser sought to re-think the dialectic, freeing it from its Hegelian moorings and supplying in its place a more properly materialist reading. This required, he argued, the replacement of the simple contradiction (which characterised, he claimed, Hegelian abstraction) by the more complex, multiple and historical contradiction (that is, an overdetermined contradiction) appropriate for a materialist or Marxist theorisation. The problem was not to stand Hegel on his head – to 'invert' his propositions – but actively to recast his philosophy in a fully materialist mode.

But there are surprises. Just as in Freud, so too in Althusser, the concept of overdetermination is intimately connected to the work of memory.

There are three aspects to Althusser's argument that I'm concerned with here. The first is his discussion of the inner complexities of historical time, in its world aspects. This took him back to the Marxist debates about the historical location of Russia at the opening of the twentieth century. Why, asked Althusser, was Russia the decisive arena of socialist revolution? This was not, he explains, because it was there that the antagonism between capital and labour was at its most pure. On the contrary, it was the very unevenness of historical development, the cataclysmic meeting of opposites, in which the most 'backward' historical forces combined with the most 'advanced': *this* – evident of history moving by its profane, 'bad side', as opposed to the neat expectations of a given teleology – is how, he insisted, history works in real time. He cited Lenin's *Letters from Afar*:

That the revolution succeeded so quickly ... is only due to the fact that, as a result of an extremely unique historical situation, *absolutely dissimilar currents*, *absolutely heterogeneous* class interest, *absolutely contrary* political and social strivings have *merged*... in a strikingly 'harmonious' manner.

Thus it was in Russia that social antagonisms accumulated to the greatest degree, and 'fused' to create the crisis from which the revolution emerged. This recuperation of Lenin provided an incisive edge to the familiar Braudelian or *annaliste* schemas, giving greater conceptual prominence to a specifically

143

conjunctural history. But the interplay of historical times – between 'backward' and 'advanced' – remained, if not unexplored, then arguably more open an issue than Althusser had bargained. Clearly, it describes historical realities, in the sense that the giant Putilov factory in St Petersburg, for example, coexisted with the 'medieval' conditions of the countryside. But, as Althusser himself noted, this was an interpretation which, in turn, raised further questions about historical 'survivals', about the effectivity of 'the national past', about 'customs' and 'habits', and – more generally – about the past in the present. In consequence he felt obliged to pose the question: 'What is a "*survival*"? What is its theoretical status? Is it essentially social or "psychological"?' To this he offered no answer.[28]

Second, this problem of the past in the present, pressing, difficult, resistant to a materialist orthodoxy, pulled him back to Hegel – from whom (we recall) he was seeking to escape. By and large Althusser's misgivings rehearsed the conventional Marxist critique of Hegel's idealism. Focusing on Hegel's *Phenomenology of Mind*, Althusser argued that, in Hegel, contradiction (or the dialectic) is only seemingly a complex matter. Its simplicity or essentialism derived from the fact that, in the Hegelian system, contradictions were phenomena that occurred solely as part of human consciousness. In other words, contradiction was subject to a process of '*internalisation*' alone. While this may connect the past with the present in an apparent dialectical unity, it does so only at the cost of ignoring other material social relations. 'Every consciousness', Althusser concluded, summarising the Hegelian reading, 'has a suppressed-conserved (*aufgehoben*) past even in its present …'. Read like this, he insisted, the past registers in the present merely as an 'echo', as 'memories', touching the present only by presenting it with 'phantoms of its historicity'.[29]

Third, at the end of the essay, Althusser returned to the question of historical 'survivals', conscious that a theoretical resolution was a long way off. Although he appreciated the fact that 'survivals' might incorporate memory, he was reluctant to pursue the point because of what he perceived to be the Hegelian connotations embedded in the concept of memory. In Hegel, he declared, 'the survival of the past … is simply reduced to the modality of *memory*'. As he'd argued earlier, memory was too closely tied to consciousness, to subjective life, to be able to encompass the full range of historical times he believed the concept of overdetermination should deliver. In its Hegelian formulations, memory could only function as a moment in a formal metaphysics of supersession and negation or, to put this in less technical terms, as a choreographed conception of history in which the dialectic rules. Thus memory (of the past) is, in this scheme of things, 'merely the inverse' of '*anticipation*' (of the future): or, in Althusser's more poetic formulation: 'the past survives in the form of a memory of what it has been; that is, as the whispered promise of its present'. In Marx, on the other hand, according to Althusser, the past 'was no shade, not even an "objective" shade – it is a terribly positive and active structured reality, just as cold, hunger and the night are for his poor worker'. But this invocation of a materialist 'structured reality' is immediately followed by a question – by, in fact, a repetition of the earlier question: 'How, then, are we *to think these survivals*? Surely, with a number of *realities*, which are precisely *realities* for Marx, whether superstructures, ideologies, "national traditions" or the customs and "spirit" of a people, etc?' By this stage, however, Althusser was drawing his comments to a close. With his usual dose of brimstone he called for the elaboration of '*a rigorous conception of Marxist concepts*' ensuring that they could be distinguished '*once and for all from their phantoms*'. The final paragraph is emphatic:

> One phantom is more especially crucial than any other today: the shade of Hegel. To drive this phantom back into the night we need *a little more light on Marx*, or what is the same thing, *a little more Marxist light on Hegel himself*. We can then escape from the ambiguities and confusions of the 'inversion'.[30]

I hope the reason for this return to Althusser – a figure, given current fashions, who is now something of a shade or phantom himself – is clear. We can witness the same movement in Althusser as we can in Braudel, where a theory of external, historical temporality comes to confront the issues of subjective time and of memory. If Braudel hoped to exorcise the 'spells' and 'enchantments' associated with the time of memory, then in much the same way Althusser wished to drive these phantoms 'back into the night'. Each of these theoretical engagements was conducted in the name of scientific rigour, though each also gives an indication of being troubled by the realm of subjective time, recognising that further conceptual elaboration was necessary. What kind of conceptual elaboration, however, remained an open matter. (Social or 'psychological'?) Althusser's critique of Hegel's choreographed conception of history is convincing, just as he is right to reject a conception of historical time in which *everything* is reduced to subjective consciousness. (To reiterate: history and memory are not the same.) But the problem is more compacted, or at least less polarised, than these points suggest.

Althusser's stated purpose was to purify Marxist concepts in order that they would shed their Hegelian 'contaminations'. My intention is to follow a different tack. It's to suggest that, when we investigate relations between memory and historical time, it is precisely these apparently anti- or pre-materialist insights – Hegelian or Freudian, phenomenological or psychoanalytical – to which we need to attend most carefully.[31] It is these that offer the most profound way into subjective time, without which memory cannot be reached. These impure concepts may come attired in a disturbingly pre-secular ragbag of cast-offs, inviting us to enter a world composed of spells and phantoms. Or at least, so we are told. But in so doing they attest to a human consciousness in which memories of the past remain stubbornly unappeased. There are moments when it looks as if Braudel and (more particularly) Althusser were ready to concede something of the sort. In this respect, their troubled encounters with the interior dimensions of time are revealing. In the end, however, they never cross the threshold. But how else are we to grasp the irreducibly human dimensions of historical reality?

There are many other issues. It's tempting to carry these themes forward in order to address contemporary concerns about postmodernity and (especially) about the consequent presentiments that we live in a time marked by a deep amnesia, in which memory itself can no longer apprehend a historical past. But, in the spirit of my earlier comments, I'll close by looking back to the moment of modernism. In particular, it's necessary to say a word about narrative.

I can be brief. Braudel himself was convinced that historical narrative itself constituted a theoretical issue. Narrative is not a matter of technique, or method, he cautioned, but embodies an entire 'philosophy of history'.[32] His own history of the Mediterranean can be seen, among other things, as an experiment in historical narrative. He was clearly convinced that composite historical times need to be represented by commensurately 'composite' historical narratives, in which differentiated temporal speeds can be conveyed in all their heterogeneous complexities. There were, though, few conventions in the historiography of the period that could serve as a model. But if the historiography was deficient in this respect there was – close by, as it were, in Paris or London or Dublin – an entire tradition of high modernist literature which devoted its greatest energies to devising narrative forms which could reproduce time moving at different speeds. Much of the modernist canon was preoccupied with time as a phenomenon which existed only in its displacements and condensations, only *able* to work (to continue the metaphor) in its contaminated forms. One can suppose that the silence in Braudel's own historical writings about these parallel experiments in temporality derived from the fact that he perceived the fiction-writers (as he did the philosophers) to be imprisoned by a conception of time he deemed to be historically 'weightless', capable only of understanding subjective time at the expense of temporalities located socially and externally. Yet what Braudel might have perceived as an inhibition we, in retrospect, might imagine to be a virtue. For a range of modernist writers not only investigated the properties of subjective time, and of memory pre-eminently. They also explored the *transactions* between internal and external times, showing that subjective time does indeed live within reach of conventional historical time. To ignore the modernists in the supposition that their conceptions of temporality defied the gravitational pull of external histories is to miss too much.

There are many places we might look to demonstrate this. Most compelling of all, to my mind, is *To the Lighthouse*, in which the emotional and psychic conditions of interior time are portrayed with incomparable beauty.[33] The fact that social time appears, throughout, in minor key shouldn't allow us to think that it is absent. To propose Woolf's text, or other comparable modernist fictions, as a model for historiographical narration in the twenty-first century is not, I know, likely to win universal acclaim.[34] General observations on historical narrative, in any case, are only of limited value, as the requirements for each particular object of study differ so markedly. Even so, we can say something. If one turns to

Woolf's own reflections on narrative it's worth asking whether there may not be insights that could be appropriated and smuggled across the border into the altogether stricter domain of historiography.

Woolf felt herself having to write against a generation of forbears whose perception of the external world gave every indication of being entirely unproblematic. All they believed they needed to do (she claimed) was to accumulate sufficient detail, with ever greater degrees of refinement, and – *hélas!* – the material world, in all its historical veracity, would finally take observable shape. In such settings, the novel's characters were not so much rounded (to use E.M. Forster's term) as rooted exactly in their appropriate social stratum. By such narrative technique Messrs Bennett, Wells and Galsworthy (Woolf's favoured adversaries) endeavoured to get their characters safely 'from lunch to dinner'.[35] There was humour, as well as provocation, in Woolf's rebellion against the falsity of these naturalistic truths, apparently so indomitable. To get one of her own characters through to dinner, she implied, was a minor triumph. In any single human imagination there was, Woolf knew, even in the course of a few hours, an infinity of interruptions to confront, the passage between external occurrence and internal thought impossibly complex. How could *this* reality be represented? The slightest acquaintance with her own fiction will persuade readers that, in order for this inner time to be told, the composite narrative structure of the novel is quite different from the naturalism of a Bennett or a Wells. Displacement and condensation of competing temporalities are achieved *in the narrative itself*. And, in consequence, the obvious fixity of the external world – the table, the rock on the beach against which one stubs one's toe, a dinner party, the present, the past – never turns out to be quite as obvious as it first seems.

Insofar as Woolf deployed a choice, favouring one narrative rather than another, it was a tactical argument about the appropriateness of specific literary, narrational conventions. The crisis she identified in her own generation of writers was not initially or in essence an abstract, theoretical one. It came about, she observed, simply because they knew that they couldn't go on writing as those before them had done. The inherited literary codes, far from being productive, had become an obstacle. And once this perception had taken hold, it transpired that they – Woolf's own generation of 'moderns' – had no 'conventions' they could call upon. This explained, she believed, the 'difficulty' of so much of the literature she and her contemporaries produced: 'where so much strength is spent on finding a way of telling the truth, the truth itself is bound to reach us in rather an exhausted and chaotic condition'. This was the cost of shaping new ways of writing. But if this was the cost, the promise was something much greater: that out of exhaustion and chaos a more profound, a more complex and a more passionate realism might be imagined, which – fleetingly – would have the capacities to 'catch the phantom' of the real.[36]

I'm not proposing that a historiography be cast in the image of Woolf or Joyce; nor, for that matter, in the image of Husserl or Heidegger. My concern, like Woolf's, is simply with current conventions and with what occurs when these

conventions cease quite to work. Woolf's description of the naturalistic predispositions of her literary forbears is still a recognisable attribute of historians a
century later. Historians, I'm sure, can learn from many sources. I see no reason
why the complex realism imagined by Woolf, seeking to 'catch the phantom',
couldn't (in some – not all – circumstances) serve the kind of realist narrative
required by historians.

I've suggested that historical practice has been resistant to some of the great
breakthroughs of twentieth-century intellectual life, particularly those innova-
tions in cognate disciplines most concerned with temporality. Psychoanalytical
investigation into the interior workings of mental life; phenomenological interpretation of the interconnections between external and internal time; high
modernist narrative forms; even Braudel's historiographical discovery of differential temporality: the insights deriving from these varied paradigm-shifts have
only registered weakly within the common practices of historiography. The anti-
empirical force of these shifts does not lend itself to a happy rendezvous with the
necessarily empirical practice of historiography. Nor does the fact each points to
different methods of working make the matter any easier. (The common *historical*
origins of these very different theorisations of temporality are, however, of great
interest.) But if much of the historiography has been resistant it hasn't been
immune. A historical reconstruction of the historiography would present a more
nuanced, more fascinating story than I can present here. Much still turns on the
question of memory. How these philosophical and literary insights can be translated into a properly historiographical conceptual practice is not easy to imagine,
though there are now many hints. The renovation of historiography along these
lines is, one could claim, inaugurating a new poetics of the historical imagination, in which – at last – the study of history is catching up with its modernist
past.

Notes

With thanks to Sally Alexander and Susannah Radstone.

1 Peter Burke, *The French Historical Revolution: The Annales School, 1929–89*, Cambridge:
Polity, 1990, p. 39.
2 Eric Hobsbawm, *Age of Extremes: The Short Twentieth Century, 1914–1991*, London:
Michael Joseph, 1994, pp. 534–5.
3 This was the reasoning, in part, behind Julia Kristeva's essay, 'Women's Time', republished in Toril Moi (ed.) *The Kristeva Reader*, New York: Columbia University Press,
1986.
4 Fernand Braudel, *The Mediterranean and the Mediterranean World at the Time of Philip II*,
Vol. I, London: Collins, 1972, pp. 17–22. The original Preface is dated May 1946. It is
an ambiguous piece of writing for it is not clear the degree to which Braudel believed
these historical times were those of the particular study in hand (the Mediterranean
in the sixteenth century) or whether they had a greater, universal significance.
5 The best analysis, not only of Braudel's programmatic statements but also of his
concrete historical narratives, is by a philosopher and appears in the first volume of
Paul Ricoeur's *Time and Narrative*, 3 vols, Chicago: University of Chicago Press, 1984,

1985 and 1988, pp. 101ff and 209ff. Ricoeur argues that Braudel's historical practice does not conform to his programmatic formulations; that the category of 'the event' furtively touches every part of his historical explanation, and that this is because the workings of 'the event' define the specificities of a historian's concerns with structures; and that (unexpectedly, given his declared protocols) the imperatives of 'mortal time' interpose themselves into his larger account of the Mediterranean. There is much to absorb in these comments. I came to Ricoeur after I had drafted this chapter. But the movement of his argument – from the structuralism of the *annalistes*, to Husserl and the phenomenologists, to the narrative strategies of high modernism (Virginia Woolf in particular) is precisely the movement I follow here.

6 Drawing from mathematics, he distinguished different registers of truth, identifying for example 'the language of conditioned facts – neither determined nor accidental, but subject to certain constraints and certain rules', Fernand Braudel, 'History and the Social Sciences', in Peter Burke (ed.) *Economy and Society in Early Modern Europe: Essays from Annales*, London: Routledge and Kegan Paul, 1972, p. 29. It is in this anti-positivist, conventionalist spirit that Braudel's commitments to historical truth can be identified as 'relativist'. I should add that I make much use of this article, which was first published in *Annales* in 1958. It deals with both Sartre and Lévi-Strauss and thus, for my purposes, stands in a pivotal historical moment of philosophical debate, which bears directly on my argument. This essay is republished, alongside other essays on the same theme, as Part I ('Time in History') of Fernand Braudel, *On History*, Chicago: University of Chicago Press, 1980.

7 Especially Fernand Braudel, *Capitalism and Material Life, 1400–1800*, London: Weidenfeld and Nicolson, 1973.

8 Braudel, 'History and the Social Sciences', op. cit., p. 16.

9 Fernand Braudel, *The Mediterranean and the Mediterranean World at the time of Philip II, Vol. II*, London: Collins, 1973, p. 1244.

10 Most of all Louis Althusser, 'Contradiction and Overdetermination' (first published in 1962) in his *For Marx*, London: Allen Lane, 1969; and his 'The Errors of Classical Economics: An Outline for a Concept of Historical Time', in Louis Althusser and Etienne Balibar, *Reading Capital*, London: New Left Books, 1970.

11 For example, Pierre Vilar, 'Marxist History, a History in the Making: Towards a Dialogue with Althusser', *New Left Review* series I, 80, 1973. Relevant too is Braudel's own theoretical commitment to the concept of conjuncture, explicitly addressed in the section entitled 'Conjuncture and Conjunctures', *The Mediterranean, Vol. II*, op. cit., pp. 892–900. Althusser, certainly, was reading Braudel, and (despite the differences), was ready to place on record his debt to him: *Reading Capital*, op. cit., p. 96.

12 Braudel believed that Marx's 'genius' derived from the fact that it was he, Marx, who had first discovered the historical temporality of the long duration: 'History and the Social Sciences', op. cit., p. 39. Arguably, though, Marx's *Eighteenth Brumaire* represents the founding theoretical text in this field of enquiry.

13 These movements in intellectual thought can be traced from Lenin's *Development of Capitalism in Russia*, first published in 1899 (*The Collected Works of V.I. Lenin, Vol. III*, Moscow: Progress Publishers, 1972) to Trotsky's *History of the Revolution in Russia*, especially the Preface to the first volume, which was first published in English in 1932 (London: Sphere, 1969). These debates continued through the twentieth century as a sub-field of the larger Marxisant theorisation of colonialism and imperialism, most fruitfully in relation to Latin America and the Caribbean.

14 Braudel, *The Mediterranean, Vol. I*, op. cit., p. 20.

15 Ibid., p. 21. He writes in the same passage that this is a historical time composed of 'nervous fluctuations' and that it brings, too, the 'anger, dreams or illusions' of those historical individuals who make it move.

16 Braudel, 'History and the Social Sciences', op. cit., pp. 13 and 26.

17 Eric Hobsbawm, *On History*, London: Weidenfeld and Nicolson, 1997.

18 Having written these words I was startled to fall upon a new publication of an old Braudel manuscript entitled *Memory and the Mediterranean* (New York: Knopf, 2001). It transpires that this is effectively a prelude to his Mediterranean volumes, exploring the archaeology of the region. Despite the title, it bears only obliquely on questions of memory.

19 There is an argument that the velocity of interior time has accelerated as a consequence of the increasingly profound and rapid mediation of social relations (television, MTV, CNN, digitalised media and so forth). An alternative, but not I think incompatible reading, draws attention to the fact that the repetitive time of the unconscious – that which is acted out as opposed to that which is remembered – has a primordial quality in which the tempo slows. As Sally Alexander comments: 'The human subject is formed through fantasy and identification, processes as historically resonant as Fernand Braudel's *longue duree* and as slow to change… repetition is the time of the unconscious…', completing the sentence by observing, 'which is only ever one of the composite times of history', 'Feminism, History, Repetition' in her *Becoming a Woman*, London: Virago, 1996, p. 247. With great insight this brings together Althusser's (and Freud's) 'time of the unconscious' (*Reading Capital*, op. cit., p. 103) with Braudel's 'history of constant repetition'.

20 I'm thinking especially of work which first grew out of historiography (oral history most of all, feminist history to a degree), which took many different forms, and which in Europe is associated with such diverse names as Luisa Passerini, Alessandro Portelli, Sally Alexander, Carolyn Steedman and Ronald Fraser. An interesting early attempt to locate the specifically autobiographical dimensions of these investigations was Laura Marcus's, ' "Enough about You, Let's Talk about Me": Recent Autobiographical Work', *New Formations* 1, 1987. As her title indicates, she adopted a more negative stance than the one I follow here. In part, I think this was because her concern with autobiography occluded what I take to be most impressive about this corpus: its *explicit* concerns with the transactions between external and internal times, and its consequent interrogation of the foundations of external time. But she also upbraided those whom she regarded as insufficiently deconstructive. Thus, in discussing Ronald Fraser's influential book, *In Search of a Past: The Manor House, Amnersfield, 1933–1945* (London: Verso, 1984), she was sceptical about the value of his recourse to a Sartrean phenomenology, believing this undid much of what the author was trying to achieve. Maybe so. But as I suggest below, I would guess that this was probably a necessary route through which these questions about interior historical time could (once more) be opened up. For Fraser's own perspective on the influence of Sartre, '*In Search of a Past*: A Dialogue with Ronald Fraser', *History Workshop Journal* 20, 1985, p. 187. And, nearly twenty years on, for a more contemporary engagement with these issues in both Fraser and Steedman, Nicola King, *Memory, Narrative, Identity: Remembering the Self*, Edinburgh: Edinburgh University Press, 2000.

21 In fact, in an interesting mutation, there is evidence that a new genre of 'memory-texts', of popular not academic provenance, is directly addressing the time of politics in these terms: for example (on Ireland and Turkey) Joseph O'Neill, *Blood-Dark Track: A Family History*, London: Granta, 2001 and (on South Africa) Henk van Woerden, *A Mouthful of Glass*, London: Granta, 2000. They convey a sense of history as embodying – not truth, nor universal retribution or redemption – but only the 'quiet force of the possible'. The phrase, famously, comes from Heidegger's *Being and Time*, Oxford: Blackwell, 1962, p. 446.

22 This is deliberately polemical. It reflects my enthusiasm for the old, but still engaging, study by H. Stuart Hughes, *Consciousness and Society*, New York: Knopf, 1958; and, in a rather different vein, it reminds us of the historical transformations in historical time

in this period, for which see Stephen Kern, *The Culture of Time and Space, 1880–1918*, London: Weidenfeld and Nicolson, 1983.

23 Edmund Husserl, *The Phenomenology of Internal Time-Consciousness*, Bloomington: Indiana University Press, 1964, p. 22. I don't mean to imply that this represented an unknown terrain for Braudel. It's clear that he was familiar, if not with Husserl himself, then certainly with the positions he represented. 'The philosopher', he noted, 'being attentive to the subjective, interior aspect of the concept of time, never feels the weight of historical time in this concrete and universal sense', 'History and the Social Sciences', op. cit., p. 36. It is simply that he couldn't find a way of comprehending this 'interior aspect' of time as historical. In this lies the contrast between his theorisations of the 1960s, and those which preoccupy us today.

24 Peter Osborne discusses key elements of this body of work in his *Politics of Time*, London: Verso, 1995.

25 Inevitably, there are unanticipated connections. One of his first published writings, which appeared in 1955, was an open letter to Paul Ricoeur entitled 'On the Objectivity of History', in which Althusser *commended* Ricoeur for arguing that historical knowledge, above all else, was a science (on the model of the natural sciences) and not merely a matter of 'immediate experience'. For this episode, Gregory Elliott, *Althusser: The Detour of Theory*, London: Verso, 1987, pp. 29–30.

26 Instructive in this respect is David Macey, 'Thinking with Borrowed Concepts: Althusser and Lacan', in Gregory Elliott (ed.) *Althusser: A Critical Reader*, Oxford: Blackwell, 1994.

27 When Althusser championed his own idea of historical time he emphasised that it created the possibilities for reaching 'invisible times', 'the invisible rhythms and punctuations concealed beneath the surface of each visible time', *Reading Capital*, op. cit., p. 101. Whatever these claims of Althusser, this was pure Braudel.

28 Althusser, 'Contradiction and Overdetermination', op. cit., pp. 94–101, 106 and 114. The quote from Lenin comes from V.I. Lenin, *Selected Works, Vol. II*, Moscow: Progress Publishers, 1963, p. 35.

29 Althusser, 'Contradiction and Overdetermination', op. cit., pp. 101–2.

30 Ibid., pp. 115–16.

31 And actually, even within Althusser's own problematic, the 'contaminations' lie near the centre of things. His critique of historicism developed from certain currents within phenomenology, while Peter Osborne notes that 'the Heideggerian roots of Althusser's discussion of differential temporality are rarely appreciated', 'The Politics of Time', *Radical Philosophy* 68, 1994, p. 8.

32 Braudel, 'History and the Social Sciences', op. cit., p. 21.

33 For Ricoeur's fine reading of Woolf's *Mrs Dalloway*, see the second volume of *Time and Narrative*, op. cit., pp. 101ff. In a different context we might note that the famous passage of the novel which reflects on 'the ruins of time' (Harmondsworth: Penguin 1996, p. 19) touched Gabriel García Márquez so deeply that he claimed this single sentence 'transformed my sense of time' and served as the trigger for *One Hundred Years of Solitude*. See Plinio Ayuleyo Mendoza and Gabriel García Márquez, *The Fragrance of Guava*, London: Verso, 1982, p. 48.

34 Though see Carlo Ginzburg's riveting discussion of the narrative structure of *Sentimental Education* in his *History, Rhetoric, Proof: The Menahem Stern Jerusalem Lectures*, Hanover, NH: University Press of New England, 1999.

35 Virginia Woolf, *A Writer's Diary*, London: Hogarth Press, 1953, p. 139.

36 Virginia Woolf, 'Mr Bennett and Mrs Brown' in her *A Woman's Essays: Selected Essays, Vol. I*, ed. Rachel Bowlby, Harmondsworth: Penguin, 1992, pp. 84, 86 and 89. Eric Auerbach, in his commentary on *To the Lighthouse*, argues that this allows us 'to fathom a more genuine, a deeper, and indeed a more real reality', *Mimesis: The Representation of Reality in Western Literature*, Princeton, NJ: Princeton University Press, 1968, p. 540.

8

GETTING TO THE BEGINNING

Identification and concrete thinking in historical consciousness

Karl Figlio

The idea that we have roots in human activity similar to our own, rather than in myth, seems to be intrinsic to modern secular culture. That is what we mean by history, and I will call it a 'historical consciousness'. Historical consciousness acknowledges the reality of the past as a culture in its own right, and historical enquiry proceeds objectively and empirically. Nonetheless, the urge for historical knowledge is also driven by a wish to go back, to get to and be at the beginning, as if it were a wish that could be fulfilled.

In this chapter, I would like to explore the way wish-fulfilment, understood psychoanalytically, informs our sense of history. In my view, modern culture tends towards concrete thinking, which treats memories and historical situations as if they were objects. It can invest these objects, which are phantasies, in actual, present objects, and collect them, preserve them, destroy them and restore them.[1] Time simply marks the changes in, or re-arrangements of, these objects, so we can lapse into the belief, largely unconscious and under the sway of wish-fulfilment, that we can enter into history by literally reversing time.

In psychoanalytic thinking, wish-fulfilment happens in dreams and in phantasy, where checking against external reality is suspended. Projected into external reality, phantasy then informs and animates the sense of empirical reality. In my view, the phantasy of a beginning at which one is present drives and colours historical consciousness and historical enquiry in secular culture. Moreover, the linear time that permeates such a culture lends an uncanny concrete reality to this phantasy.

From a psychoanalytic point of view, all beginnings ultimately lie in an originating scenario. The classic originating scenario is the primal scene of parental intercourse, which underlies the Oedipus complex. One aspect of the classic male Oedipus complex is the wish to displace father, born not just of jealousy of father's intercourse with mother, but of the child's (unconscious) wish to give his mother himself as her child – in effect, to be his own father.[2] But there are more primitive moments of origination, in what I have elsewhere called the 'beginning of the beginning'.[3] The urge to get to the beginning becomes the wish to be inside the primal scene and also its more primitive antecedents; to merge with mother's reproductive capacity. At least three displacements of external reality by phantasy are necessary to underwrite the fulfilment of this wish. First, the difference between generations must be elided. Second, the difference between the sexes must be eliminated. Third, the idea of two parents must be replaced by the (unconscious) belief that one parent can bear children alone.[4]

The significance of these manoeuvres resides in the omnipotence of the phantasies that underpin them. The difference between generations must be elided, in order to blur the boundary between parents and children, to push from sight the maturational tasks on the path to adulthood and to install the child as parent. The difference between the sexes must be eliminated because, as a marker of what the ego must attend to, it stands in the way of omnipotent total-ising phantasies. These illusions are completed by the third displacement of reality, in which children are produced by one parent alone, especially the father; now the child, confused with this parent, replaces the humble role of two, incomplete, procreative parents.[5]

So, a historically conscious culture is driven by the need to deepen its knowl-edge by empirical methods, but it is also preoccupied with phantasies of pre-empting beginnings. In this dual enterprise, it condenses two contradictory currents. We investigate nature and our past; we discover the sources of natural and social processes. But the drive to get to the source also harnesses our empiri-cism to the phantasy of infiltrating the inside of the object, to be at the beginning.

The particular form into which the phantasy is pressed by the idea of time – specifically linear time – is intriguing. Linear time represents difference concretely as distance. Spreading into every aspect of everyday consciousness, linear time carries with it the idea that historical difference is a matter of time. The 'back to the future' type of science fiction – beginning with *The Time Machine* by H.G. Wells (1895) – will serve as an illustration from popular culture. In such a story, including the films in this genre, the hero is tempted to find a way into the past, aiming to change it. Literally, the son becomes father to the man, as he restructures his father's own childhood.

In another version of this narrative, time itself takes over. In the film *Groundhog Day* (Harold Ramis, US, 1993), a self-important TV presenter covers this annual vigil, and is trapped in a repetition of the morning when either spring will begin or winter will persist. The theme is narcissism, in which loving oneself, rather than loving another, becomes a deadening repetition. The impulse is the same as in the back-to-the-future theme – to insert oneself into the other (love object, nature, history); the motive varies, from the extreme of controlling the other to the point of making it into oneself, to affecting the other in a more benevolent way. The cost of total control, paid by the narcissistic TV presenter, was to be caught in an object (life, time, the season – a woman) that had been deadened by his narcissism. He was frozen in it, as in winter, by his deadening narcissism, until he was freed by loving it (similarly, the past in *The Time Machine* was terrorising).

The 'back-to-future' theme gives an apparent agency to the future. The way things happen can be bent round and inserted into the past, to become a cause. To reverse time, as a current of events, means concretely to be able to return to any point in time, not as an imitation or replica, but as the original instance. Disdain for the whim or the intuition of the groundhog – nature's move to restore life in spring – is equivalent to controlling the movement from the past through the present into the future.

The phantasy of recovering the past by time reversal is a concretely material version of the relationship that a culture has with its past and future. Changing ideas about causality have contributed to this material version of our relationship to the past and the future. In pre-modern (Aristotelian) metaphysics, purpose was immanent in everything that changed. Everything was a coming into existence or a passing away: part of a whole, in which purpose was indwelling, not the product of a separate organising power. Aristotle called it the 'final cause'. Thinking in terms of causality, one would say that the cause was always greater than the effect: that events were embraced by their causes and fulfilled in them.

In the natural philosophy of early modern Christian culture, God as a super-natural architect, separate from creation, contained the final cause and created the world in such a way that events unfolded from its constitution. Modern meta-physics, by contrast, has ignored the final cause altogether. Events are now produced: by nature, by us. We are left with matter in motion, and have lost the vocabulary to convey the notion of purpose, except as a form of production.[6] So what is the future? It is the material consequence of events in the present, as the present is the material consequence of events in the past. We are left with a depleted, concrete form of thinking. We are also left with the puzzling idea that having the future in mind implies the literal possibility that, by time-reversal, it could insert itself into the past as a physical cause.

A variant of a final cause does remain in psychoanalytic thinking. Freud invented the term *Nachträglichkeit* to refer to the revision of the past; and if this process is continuous, then consciousness becomes revision itself, as thinking itself becomes *nachträglich*. Memory becomes akin to imagination rather than to an assemblage or recollection of objects in the mind. What spares thinking *nachträglich* from omnipotence of thought is the grit in the system. A perception is usually registered differently from a memory. Typically, it conserves its firm, exterior nature, while a memory, often seeming similarly beyond confusion with the present, is revised by later experiences, thoughts or phantasies, right up to 'now'. The words through which we access memory and organise perceptions normally refer to things without being identical to them. To say 'that is a dog' does not create a dog, nor does saying 'I am happy' normally produce the feeling of happiness.[7]

Melanie Klein expressed the revision of the past in terms of an urge to re-do it, in her concept of reparation. She also distinguished the reparative engagement with the external and internal worlds from manic reparation, which is a magical act of re-animating dead or damaged internal (mental) objects. This distinction, which is similar to that between *Nachträglichkeit* and omnipotence of thought, is important to historical enquiry. The concern for others whom we have wounded can shift to intolerance, and the gratitude for one's life can shift to seeking to remake the past without unwanted features. Through reparation we shoulder responsibility for the past. It binds us into history, and makes us into historical agents. In distinguishing it from manic reparation, we strengthen the disposition towards accountability, guilt and concern, and against the need to remake the past into our own creation. Reparation flows from love and from identification with the good object, and tends to retain and restore internal objects; manic reparation flows from magic and intends omnipotently to control internal objects.[8]

We live in the past as a relationship with internal figures – not the past as an experience of an earlier external reality. The figures of this internal world are generated in internal object relations rather than through ego-based perception of external figures. In object-relational terms, remembering is a form of phantasying, primarily working over the disturbing aspects of internal objects. The most important question is not the representational accuracy of a recollection, but the nature of the object relations: whether loving or hating, beneficent or malevolent, permissive or punitive, tolerant or controlling; and whether they embody, as an attitude towards what has happened, a reparative or a manic reparative disposition.

Understanding the process of reparation suggests one reason why we are so involved with the past, why history has continually to be rewritten and why it must take an expressive, narrative form. We are engaged with the past as with important internal figures, and we re-write history, not just because there is more to be discovered, in order more accurately to depict a historical situation, but because these past relationships have to be worked over again and again. The past-in-the-present has to be revivified, restored, repaired. It is a matter of preserving and restoring internal objects, and it has implications for all forms of preservation, whether of documents, artefacts, buildings, sites of special scientific interest or accounts of the past.[9]

We can bracket the past-in-the-present between two poles. At one extreme, the past burdens the present with the heavy weight of parental authority; at the other, it is a child whom the present tries to mould. These two forms turn around a common core. Think of how children at play make their parents into their children, or put dolls or playmates into the role of children. They gain control over their parents by reincarnating them, in phantasy, as their children, and handing on what they were subjected to. In a collective phantasy, we try to remake the past in the way we treat what it has left us. We may, that is, adopt an attitude towards the past as if it were the present, containing the germ of the future, and had taken the form of children that we could make into whatever we wanted.

Freud said that parents act towards their children as their own parents acted towards them. Since their own parents formed the nucleus of their superegos, they raise their children in line with their superegos and not in conformity with their (ego) experience. Children therefore inherit not their parents' ego-orientation to the world, but that of their parents' superegos.

> As a rule, parents and authorities analogous to them follow the precepts of their own superegos in educating children. Whatever understanding their ego may have come to with their superego, they are severe and exacting in educating children. They have forgotten the difficulties of their own childhood and they are glad to be able now to identify themselves fully with their own parents who in the past laid such severe restrictions upon them. Thus a child's superego is in fact constructed on the model not of its parents but of its parents' superego; the contents which fill it are the same and it becomes the vehicle of tradition and of all the time-resisting judgements of value which have propagated themselves in this manner from generation to generation.[10]

From this perspective, the past lives in the present as a stable tradition, as continuity through the lineage of the superego, despite the beliefs and wishes of the present. Tradition bears the unrealistic authority of the superego, insulated from the ego's function of living in the present, dealing with situations in their current significance, and relating to contemporary figures on a mutual footing and on the basis of reality-orientated judgement. Freud says that each generation unburdens itself of the humiliation of continuing domination by the superego, by identifying with it and treating the next generation as it experienced its own upbringing. Each generation struggles with its own conscience (superego) as it struggles with its history.[11]

Ernest Jones makes the linkage explicit: children reincarnate their grandparents, and each generation seeks to reverse the injury done to it, by transferring its parental figures into its children. According to Jones, there is:

> a peculiar phantasy …to the effect that as [children] grow older and bigger their relative position to their parents will be gradually reversed, so that finally they will become the parents and their parents the children…. It should be noted that there are several component parts, or degrees, of the phantasy – the gradual reversal in size, the extension of this to the belief that the child is in imagination the actual parent of its parents – i.e., equivalent to its own grandfather…. The logical consequence of this phantasy … is that the relative positions are so completely reversed that the child becomes the actual parent of his parents…. Another way of stating this conclusion is that the child becomes identified with his grandfather.[12]

A benign version of the phantasy that later generations treat earlier generations as children may underlie the interest in discovering – with amazement – how much earlier generations knew. It is as if, next to us, they were children. If they were children, our surprise would be at the cleverness of our children, and our amazement would suggest a veiled denigration. Our surprise at how they managed, at how much they knew, would displace on to them the insecurity in our own capacities and the child-like helplessness of our situation, which we would hand on by reversing the generations and thinking of ourselves as older and wiser than they. And because the benevolent interest also covers denigration, there would be a continual need to go over the past, to protect it from belittlement or to propitiate it, as if it were also a retaliating belittled parental figure.[13]

I suggest that we apply the reversal of which Jones spoke to the projects and plans of the present generation. In my view these projects contain phantasies of revenge on the parents. This condensation of planning for the future and taking revenge on the past, revokes the past by projecting it into the future with the aim of re-doing it, as if it were not parental, but amenable to domination as if it were a child. The striking concreteness of such a project is consistent with primitive phantasies that magically control internal objects – objects that bear no relation to external reality, are very black or white, and are neither the objects of, nor the bearers of, concern.

This sort of object relation is favoured in a modern culture of scientific naturalism, because the omnipotence of the drive to get to the beginning gives an impetus to concrete thinking as a social form. For example, the organised scientific enterprise so typical of such a culture contains this sort of omnipotent drive, which both adds to the momentum of scientific work and haunts the culture with magical fears.[14] It is a curious paradox that a historical culture, with its keen sense of a past in time – that is, a past in which events build one upon the other just as they do in the present – also elides the difference between generations, and even reverses them. Surely, we might think, if the present is the accretion of everything that went before, layer upon layer, then the past could be found, quite distinctly, in earlier layers, just as in archaeological strata. Indeed, depth in strata would be equivalent to time and to the numbering of generations.

Freud tells a different story, one consistent with an uncanny sense that different generations keep an eye on, and act on, each other, because the co-presence of all times implies no time. In his analogy between the unconscious and the archaeology of Rome, all the structures from the past are intact – all coexist. The past is eternally present.[15]

Freud's archaeological metaphor makes the case that an archaic oceanic feeling can exist next to reality-orientation, including the recognition of threat from the external world. The archaic moment of total immersion in a cosmic unity, along with an ego awareness of threat from an external reality, is an abject moment, a condition of absolute need. The religious impulse is born, Freud argues, not of oceanic feeling, but of this need. It promises a way out of harsh reality through an illusion of a parental presence, and finds no security in the Enlightenment ideal of freedom in the naturalism of science and in the secularism of scholarship – especially historical scholarship, which puts the past safely in the past.

The confusion of an eternal past with the actuality of the present, as in Freud's archaeology, means that nothing is ever lost, and the past is included in the present. The Rome that Freud imagines can never be seen, but it endures as an elusive memory. The historically orientated mind reflects on objects that are not there, and believes that they exist as solidly as anything one could touch, while knowing that they cannot be touched – not because of practical limitations, such as distance in space, but as an intrinsic impossibility. Living in history and thinking historically forces us to acknowledge that, in the very moment of grasping the past, it is utterly unreachable. And just as fundamentally does the historical mind repudiate this impossibility, making it, instead, just a matter of time.

On the underbelly of the Enlightenment ideal, the very linearity of time, on which both scientific naturalism and historical secularism depend, engenders phantasies of meddling with the past and primitive fears of retaliation by it. This idea – that it is just a matter of time – is distinctly modern. Einstein's theory of relativity, in which time is no longer the universal constant of Newtonian mechanics, fascinates us because it invites us to breach the barrier between now and then, self and other, as if time stood for an injunction that could be transgressed.

The invitation to breach the time barrier is a temptation to breach the difference between the generations. To think that history is a matter of time is equivalent to the temptation to 'just go back in time': the phantasy into which the 'back to the future' films invite us. Time becomes a material cause that moves events, or their imprint. Time is the film that moves through a projector, and history is the imprint of the movement of events. Time is the dimension in which reality accretes. It is not just an abstract space of reality, as in a Newtonian universe; it is the accretion of material reality, so moving in time alters material reality. Whatever happens can be re-done, re-run, moved backwards and forwards. If time is the material record of movement along an axis, then why not move in either direction?

I will illustrate the phantasy of the reversal of generations with a psychoanalytic case presentation by Gabriel Sapisochin, an Argentinean psychoanalyst living and working in Spain.[16] His patient, a woman whom he called 'L', had assumed from the outset that he knew that she was aware of his Argentinian origins; and, although Spanish herself, she had used characteristic Argentinian expressions. During the sessions, Sapisochin also noticed a compelling homely feeling, including reminiscences of particular Argentinian foods. It was as if she were unconsciously feeding him an unconscious residue of his childhood self, and conveying to him a belief that he felt known by her as a mother would know her son. In his dreaminess and reminiscences, he unconsciously agreed.

L remembered that her father, an Italian, 'was "*amazed*" to hear her perfect pronunciation of the dialect of a certain region of Italy'.[17] She also reported a ceremony she used to perform, which had been so unexceptional to her that she never thought of mentioning it. Every night, she needed to turn down the bedcovers, on which the family initials were embroidered, in a particular way. She remembered that, when she was very young, 'Daddy said to me: "When I see you arranging the turndown like that, I see my mother."' She went on to say that her father had lost his mother when he had been very small. He had been close to her emotionally; indeed, she had been more important to him than his wife, L's mother, and he used to flirt with women who were like his mother.

What characterised the clinical situation was L's attempt to seduce the analyst into accepting her as his mother, which would have reproduced the situation with her father, but reversing the agency along with the reversed generations. As a child, she was seduced into the '*amazing*' phantasy that she was her father's mother (not, as in an Oedipal scenario, his wife). Now, with her analyst, she adopted the seductive aim herself, and drew the analyst into an unconscious belief that she was his mother.

Together, the father and the daughter colluded to escape the Oedipus complex. She avoided Oedipal exclusion from the parental couple by becoming her father's mother: the object of *his* most intense, Oedipal love. The father avoided Oedipal exclusion by *creating* the mother from whom he had been excluded, in the form of his daughter, whom he fashioned into a replica of her. Their collusion also dampened the transgressive aspect, if only in part: the daughter enacted her Oedipal wishes towards her father indirectly, by becoming the mother. The father enacted his Oedipal wishes towards his mother indirectly through his daughter. Their Oedipal collusion confused the generations, as the daughter became the mother and the father became the son.

How does history come into it? The historical mentality reconstructs the past. We are invited to 'remember' it, but remembering is filtered through unconscious processes, through phantasies of parenthood and childhood, including Oedipal scenarios. A historical consciousness, underwritten by historical scholarship, establishes the past in its own right, but it also calls up the phantasy that the past lives in us and we live in the past. While the historical process puts things clearly in the past, it instigates the contradictory aim of confusing ourselves with it.

Partly, we confuse ourselves with the past for the same reason that L confused herself with her grandmother: to avoid Oedipal exclusion, to confuse the generations, to violate the incest taboo. The clinical example emphasised the transgressive core to the phantasy of confusing generations, but there is another dimension. Riding on the back of the seductive relationship between father and daughter was the fact that her father lost his mother when he was very young, and his daughter filled in for that loss. Even though she fell in with a seductive scenario that confused the generations, L may have borne reparative wishes towards her father. Similarly, historical interest bears a reparative aim, though the mode may be perverse, in enacting Oedipal phantasies.[18]

In our historical mentality, we bear reparative wishes towards the parental past, but we also transgress Oedipal-generation boundaries. Tradition, which Freud described as a parental superego, is like a parent carried inside the psyche. The burden of tradition can be lightened by the phantasy of becoming that parental superego, that is, by reversing the generations, as Jones described it. A seductive relationship can undermine the difference between generations, as in the clinical example, but can contribute to reparative aims as well as to the confusion of generations by going back into the past. It can allow one to work over historical reality, to put more into the past as memory, and do what can be done to improve one's lot without compulsive actions or bondage to the past, just as L's positioning the turndown of the bedcovers 'lost its obsessional quality when [she] was able to make contact with [her] living-dead paternal grandmother ... who had taken possession of her psyche like an intruder'.[19]

Part of the drive to write more history is to overcome the conflict between the reparative and the perverse relationships with the past. Historians rely on collecting, authenticating, classifying and comparing documents, and correlating variables, but they also identify with the objects of their enquiry (as implied in Dilthey's notion of *Verstehen* as the defining methodology of the human sciences).[20] Although they re-work their narratives in the light of new discoveries, they also do it because the re-working itself is the primary task. It must be re-done as a continuous reparative task, and because the narrated past is continually infiltrated by phantasies that undermine and damage it, and make it persecutory.

In this chapter, I have had in mind principally phantasies related to the confusion and reversal of generations, in relation to linear time. Time is the path by which the future (anticipation, hope) moves through the present and into the past. It is a meeting-point between wishing, experiencing and losing, and an occasion for merging and identifying. Linear time reduces the dimensionality of whatever it measures. It erodes the sense of qualitative difference, which then builds up as a quantitative movement in time. This sense of time promotes a particular form of identificatory relationship between the present and the past, which seizes the past or the future by moving into it.[21]

A bit of general background will make this form of identification clear. Identification is the mode of relating to what is not there. In everyday life, we take on characteristics of loved ones when they are absent. It is the process of assimilation of oneself to another, as well as of reflection and differentiation. It is as essential to human understanding as time is to physics and ordinary life, but it also undermines objectivity, because it merges self and other. In historical imagination, the absent other is the past, which we cannot experience in external reality. As Collingwood pointed out, the object of historical enquiry is not present, and must be raised in the imagination. Thus the identification must be formed through inserting imagination – phantasy – into it.[22]

On the one hand, historical consciousness involves an awareness of a past, which is equivalent to an awareness of difference between one person and another, between an event and one's experience, between then and now, between an external reality and a phantasy. Indeed, it is a mode of thought in which an other (which includes an event) has boundaries. On the other hand, the very absence of the past fuels an unconscious relationship to it, which is driven by longings like those, in the clinical example above, that were evoked in the analyst by his patient, or in her by her father, or in her father by his mother. Linear time only appears to establish the future as the future, differentiated from the past. In reality, it generates an uncanny sense that, though the past and the future are quite distinct, they are also merged or co-present, and one can – though one ought not – move between them. As one travels in time, one becomes a voyeur of the past or the future.

Originally, Freud equated identification with incorporation, that is, with eating and assimilating the properties of the object as if they were food: one eats what one likes, and spits out what one does not like. But one can incorporate the object with different aims. One obvious wish is to keep the other alive through assimilation to one's own life, such as occurs when someone is absent, and one notices the other in one's own behaviour and thinking. Identifications range in the extent of confusion, the intensity and kind of affect, and the extent to which the object is nourished and nourishing, or controlled and controlling. They can range from enrichment by the other to destroying it, loving it to hating it, but always charged with ambivalence. In one extreme form of confusion, parts of the ego, in phantasy, enter the object to observe and control it, like an internal voyeur. Melanie Klein called the phantasy of intruding parts of the ego into the object, 'projective identification', by contrast with the 'introjective identification' mentioned above, which referred to an enriching assimilation of the object.[23]

The same modes of identification must be active in relation to the past as to any other object. They include the wish to keep the past alive, but also the range of aims towards the object whose life is sustained through contact with oneself: loving, sustaining, enriching, hating, punishing, controlling, monitoring, fearing. It is the past that we keep alive in the present, and towards which we express these aims. That is why, no matter how useful the methods of sociology, demography, economics or intuition may be to the historian, at the core there remains a historical consciousness based on identifications, including the primitive core identifications, such as those between child and parent. The varied identifications of individual historians and groups of historians bring alive in the present the complexity of these past lives and events.[24]

Knowing the past builds on a dialectic between conscious intentions, including scholarly and scientific knowledge, and unconscious aims, including the temptation towards incestuous involvement, as in L's wishes towards her father. Keeping the past alive also invites an uncanny presence in the past, with the aim of monitoring and controlling it from the inside by projective identification. And it will be matched by an uncanny presence of the past in the present, calling for revenge, respect, preservation, restoration.

The historian represents the past as a situation with its own character, researched and ever more accurately known in its own right, as in Leopold von Ranke's founding dictum for professional history: '*wie es eigentlich gewesen ist*' (as it essentially was).[25] But the idea that we are in the present, while those whom we study were in the past, puts the current generation into a superior position, as

161

Jones says of the reversal of generations. At the same time, the same historical figures fascinate us with the mystery of an earlier time, and draw us into the phantasy that we will discover their essence and empty them of it or appropriate it. As an actualisation of incestuous phantasies, historical work intrudes into its objects: at one extreme, to dominate them; at the other, to relate to them generously and gratefully, so that life can be lived free from bondage to them.

Linear time fuels this contradictory relationship to the past. Measurement allows precise specification, but it also makes qualitative difference into a quantitative movement. It merges while it separates. The phantasies that fill in this abstract formulation include setting boundaries, guarded by taboos, and the temptation to breach taboos. The historical mentality, which considers the past as identical to the present, that is, in the same dimension and only separated by time, promotes primitive phantasies, including primal scene phantasies.

The temptation to breach the time barrier becomes a form of incestuous relationship between the present and the past. It gives a particular form to the view proposed by Samuel:

> Our time-reckonings, too, though apparently adopted for purposes of expository common sense, occupy an imaginative as well as a chronological space. Days, as well as offering mnemonic devices to the teacher, and precise locations to the stickler for accuracy, also serve as choreographic devices; investing events with dramatic and historical pattern; characterising and ordering what might otherwise seem formless; and creating the space in which notions of linear progression can have free play.[26]

The clearest example of these processes at work would probably be found in the history of science. We know better than historical figures, but are nonetheless fascinated by their lives, of which we have little knowledge. We know better than they, in practical, theoretical and objective ways: we can manage some areas of experience, particularly in relation to the natural world, better than they could. Yet we are as drawn to their intimate lives and private thoughts as we are to the lives of politicians or poets. We want to prove them right or wrong, as surely as if they were our parents; and to be as interesting to ourselves and to others as they are to us. Moreover, when science is right, it need no longer recognise the past on that issue, and when it is wrong, it remains dependent on the past. The scientist with new knowledge is therefore like an Oedipal hero, born without a father and possibly without a mother as well.[27]

More generally, the way we treat artefacts, relics, monuments, records – all the traces of the past – expresses the continuous process of invading, destroying, rebuilding, fearing, loving, respecting, repairing. To preserve a moment of the past is to infiltrate it at the same time as to keep it alive. This conflict will never end. No doubt it fuels the never-ending proliferation of historical controversy.

162

Notes

1 In Kleinian thinking, which is the basis of my approach, phantasies are the unconscious psychological aspects of basic impulses, such as feeding from the breast, as opposed to conscious fantasies, as in daydreams. See R. Hinshelwood, *A Dictionary of Kleinian Thought*, 2nd edn, London: Free Association Books, 1991.

2 Freud made this interpretation in 'A Special Type of Choice of Object Made by Men (Contributions to the Psychology of Love I)', 1910, in *The Standard Edition of the Complete Psychological Works of Sigmund Freud*, London: Hogarth and the Institute of Psycho-Analysis, Vol. 11, p. 173.

3 I have explored in detail the urge to get to the beginning, mainly with respect to science, in K. Figlio, *Psychoanalysis, Science and Masculinity*, London: Whurr, 2000; Philadelphia, PA: Brunner-Routledge, 2001.

4 On the first two displacements, see J. Chasseguet-Smirgel, *Creativity and Perversion*, London: Free Association Books, 1985; on the production of children, see Figlio, *Psychoanalysis* op. cit.

5 ' "[C]reativity" is a function of the internal parents, or the gods, in earlier terminology. Only "discovery" is vouchsafed to the mortals.... Parents, like artists, feel that they have "found", not "created", their children', D. Meltzer, *Sexual States of Mind*, Strath Tay: Clunie, 1973, p. 85. I have explored the phantasy that knowing has become an omnipotent production in *Psychoanalysis, Science and Masculinity*, op. cit.

6 Hans Jonas speaks of an '*ontological reduction* of nature', in which

> wholeness as an autonomous cause with respect to its component parts, and therefore the ground of its own becoming, shared the fate of final causes.... The presence of the future, formerly conceived as potentiality of becoming, consists now in the calculability of the operation of the forces discernible in a given configuration.... Thus for purposes of explanation the parts are called upon to account for the whole, and that means the primitive has to account for the more articulated, or, in older parlance, *the lower for the higher*.
> (H. Jonas, *The Phenomenon of Life: Toward a Philosophical Biology*, New York: Harper and Row, 1966, pp. 200–1 [author's emphasis])

7 K. Figlio, 'Historical Imagination/Psychoanalytic Imagination', *History Workshop Journal* 45, 1998, pp. 199–221; on *Nachträglichkeit*, see S. Freud, *From the History of an Infantile Neurosis*, 1918, in *Standard Edition*, Vol. 17, pp. 1–122, see p. 38, 44, 45, 58, 77, 107, 109, 112; J. Laplanche and J.-B. Pontalis, *The Language of Psycho-Analysis*, London: Hogarth and the Institute of Psycho-Analysis, 1973, pp. 111–14. The basis of transference is confusion of the present with the past, but except in psychotic states, markers of a perception as external remain. S. Freud, 'Neurosis and Psychosis', 1924, *Standard Edition*, Vol. 19, pp. 147–53. On words and things, S. Freud, 'The Unconscious', 1915, *Standard Edition*, Vol. 14, pp. 161–215; esp. pp. 201–4, 209–15.

8 In Klein's thinking, the reparative urge arises from 'depressive anxiety'. Depressive anxiety arises from the phantasy of damaging and losing a good object, with an associated dread of accumulating damaged and dead objects in the internal world. It stimulates an urge to repair the damaged objects; see M. Klein, 'The Early Development of Conscience in the Child', 1933, in *Love, Guilt and Reparation and Other Works 1921–1945*, London: Hogarth/Institute of Psycho-Analysis, 1975, pp. 248–57, esp. p. 255. On manic reparation, see Klein, 'A Contribution to the Psychogenesis of Manic-depressive States', 1935, in *Love, Guilt* ... pp. 262–89, esp. pp. 277, 278. For an overview of reparation and manic reparation, see R. Hinshelwood, *A Dictionary* ..., op. cit.

9 I have explored this theme in 'Historical Imagination', op. cit.

10 S. Freud, 1933 (1932), in *New Introductory Lectures, Standard Edition*, Vol. 22, pp. 1–182, see p. 69.

11 Robert Hinshelwood has studied the dynamics of groups in terms of 'handing on', in *What Happens in Groups: Psychoanalysis, the Individual and the Community*, London: Free Association Books, 1987. This understanding of groups, in which they exist partly as active systems for defending their members from mental pain, has become known as the analysis of social defence systems. See this entry in Hinshelwood, *A Dictionary ...*, op. cit.

12 E. Jones, 'The Phantasy of the Reversal of Generations', 1913, in *Papers on Psychoanalysis*, 5th edn, London: Bailliere, Tindall and Cox, 1948; Karnac, 1977, pp. 407–12; see pp. 407, 409, 411. I have called this theme the 'Perseus complex', because in Greek mythology, Perseus killed his grandfather 'by accident', in the way Oedipus killed his father 'by accident'. The Perseus complex refers to an unconscious wish to displace and replace a grandparent, in the way the Oedipus complex refers to the unconscious wish to displace and replace a parent. Figlio *Psychoanalysis*, op. cit., pp. 164–85.

13 Raphael Samuel says:

> Ancestor-worship is arguably a potential element in any historical project, while the idea of keeping faith with the past, or being 'true' to it, is the driving force or animating spirit in restoration work of all kinds. Solidarity with the dead – or an act of reparation towards them – has been a leading motive in many of these do-it-yourself retrieval projects which have as their object honouring the hardship and sufferings of those who have been hidden from history in the past.
>
> (R. Samuel, *Theatres of Memory, Vol. 1, Past and Present in Contemporary Culture*, London/New York: Verso, 1994, p. 230)

I would add to ancestor worship and keeping faith with the past the phantasy of intrusion into the past by identifying it with unwanted aspects of the present, with the aim of controlling them. We then have repetitively to restore and assuage this damaged and retaliatory past. Also, see note 18.

14 I have explored this theme in detail in Figlio, *Psychoanalysis*, op. cit.

15 *Civilization and Its Discontents, Standard Edition*, Vol. 21, pp. 57–145; see p. 70.

16 G. Sapisochin, '"My Heart Belongs to Daddy": Some Reflections on the Difference between Generations as the Organiser of the Triangular Structure of the Mind', *International Journal of Psychoanalysis* 80, 1999, pp. 755–67.

17 Ibid., p. 758.

18 I have explored the idea that historical research and writing have a reparative aim in 'Historical Imagination', op. cit.; also, see Samuel, *Theatres of Memory*, op. cit. and note 13.

19 Sapisochin, '"My Heart Belongs to Daddy"', op. cit., p. 759.

20 W. Dilthey, *Introduction to the Human Sciences: An Attempt to Lay the Foundations for the Study of Society and History*, 1883, London: Harvester Wheatsheaf, 1988, see 'Human Sciences'.

21 I have to leave aside the question as to whether linear time is uniquely a Western modern epistemic principle. The classical view, proposed by Mircea Eliade, was that modern Western cultures lived in linear time, and other cultures lived in circular time, in which events recurred. This distinction is bolstered by noting that science does not rest with recognising recurrences of phenomena: it drives relentlessly to get to the beginning and to move back and forth in time, in its theoretical imagination. I have explored this scientific drive psychoanalytically, in *Psychoanalysis*, op. cit.; on circular

and linear time, see Mircea Eliade, *Cosmos and History: The Myth of the Eternal Return*, New York: Harper and Row, 1954; Bollingen Library, 1959.

22 R.G. Collingwood said of historical imagination:

> The historical imagination differs from [the artist's imagination and Kant's analysis of perception] not in being *a priori*, but in having as its special task to imagine the past: not an object of possible perception, since it does not now exist, but able through this activity to become an object of our thought.... The criterion [of historical truth] is the idea of history itself: the idea of an imaginary picture of the past.
>
> (R.G. Collingwood, *The Idea of History*, 1946, Oxford: Oxford University Press, 1993, pp. 242, 248)

23 On identification and incorporation, see S. Freud, 'Instincts and their Vicissitudes', 1915, in *Standard Edition*, Vol. 14, pp. 109–40, esp. pp. 134–6. On projective identification, see R. Hinshelwood, *A Dictionary* ..., op. cit., pp. 79–208; M. Klein, 'Notes on Some Schizoid Mechanisms', 1946, in *Envy and Gratitude and Other Works 1946–1963*, Hogarth/Institute of Psycho-Analysis, 1975, pp. 1–24, especially p. 12. Freud analysed the extremes of enrichment and of harassment, in the extremes of mourning and melancholia, 'Mourning and Melancholia', 1917, in *Standard Edition*, Vol. 14, pp. 237–58.

24 In the minutiae of the clinical situation, one can get a sense of the way the past is thrown up like a wake behind the moving present, with all its turbulence. This disturbed relationship between an individual's present and past can be observed in the transference, and interpreted in object-relational terms from moment to moment, as, for example, an Oedipal phantasy from which one, in the present, is excluded, or the reverse. The historical narrative, by contrast, has been smoothed and turned into an account presented by a coherent author (whether a historical actor or a historian). But that author is then read by readers who identify, for example, with underplayed parts of the narrative, as if they too feel under-represented or excluded. The totality of the historical enquiry then becomes conflicted, and it is there that we must look for the unconscious themes.

> [T]here are no historical propositions which are insulated from contrary readings. If radicals are fearful that resurrection domesticates the past, and by making it too familiar robs history of its terrors, there are others, at the opposite end of the political or pedagogical spectrum, who are no less convinced that the new history is turning out a nation of subversives.
>
> (Samuel, *Theatres*, op. cit., p. 164)

I would say that these readings are based on identifications. No one historical narrative necessarily shows the conflicted nature of this relationship, but the inevitable eruption of conflicting interpretations suggests it, when taken together.

25 This expression has become part of the vocabulary of the historian, as identified with Ranke as 'repression' or 'wish-fulfilment' is with Freud. Collingwood, in *The Idea*, op. cit., p. 130, n. 1, attributes it to the preface of Ranke's *Geschichte der romanischen und germanischen Völker*, 1874.

26 Samuel, *Theatres*, op. cit., pp. 435–6.

27 Whether science, by contrast with the humanities, generates knowledge as absolute truth is the subject of a vast literature into which we will not venture. It is enough to say that science is the principal social form through which this idea is expressed in a secular culture. Leonardo da Vinci was a hero of science for Freud, who said of him

165

that his scientific curiosity was liberated by the absence of a father; see *Leonardo da Vinci and a Memory of his Childhood*, 1910, in *Standard Edition*, Vol. 12, pp. 57–137, esp. p. 122. I have explored the theme of the scientist as an oedipal hero in *Psychoanalysis*, op. cit., which includes a psychoanalytic case study of an important figure in early modern science, Robert Boyle, pp. 186–209.

Part V

MEMORY BEYOND THE MODERN

Introduction

Susannah Radstone and Katharine Hodgkin

The three chapters in this section are all concerned with delineating the contours of a map of memory that stretches beyond the modern. Esther Leslie's chapter focuses on the modernist understandings of memory as they emerged during the late nineteenth and early twentieth centuries, in which the emphasis fell on the relations between consciousness and forgetting. Richard Terdiman's concern is with the relations between memory and postmodernity. His chapter focuses on two phenomena commonly associated with postmodernity: the speed and negation of distance achieved by electronic communications, and the rapid political transformations undergone in Eastern Europe. As a result of these developments, Terdiman argues, in postmodernity, everyday life is 'catching up with' memory. Michael Lambek, too, looks beyond modernity, to a culture within which the modern, Western division of memory from history does not apply. Focusing on spirit possession in Madagascar, Lambek suggests that the reach of modern, Western regimes of memory is by no means universal, and that much can be learnt about those regimes by studying domains beyond their influence.

The ground shared by the chapters in this section extends beyond a common concern with alternatives to modern regimes of memory. Two further concerns emerge in each of these chapters. First, all three are concerned with difference. Esther Leslie's essay suggests that, for modernism, memory constituted a difference beyond modernity's consciousness. Modernist accounts of this difference 'within' modernity and within individual subjects suggested that it could be figured by new technologies of the visible. Richard Terdiman focuses on memory's associational leaps. He suggests that while the connections memory makes between one thing and another might be based on shared elements – on sameness – memory's associations also reveal that memory is inextricably bound up with relations of difference. Michael Lambek's chapter looks to a culture

167

within which an almost entirely different understanding of temporal relations and of people's relation to the past pertains. Lambek suggests, moreover, that different conceptions of social personhood give rise to alternatives to 'memory' as it is conceived of in Western modernity.

A further concern of this section as a whole is with the relation between regimes of memory and broader theoretical and philosophical questions. Each of these chapters suggests, indeed, that an entire edifice of theory and philosophy might be challenged by questioning particular regimes of memory. Leslie's and Terdiman's positions share some of the same ground here. Leslie's discussion of modernist conceptions of memory leads to a questioning of the inevitability of certain postmodernist views concerning the contemporary impossibility of representing actuality. Richard Terdiman suggests that an understanding of the limits of memory's associational leaps might temper the relativism associated with postmodern theory. Both Leslie and Terdiman argue that contemporary theory has much to gain by sustaining an understanding of memory that includes, but is not limited to, its motivated *conservation* or *retention* of traces. Finally Michael Lambek suggests that the study of alternatives to contemporary Western regimes of memory/history might correct a current academic tendency to romanticise and objectify memory.

Memory's relation to the media of photography and film has been the subject of much recent discussion.[1] Leslie's chapter demonstrates that photography and other technologies of the visual were central to modernist regimes of memory. She identifies two modes of modernist association between visual technologies and memory. First, during this period, relations between memory, consciousness and forgetting came to be figured by analogy with visual technologies. Second, at the same time, visual technologies such as film and photography came to figure a broader modern 'technologisation' of memory. In other words, modernism suggested that in modernity, the subject remembers *differently*. Meanwhile Leslie identifies two apparently contradictory tendencies within modernism's 'politics' of memory. Modernism urged that memory should be wiped away and the past forgotten, while simultaneously invoking the authenticity of past, primitive or pre-modern modes of being, and the significance and permanence of the memory trace. Leslie shows that visual technologies allowed for the figuration of these complex, rather than contradictory, modernist regimes of memory.

Leslie's chapter is centrally concerned with the modernist analogies between consciousness and optical devices found in the works of Walter Benjamin and Sigmund Freud. Through these analogies, she suggests, something can be grasped of modernism's challenges to established understandings of history, memory and time. Central to the differently nuanced modernisms of Benjamin and Freud was a view of memory as a hidden substratum whose meanings might run counter to those of surface understanding – of ideology, or of consciousness. Both thinkers strove to penetrate this hidden substrate. While for Freud, this probing was undertaken through psychoanalysis, which aimed to reveal the links between surface disturbances and buried traces, Benjamin believed that photography and film might provide access to an optical unconscious. For both Freud and Benjamin, it is the relations between consciousness, memory and forgetting that are central. One might say, indeed, that modernism proposed that consciousness had limits, thus highlighting the limits of a certain positivism associated with Enlightenment thinking. Events 'pass through' and are forgotten by consciousness, but leave their traces in memory. Leslie's chapter concludes with a consideration of postmodernist tenets concerning the relation between new electronic technologies and memory. As Leslie explains, on postmodernist accounts, the contemporary unrepresentability of truth and actuality is confirmed by analogy with virtual technologies, which allow for the unlimited manipulation of the image, while leaving no room for an optical unconscious. On these accounts, any belief in the relation between actuality and the trace has to be abandoned. Leslie refutes, however, the inevitability of this move. Instead, she suggests that the relation between representation, actuality and the trace might be revivified by analogy with the retention of traces by computer memory. Leslie proposes, then, that modernist regimes of memory may have life in them yet and that new technological developments do not inevitably dictate the abandonment of the insights they offered concerning relations between actuality, consciousness and memory. In short, Leslie proposes that memory need not be uncoupled from its connection with actuality.

As Leslie's chapter demonstrates, it is often via discussions of memory's mediation by electronic communications, computers and digital media that arguments concerning the relation between modern and postmodern regimes of memory are currently formulated. Richard Terdiman's chapter opens, indeed, precisely in the place that Leslie's concludes, with a consideration of memory's relation to these new electronic technologies. Terdiman's suggestion is not, however, that these new technologies are transforming memory, but rather that they can help us to reformulate our own understandings of the ways in which memory has always functioned.

Terdiman's account of memory proceeds by way of analogy with his own recent journeys to the Isle of Skye, to London, to Poland. These journeys, he suggests, were the prompts for memory associations to other places (while in Poland, for instance, he found himself remembering a book about Los Angeles) just as Internet search engines offer up a flood of associational leaps to whatever prompts they are offered. Terdiman builds on these points to offer a description of memory that foregrounds its twin tendencies: memory, in Terdiman's view, conserves *and* transforms, it reproduces the same while also mediating the experience of difference through the imagination of 'something else'. Terdiman suggests that both electronic communication and the rapid transformations that characterise contemporary history illustrate well what he calls the 'associational leaps' that have always been true of memory. And his insistence on memory's twin tendencies of conservation and transformation leads him to question the current theoretical tendency towards relativism. This tendency springs in part, from that association of postmodernism with only one aspect of memory's twin tendencies: with transformation rather than with conservation, with the construction of difference, rather than with the reproduction of the same. Here Terdiman's project finds a common ground with Leslie's, in their wish to retain relations between memory and trace, memory and actuality, memory and motivation, while acknowledging that memory is also the agent of transformation.

Michael Lambek's chapter, which concludes *Regimes of Memory*'s final section, offers a radically decentring view of contemporary Western regimes of memory, by contrasting them with a culture within which the Western conception of memory does not apply. Though Lambek does suggest, in passing, that 'Western media do offer some points of comparison with spirit mediums' (p. 209) his chapter does not share Leslie's or Terdiman's concern with media and memory. Instead, he focuses on practices of spirit possession in north-western Madagascar, describing a way of life in which the current generation lives with and communes with its ancestors, with its past. This communing with the past is achieved via spirit mediums who give access to one or more of these ancestors. Lambek draws on Marcel Mauss's concept of the '*personnage*' to describe the spirits who inhabit their Sakalava mediums. Like personages, spirit possession reproduces social roles that endure beyond mortal time-spans. In Madagascar, Lambek suggests, the lively relations between spirits and mediums, between ancestors and present generations, render the distinction between history and memory inappropriate.

Lambek's main argument, then, is that conceptualisations of memory and history are dependent on conceptualisations of social persons. In a society in which possessive individualism does not hold sway, and in which it remains unclear whether spirits possess mediums, or mediums possess spirits, then memories are not carried as 'things'. Instead, the boundaries between what the West knows as history and memory do not pertain. In their place is a practice of intersubjectivity in which present and past lives converse.

Lambek suggests, finally, that the Sakalava practices to which he draws our attention can be counterposed to the romantic objectification of memory that he critiques. In the West, he argues, memory is indissociable from the extreme individualism characteristic of modernity. For Lambek, the romantic objectification of memory follows the logic of possessive individualism, for memory takes on the qualities of the individual: boundedness, homogeneity and continuity. In conclusion, Lambek offers up Sakalava practices as an aid to imagining an alternative to this Western regime of subjectivity/memory, and suggests that memory might be seen, not as something possessed by individuals, but as something shared between subjects: as practical and relational.

This journey through memory concludes, then, with the reminder that the study of memory risks adding to its romantic objectification. Lambek suggests that it is by exploring practices that fall outside modern, Western regimes that this tendency can best be avoided. Yet Leslie and Terdiman warn, too, of the risks of relativism – risks that are arguably embedded in postmodernist accounts of memory's sundering from actuality. Perhaps what this leaves us with is a question: can studies of memory avoid the risks both of romantic objectification and relativism? This is the challenge posed by this final section of *Regimes of Memory*.

Note

1   See, for instance, Vivian Sobchack (ed.) *The Persistence of History: Cinema, Television and the Modern Event*, New York and London: Routledge, 1996; Marianne Hirsch, *Family Frames: Photography, Narrative and Postmemory*, Cambridge, MA and London: Harvard University Press, 1997; Marcia Landy, *The Historical Film: History and Memory in Media*, London: The Athlone Press, 2001.

9

ABSENT-MINDED PROFESSORS

Etch-a-sketching academic forgetting

Esther Leslie

Traces of the modern

Modernist aesthetics in the 1920s frequently invoke the processes of remembering and forgetting. This is apparent in the exhortations to wipe away traces of a previous epoch or previous styles. In polemical form, typically, avant-garde groups propose the negation of all that has gone before. Also common is the seemingly contradictory impulsion to invoke 'primitivist' or 'naïve' prototypes, regarded as a more authentic mode of being and accessible to our own archaic memory, once the civilisational carapace has been stripped away. Such concerns about negation, memory and forgetting, and layers of the self and psyche are explored in Freud's essays of the 1920s.

In his essay 'A Note Upon the Mystic Writing Pad', written around 1924 and published in 1925, Freud outlines the workings of consciousness. It is a peculiarly self-conscious essay, right down to the punning title. Freud puts his own notes upon the mystic writing pad.[1] He sketches out a model of consciousness and forgetting, and thereby adds another layer to his intricate model of the psyche. In the process, he overwrites what has been assumed till now. 'A Note Upon the Mystic Writing Pad' elaborates a psychic apparatus that 'has an unlimited receptive capacity for new perceptions and nevertheless lays down permanent – though not unalterable – memory traces of them'.[2] He then refers to his earlier work in *The Interpretation of Dreams*, from the turn of the century. Here he observed a system of perceptual consciousness, which receives perceptions but retains no trace of them, so that it can react like a clean sheet to each new input of data. It seems that experience lands on an ever-wiped table. However, the permanent traces of the excitations that have been received (the crumbs, the stains, the mess) are preserved elsewhere, in 'mnemic systems' that lie beneath or behind the perceptual system.

In *Beyond the Pleasure Principle* (1921) Freud refined this model, according to Walter Benjamin's reading of Freud in his writings on Baudelaire. Benjamin notes that Freud makes a distinction between unconscious memory and the role of consciousness in shielding the self against stimuli, by blocking retention, acting to counter the leaving of an impression. Consciousness, in acting as a buffer, counteracts what unconscious memory attempts to procure and conserve – the trace. Consciousness appears in the system of perception in place of the memory traces, because 'becoming conscious and the leaving behind of a memory trace are processes incompatible with each other in one and the same system'.[3] Trace memory fragments are all the more powerful when the incident that brought them into being never in fact passed through consciousness. That which is dimly felt, but not fully confronted, grips the person more tightly because it is only partially known. The shocks occur but are not consciously perceived. Consciousness is engaged in a damage-limitation exercise. Consciousness swaddles the organism against shocks from the external environment, diverting abrupt or abrasive sensations elsewhere, away from the surface. But once the protector is off its guard, when the person dreams or suffers mental trauma, the shocks, the traces re-emerge into consciousness unbidden. Or that which has been repressed might be called forth by the analytic process. Dreams and analyst get to that somewhere 'behind' consciousness or, rather, open up a channel through which repressed contents come to expression.

In 'A Note Upon the Mystic Writing Pad' Freud further elaborates the workings of the psyche to reveal the real wonder, the *raison d'être* of the essay. He has found a commercial expression of the model of consciousness and its hinterland. An apparatus has appeared on the market and its functioning perfectly replicates the operation of the psychic system. The apparatus is the *Wunderblock*, the 'mystic writing pad'. Freud goes to some length to describe this device, a toy that clearly excites him in the way that a new toy enchants a child. The *Wunderblock* is a writing tablet from which notes can be erased by an easy movement of the hand while permanent traces of all the etchings that have been made on it are retained elsewhere. Freud details the apparatus's structure and its components, which are wax, translucent paper and celluloid. A pointed stylus scratches the surface, making impressions on the waxed paper. This writing or marking stands out because it is darker than the surrounding grey. Freud even troubles to tell us that the latest version of the device works slightly differently but is in principle the same apparatus, and so the analogy still holds. The device's celluloid sheath protects the paper that receives the impressions. When the top sheet is lifted and cleared a permanent trace remains on the underlying wax slab. This is legible in certain lights. It is unlike paper, which can only be used once and whose traces are retained on its surface, subject only to fading through the passage of light-imbued time or conscious erasure or obliteration. It is unlike a blackboard, which is permanently rewritable but the previous expressions are lost forever once wiped away. In the mystic writing pad there is both erasure and retention.

The mode of operation of this device mirrors the workings of consciousness, which also divides the functions of receipt and preservation between two types of consciousness. Freud is constantly concerned with the appropriateness of his analogy. He worries about the fact that no use is made of the permanent traces of impression on the wax block, but then insists that indeed it is not of great importance. It does not matter for the use of the writing pad, which truly would be mystical were it able to 'reproduce' the writing from within. Memory can, however, do this. Memory can reproduce the 'writing', the traces, from within.

Freud then pushes the analogy even further, revealing that it agrees with a notion he hitherto kept to himself but can now divulge. This relates to the way in which consciousness, like the writing pad, constantly stretches out to the world and receives impressions, only then to recoil, to withdraw once the excitations are sampled. Indeed the inanimate pad and consciousness are both active, opening onto the world, and then shutting down.

This particular idea is invoked again in the 1925 essay 'Negation' where, altering his terminology ever so slightly, Freud asserts that the ego periodically forays through the perceptual system to sample external stimuli, only then to withdraw.[4] The unconscious never admits negation, but the unconscious is revealed by negation constantly. Repression works in so devious a way. Freud also asserts the way in which the perception of real objects can be an internal process. It is not a checking that an object exists in reality, but rather a re-finding of the object in memory in order to assure oneself that it is truly real.[5] The external world is verified in memory. The machinery of memory guarantees the actuality of the event. Memory precedes experience, in a sense. Chronology is sent into reverse, in order, notes Freud, that time might be experienced.[6]

Freud's analogy between consciousness and an optical device did not come out of the blue. Various theorists in and of the modern epoch associated optical devices and consciousness. Marx, for example, had evoked at different times the *camera obscura* and the *phantasmagoria* apparatuses of the nineteenth century in order to discuss the workings of consciousness and ideology, or what Lukács would later describe as false consciousness. It is important to note that though these optical machineries are put forward in order to represent illusion and miscomprehension in capitalism, Marx notes that they are not, in themselves, generators of untruths – indeed they faithfully represent things 'as they actually are', either topsy-turvy, in the case of the camera obscura, because of power imbalance in the world, or with mis-attribution of liveliness, as in the phantas-magoria, because of commodity fetishism. Such connections between optical machineries, human perception of the world and actuality continue over a period in which optical devices increasingly disseminate themselves through everyday life. Indeed, the analogy between optics, optical devices and memory, combined with Freud's interest in negation, offers a route to the core of modernist theory and aesthetics in the 1920s.

In this period the notion of recording, particularly through time, comes to the fore, alongside developments in mechanical reproduction, especially in relation to film. Concomitant with this, and tied more closely and obviously to the action of negation, is the opposite move: the injunction to wipe everything out. This erasure found most vociferous expression in European modernist movements from the Futurists, Dadaists, Constructivists and others onwards. In January 1923 a journal called *Littérature* published 'Thank you, Francis!' by the International Dadaist Francis Picabia. Railing against an 'imbecilic age' in which, since the war, 'morality' is the new contagion, and artists foolishly strive to be taken seriously, Picabia insisted:

What I like is to invent, to imagine, to make myself a new man every moment, then forget him, forget everything. We should be equipped with a special eraser, gradually effacing our works and the memory of them. Our brain should be nothing but a blackboard, or white, or, better, a mirror in which we would see ourselves for a moment, only to turn our backs on it two minutes later.[7]

Picabia flaunts speed, impermanence and the virtues of deletion. Picabia wants more forgetting and obliteration – not for him Freud's retention of traces on a block of wax, out of sight, but not out of mind. Picabia demands a real wipeout, a total eradication of the self and its illusions, preferring the blackboard, or even just the mirror, which only catches a glimpse for a moment and discards it simultaneously with the withdrawal of the image source. Picabia wants to erase his self, reinventing for each moment a new man who lives without memory. The eraser obliterates him and his works. This war on continuity and the dead weight of tradition (weighing like a nightmare on the brain of the living) is a nihilistic rejection of the trace, which means a rejection of the past and any efficacy that it might have in the present. But its productive energy comes from a desire to reset the terms of life and art, modernistically. The brain as eraser might model Hegel's description of brainwork: thinking is always the negation of what we have immediately before us.[8] Repeated deletion, considered from Hegel's dialectical point of view, leads not to nothingness but to movement – just as Freud's reiterated deletion of traces leads to the unconscious, and so to mental life. For Picabia and for Freud, deletion of traces is an activity that produces something else – movement and productivity in Picabia's terms, the possibility of going on living, in Freud's. In fact, it leads to more than that, as Freud notes, in 'A Note on the Mystic Writing Pad'. Deletion – the stretching out of consciousness and then cancellation of the gesture, this breaking of contact, a discontinuity in the functioning of the system – lies at the 'bottom of the origin of the concept of time'.[9] It is the only way in which historical experience becomes possible at all. Such a procedure also lies at the bottom of the kinetic art of film with its frame after frame. Might it be possible to say that it is not only the mystic writing pad that models the activities of consciousness and forgetting? Film too might provide such a model. At the moment of being shown, at least, as it rolls past like a mirror of the world in movement, presenting images that burst on the air, it leaves traces on our retinas (the twenty-four frames a second calibrated to our ability to string fragmentation into continuity).

Another version of the magic writing pad occurs in the work of the animator Oskar Fischinger. At the same time as Freud wrote his essay, Fischinger patented a device that cut slivers off swirled coloured waxes while a camera shutter, synchronised with the movement of the blade, filmed the changing features traced by the multicoloured whorls and striations of wax. In projection, the wax came to life in extraordinary ways; the frame-by-frame record flowed into continuous animation. The wax patterns twisted and twirled and grew and shrank. The history and development of their traces and their negation could be followed up by concentration on the source of the illusion: the filmstrip's frame-by-frame record. Fischinger's device mobilised the principle of animation (a celluloid form as old as film itself). This principle is organised around the importance of the 'between each frame', the unseen part that is the in-between on which movement, animation, is dependent. The negation in cartooning is called an in-betweening, of which the animator Norman McLaren noted:

> Animation is not the art of drawings that move, but rather the art of movements that are drawn. What happens between each frame is more important than what happens on each frame, therefore animation is the art of manipulating the invisible interstices between frames.[10]

This consciousness of negative moments, of invisible interstices, is fundamental to modernism in the years that Freud made his observations on the mystic writing pad and on negation. Dada echoed Freud's model of negation in literal terms. Hans Richter's lecture at the Dada Soirée in Zurich in April 1919 was titled 'Against Without For Dada'.[11] And while Dada may have meant refusal, in the sense that it was meaningless and embodied meaninglessness, the word itself, in Tristan Tzara's Romanian, meant yes, yes – as retort. Negation, erasure, the interstitial, all these things are pivotal; without them there is no movement, no change.

Walter Benjamin: memories and traces

Another contemporary of Freud's, Walter Benjamin, constantly evokes optical devices (and in particular their capturing of traces) in relation to thought, memory and consciousness: for example, in the section titles and thematics of his book of fragments written in 1925–6 and published in 1929, *One-way Street*. Here we find the 'Kaiser Panorama', 'Enlargements', 'Technical Aid', 'Optician', 'Stereoscope' or 'To the Planetarium'. These optical devices and scenarios become appropriate ways for focusing on questions of memory and the processing of experience. It is not surprising that Benjamin should be thinking about modes of vision and matters of perspective for, of course, *One-way Street* is all about Benjamin's own change of focus. Signalled in this book is his adoption of a new urban, political, modernist point of view, which undertakes the recovery of the extraordinary poetry of banality. In a related project, a memoir written through the late 1920s and 1930s titled *Berlin Childhood around 1900*, he wrote a short piece also called 'Imperial Panorama', which was about a favourite optical entertainment from his childhood. The Imperial Panorama had peep-holes that looked onto three-dimensional town views. His description of the viewing contraption evokes the power of the intense experience of looking at postcards of mountains, cities, railway stations and vineyards. This device teaches Benjamin something about memory and desire, and how the vividness of an experience, here a technically aided one, might, because it spoke to something so intimate and 'clichéd' and desired, be a substitute for 'true experience' and memory:

> The distant worlds were not always foreign to them [children]. It some-times happened that the longing that they aroused did not call them into the unknown but back home. And so it was that one afternoon in front of the transparency of the small town of Aix I tried to persuade myself that I had once played on the cobblestones watched over by the old plane trees on the Cours Mirabeau.[12]

In 1932, in his short speech on Proust, Benjamin alludes to a proto-cinematic device, a thumb-cinema.[13] He intended to recite this lecture on Proust on his fortieth birthday on 15 July. Diary notes and letters suggest that this day was also the day that Benjamin had nominated as the day on which to commit suicide. A letter to Gershom Scholem in June revealed that he wanted to spend his birthday in Nice with 'a quite droll fellow' whom he had often met in his life. It appears that he was referring to death.[14] He planned to kill himself in a Nice hotel. He abandoned this plan and instead wrote a lecture on memory and imaging the past. His speech touches on mortality. He talks of dying and connects this to the cliché of a proto-photographic strip of images of a life whirring through a dying person's head. The intimation is that a celluloid self lies buried in our uncon-scious. Memories are involuntarily summoned strips of montaged images, flashing past in rapid succession. The proto-cinematic device, whose functioning is aligned by Benjamin to the process of memory, appears once more in an auto-biographical entry titled 'The Little Hunchback'.[15] Our lives flit by us in a series of images, snapshots that are strung together to produce an illusion of continuity and movement. Memory itself can produce continuity, at a social level as well: 'Memory creates the chain of tradition that passes events on from generation to generation.'[16]

But this continuity comes after the event, in the re-projection of past experi-ence, as if we were equipped with a cinema inside our heads. Memory presents itself to us in pictorial form, Benjamin insisted in 1932:

> Genuine memory [yields] an image of the person who remembers, in the same way a good archaeological report not only informs us about the strata from which its findings originate, but also gives us an account of the strata which first had to be broken through.[17]

For Benjamin, the book of his childhood memoirs, like the thumb-cinema, is a series of rapidly passing images, strung together into an illusory continuity. In the closing vignette in *Berlin Childhood around 1900*, it is not Benjamin whose thumb rustles the sheaf of images in his thumb-cinema, but a little hunchback. This small demon who inhabits him is also responsible for his clumsiness, his devious-ness and his proneness to accident and failure. The demon is a kind of unconscious figure, out of control, as wily and disruptive as the id. Elsewhere Benjamin insists that the most important images in our lives are those that develop later. The darkroom where this process of development takes place is the darkroom of our subsequent lives, the 'after-life' of the moment of taking the image. The metaphor suggests that experience comes to us in the form of images that are absorbed into our memories where they then take time to develop, or do not so much take time as get shocked suddenly into the 'now of recognizability'[18], through the catalytic power of a word, a sound, a smell, an echo from past into present. That is to say, experience becomes memory, and as such does not remain a passive dormant thing, but something ever ready to burst out and scatter the fragile consensus of the present. Memory glimpses a set of flickering images that are bound up with their moment of recognition, a moment which may come unbidden or be extracted forcibly. Memories are efficacious traces.

Benjamin proposes a technologisation of memory and consciousness. But here, rather than the low-tech analogy of psyche and mystic writing pad, we get the actual assertion of a high-tech consciousness, a memory and a psyche held by technological devices. This is clearest in the 'optical unconscious' – first mentioned in 1927, when Benjamin argues that in film 'arises a new region of consciousness', through which people get to grips with the ugly hopeless world, comprehensively, ('*faßlich*'), meaningfully ('*sinnvoll*') and passionately ('*passion-ierend*').[19] New technologies of reproduction model the parameters of modern experienced reality. They reproduce experience for purposes of re-presentation (film footage, audio-recordings present modern life to viewers) but, in so mediating the world, these technologies remodel the world that is shown – becoming a fundamental part of experience, rather than just its passive representative. 'A Small History of Photography' details the 'different nature' available to machine-enhanced perception.

> A different nature speaks to the camera than speaks to the eye; most different in that in the place of a space penetrated by a person with consciousness is formed a space penetrated by the unconscious. It is already quite common that someone, for example, can give a rough account of how a person walks. But he would not be able to describe their position at the fracture of a moment of stepping out. Photographic aids: time-lapse, enlargements, unlock this for him. He discovers the optical-unconscious first of all through it, just as the drive-unconscious is discovered through psychoanalysis. Structural compositions, cell formations, with which technology and medicine deal – all this is more fundamentally allied to the camera than the atmo-spheric landscape or the emotion-steeped portrait.[20]

Whether we see better or more deeply or simply differently is not resolved. It seems to be the case that a specifically technologically enhanced vision is born with the camera. However, this vision takes us back to something we have known before: the worlds uncovered by photography may have existed before, but perhaps only in dreams. A 'scientific' way of appropriating those worlds appears to have been found. A key advance of the camera is that it allows the opportunity to understand interiority. Photography, in some sense an extremely external – because objective – art form, relates, however, to the interior. This is Benjamin's observation in an early version of 'The Work of Art in the Age of Mechanical Reproduction' when he discusses how the way of seeing that the 'optical unconscious' effects is like the mode of perception in psychoses, hallucinations and dreams. Objective camera vision links to the actual subjective human perception of non-rational types, psychotics or dreamers. Benjamin writes:

> For the manifold aspects that the recording apparatus can reclaim from reality lie for the most part only outside a *normal* spectrum of sense perceptions. Many of the deformations and stereotypes, the transformations and catastrophes, open to detection by the world of optics in film, are actually found in psychosis, in hallucinations, in dreams. And so those methods of the camera are practices, thanks to which collective perception appropriates the individual ways of seeing of the psychotic or dreamer. Film stands against the old Heraclitian truth – that those who are awake share a world, while those asleep each possess a world for themselves.[21]

Film's remarkable service is to displace an ancient 'truth' of the Greeks, and to show us that both perception and truth might be perceived in historical terms. New optical devices allow a renewed and fantastic understanding of the contents of consciousness, on the basis of negation of what simply is, through the trickery of in-betweens, the unseen gaps where and when manipulations take place, and yet always insistent on a basis in the real. This deranged world is collectively perceived in film. For Benjamin, memory is something that is held not just by humans, but by objects. The indexical trace is important here. Photography is an indexical form, in the sense that it relies on the existence of bodies in the world that impress their traces on photographic paper. The continuity with the issue of traces caught in consciousness is clear. 'Memory', then, might be held by cameras – as in the case of the 'optical unconscious' – or by objects in the world, not just the artefacts of labour, but nature too. Benjamin's 1921 essay on Goethe's novel *Elective Affinities* quotes from Goethe's scientific treatise, the *Colour Theory*. What interests Benjamin is how for the attentive spectator nature is:

> never dead or mute. It has even provided a confidant for the rigid body of the earth, a metal whose least fragment tells us about what is taking place in the entire mass.[22]

Magnetic metal speaks from the interior of the earth. It is an *Urphänomen*, and, notes Goethe, it 'reveals itself', as 'even' scientists realise in their drive to

179

construe external, visible, tangible parts as a whole, understood as indications of what is within, and so attempt to master the whole in perception. Nature as animate was not a one-off insight in Benjamin's writings. Just as the ideas of colour, play and fantasy surface again and again, so the notion of affinities between inner earth, outer space and the human body is evident across Benjamin's work, in his theories of mimetics and indexicality. Benjamin has a sense of the history of perception as a history of the body – the mode of perspective depends on how upright the gait is, the perceptual evaluation of distance depends on the amount of movement made, and so on.[23] In 1933 Benjamin wrote two articles on the mimetic capability, 'On the Mimetic Capability' and 'Doctrine of the Similar', which describe the mimetic capacity as an adaptation to the environment. These two pieces consider nature as a realm that produces similarities. This is evident, for example, in the phenomenon of mimicry. Astrology – as constellations of stars at birth – and graphology, the traces of handwriting, interested Benjamin as keys to the personality. Benjamin regards astrology as an ancient hangover of a link between humanity and the position of the stars. And words, onomatopoetics, are a form of similarity. The latest graphology is seen to teach that handwritten words are picture puzzles that conceal the unconscious of the writer. Writing is, in this sense, already the mystic writing pad of Freud. For Benjamin, mimesis is denoted as the original impulse of all creative activity.[24] A mimetic capability manifests itself in the body's imitation, in social and cultural forms, of acts that have been essential to its survival. So dancing and pictorial activity emerge in their particular forms because they relate to practical activities. In 1936 Benjamin notes that stone-age man drew the elk so incomparably because the hand that moved the drawing stick still remembered the arrow with which the beast had been brought down.[25] Drawing emerges, then, as a way of re-tracing the social activities crucial to survival. It is this originary sense of the trace, and of writing's essential and practical nature, that is repressed in 'civilisation'.

While preparing the writings on mimesis Benjamin took notes on Georg Lichtenberg, a physics lecturer who advised Goethe in his researches. Lichtenberg, reading the book of nature, finds a natural world that is alive and historical. Benjamin quotes him as follows:

> As the cuts on the surface of a tin plate relate the story of all meals in which it has participated, so too the form of each belt of land, the shape of its hills of sand and rock tells the history of the earth, each smoothed pebble thrown out by the ocean would tell of a soul which was chained to it as ours is to our mind.[26]

Historical activity imprints on the tin surface, just as photography is a chemical imprinting of a likeness, and just as the external world imprints its traces on the psyche, where they may perhaps be read, dredged up into consciousness or recognition. Benjamin's reminiscences in *Berlin Childhood around 1900* and *Berlin*

Chronicle pull photography even deeper into mimetic and mnemic reflections. In his memoirs he insists that traces of mimetic behaviour are to be found in children's pleasure at imitating things – windmills, trains – as much as they ape other people. On being photographed as a child in a studio, with a painted Alpine scene, or in the shadow of a small palm tree, clutching a straw hat, Benjamin recalls an inability to resemble himself and a desire to be identical with the embroidered cushion or the ball handed him as props.[27] (Civilisation's repressed traces are to be understood in two ways – repressed ontogenetically and phylogenetically, across vast swathes of time as well as in each lifetime as child becomes adult.)

Photography, a chemically based art, is a mimetic and a mnemic art. 'A Small History of Photography' (1931) accents the indexicality of the photograph, with its chemical connection to actuality that snatches a flash of time and exports it into the future. Just as the person imprints the world on the self by identification with its objects, so the photographic object imprints traces of the world.[28] As August Sander proclaimed, 'In photography there are no unexplained shadows!' Everything that appears is indexical and its derivation, that is, its existence, can be traced back through the process that brought it into being. Benjamin quotes Goethe in connection with August Sander's social typological images, gleaned 'from direct observation': 'There is a tender empiricism that so intimately involves itself with the object that it becomes true theory.'[29] The object speaks through its traces. Historical meaning is contained in its spoors. Recovery of that meaning might come suddenly, involuntarily, as it bursts through in a sudden moment of recognisability – what Benjamin calls involuntary memory – or it may be teased out, analysed, sifted in a more deliberate manner.

Benjamin's appeal to memory and indexicality is connected to his interest in modes of relating history and actuality. It is always a matter of how new technologies both model and enact a modern sense of time, how new technologies frame and provide a way of thinking through the current understanding of memory or consciousness. It is important that film, and photography, are perceived as truth-generating – not falsification devices – though of course, there is also a possibility, acknowledged in Benjamin's analyses, that inaccuracies and propaganda can be broadcast. When such a practice occurs, as in the Nazi use of film criticised in 'The Work of Art in the Age of its Mechanical Reproduction', Benjamin refers to it as a misuse or rape of the apparatus.[30] The apparatus is not used to reveal truth, but uses the power that clings to its apparent traces of the real to deceive.

Coda

Photography is literally writing in light. Writing, of any sort, is a trace. Handwriting's traces have been caught in graphite, ink, carbon, or scratched into pliable surfaces. More recently, through the computer, writing has become electronic (and dependent on light). The traces of words have two lives: one on the computer print-out and one on the hard disk of the word-processing machine. For the writer, in this new technological epoch, writing and reading parallel each other more closely than before. While the contemporary writer writes, the keyboard offers so easily, indeed invites and insists upon, the possibility of endless deletion, revision. The electronic text is so readily alterable, and the traces of previous formulations so quick to wipe away, seemingly permanently. The word processor offers the possibility of a perpetually alterable text, always subject to revision, the chance to change, interpolation, cut and paste. Hypertext, websites, newsgroups, new electronic forms of text hold out the promise of never-completed statements, texts without conclusion or finality.

Fast-forward, then, from Freud and Benjamin and the optical models of memory and the existence of traces, to ponder the existence of a similar parallelism in the digital era. One of postmodernism's maxims was that truth and actuality can no longer be represented. Virtual technologies arrived on the scene in order to provide the visual analogue of this statement. We can no longer trust digitalised representation to represent anything other than itself. Digitalised representations are infinitely manipulable, infinitely imitable. They are pure copy without origin, representation without represented, and so they evade the clutch of truth. This leaves no room for an optical unconscious, for that would imply a bearing of traces, an analysis of movements that have occurred in space and time. The optical unconscious relies on a guaranteed interchange between actuality as it has happened and its belated representation for analysis. This is denied by digitality's proposition of a rift between signifier and signified – or something even more insuperable than a rift – as in Jean Baudrillard's notion of the hyperreal. In Baudrillard's scenarios, computers appear to be the last word in the refinement of the hyperreal: computers are the ultimate technology of an irreversibly imploding system which has brought about the disappearance of 'the real' and meaning, and, in its place, promotes the fascination with images and, specifically, an enchantment with representation without referent. Without referent, it is as if the link to history and memory is severed in favour of a permanently overwriting present without recall.

But is it not the case that an alternative account of these technologies could come into being, that they could have been taken up differently, and in ways that extend the lineage already traced out here in which modernist analogue technologies in turn provide analogies for memory? Digital technologies inevitably become extensions of our selves – entities through which we re-think our relationship to the world and to our selves. This is already under way, given the existing metaphor of 'memory' in computer applications. The boom in 'memory studies' is perhaps evidence of this occurrence; in various scholarly contexts, there are attempts to recover all sorts of things – a type of intellectual recycling. In this, everything that has occurred, big or small, is held on to, is made significant, could qualify as the smallest detail that could alter drastically the telling of the accepted facts. The recourse to memory is often the excuse for opening up many versions, the gap between event and memory – as intriguing openness, as

access to *Geschichten*, stories, rather than to *Geschichte*, (hi)story, a singular determinate relation of cause and effect. The past is re-worked, re-told, remembered,
forgotten, mis-remembered, and subject to revision through the very fact of
memory.

Of course this has its well-founded legitimacy in memory's operation – for
perhaps all this talk of trace and recording does imply too direct a connection,
too mimetic a presence, memory as direct imprint of the world. Memories are
motile, and they relate to their causation in distorted and contorted ways, and
they change over time themselves. In relation to this point, Steven Rose has
reported that human memory and computer memory are incompatible.[31] Each
time a human remembers, the memory changes. A human memory works by
omission and lies and recontextualisations. (Here Rose concurs with Freud's
observation in 'A Note Upon the Mystic Writing Pad' of the psychic apparatus
that 'lays down permanent – though not unalterable – memory traces'.)[32] In
contrast, then, it could be said that the computer memory, despite its operational
capacity for limitless change, exemplifies infinite repeatability in self-constancy.
But does this mean there can be no psychoanalysis of computer memories, no
recovery of repressed traces of keystrokes? Our memories are partially, and to an
ever-greater degree, externalised in computer memories. Are computer memories a guarantee against forgetting, given their preservation of piles of data, of
multiple 'versions', of back-ups and utterances, with multiple existences?
Computers remember for us, and though deletion is the result of a simple set of
actions, programs tend to interrupt the process, inquiring whether we really want
to erase, whether it is not in fact a mistake. In this sense, memory and retention
are axiomatic to the computer's function. So much so, though, that this could
perhaps be taken as evidence of the contrary – that computers are, in actuality,
the endpoint of an ultimate forgetting, because memory – our memory – is here
externalised, and substituted (just like the memorial, in fact, as commentators, in
particular on Holocaust memorials, have argued)? Key ways of working with
computers could be seen to by-pass consciousness: databasing, word-searches,
search and replace, macros, templates, spellcheckers. But still within computing
the traces do remain, even after acts of erasure, though they may, by then, only
be available to specialists, forensic experts and sophisticated data programs that
take a crashed computer back to an earlier date as part of its process of recovering lost information or salvaging from computer wreckage.

The poet and librarian J.H. Prynne, archivist of many written traces, has
mused on the dilemma of archivists of the future when they inherit the hard
disks of dead poets and authors. They will be burdened by the knowledge that
nothing is lost on the hard disk, that every version, every keystroke, might be
reconstructable through data recovery, that computer memories are crowded
with ghosts. How many renderings, how many works in progress at how many
stages will be recoupable? And yet none of them will be quite as original or
auratic as scraps of manuscripts and authors' notebooks held in archives and
libraries, allowing scholars to attempt to reconstruct the processes of intellectual

production. This multiplication of traces might be burdensome, demanding too much labour and technology-enhanced sifting. Freud worked laboriously on the psyches of those who sought him out, and Oskar Fischinger struggled frame by frame to produce animations, and Benjamin winnowed painstakingly the rubble of his and Germany's past to find the causes of contemporary misery. Will it be worth it given today's mounting data pile-ups? Is there any chance of finding causes and meanings in the mounting junk of data, which, from a Baudrillard-inflected postmodern perspective, is only simulation without origin, virtuality without actuality, signifier dirempt from signified. Would it be better to abandon notions of the original, of singularity, of ultimate causation, by ridding all thought of the notion of the trace, the effective trace, and by seeking justification and solace in the fact that memories are alterable anyway, are only versions? But even if memories are alterable, do not those alterations too have causes? Is it better to dissolve memory into stories, none more significant than another, and to turn traces into arbitrary marks, no longer accountable? There is a risk in effacing the trace: if it is unhinged from its connection – however mediated – to actuality, then forgetting is all there is, and memory becomes too distant a memory. There may not be any 'recovery' for us from that.

Notes

1 The pun does not quite translate in German. The German title 'Notiz über den Wunderblock' does not suggest the same sense of writing 'on to' the toy.
2 S. Freud, *Selected Works*, Vol. 11, Harmondsworth: Penguin, 1984, p. 430.
3 Freud's 'Beyond the Pleasure Principle' is quoted in Walter Benjamin's 'Some Motifs in Baudelaire' in his *Charles Baudelaire: A Lyric Poet in the Era of High Capitalism*, London: New Left Books, 1973, p. 114. The extract can be found in context in S. Freud, 'Beyond the Pleasure Principle', in Freud, *Selected Works*, Vol. 11, op. cit., p. 296.
4 Freud, *Selected Works* Vol. 11, op. cit., p. 441.
5 Ibid., p. 440.
6 Ibid., p. 433.
7 *Littérature*, new series no. 8, Paris, January 1923, reprinted in Charles Harrison and Paul Wood (eds) *Art in Theory*, Oxford: Blackwell, p. 272.
8 G.W.F. Hegel, *Logic*, ed. W. Wallace and J.N. Findlay, Oxford: Oxford University Press, 1975, p. 17.
9 Freud, *Selected Works*, Vol. 11, op. cit., p. 433.
10 Quoted in Vanda Carter, 'Animation: Making and Meaning', in *Boiling*, 1, 1998, p. 10.
11 In English in *Hans Richter by Hans Richter*, ed. Cleve Gray, London: Thames and Hudson, 1971, p. 96.
12 Walter Benjamin, 'Berliner Kindheit um neunzehnhundert', *Gesammelte Schriften*, Vol. 7, part 1, pp. 388–9.
13 See 'Aus einer kleinen Rede über Proust, an meinem vierzigsten Geburtstag gehalten' [1932] *Gesammelte Schriften*, Vol. 2, part 3, p. 1064.
14 See letter to Gershom Scholem (25 June 1932) quoted in *Briefwechsel: 1933–1940*, ed. Gershom Scholem, Frankfurt/Main: Suhrkamp, 1980, p. 17. *The Correspondence of Walter Benjamin and Gershom Scholem 1932–1940*, New York: Schocken Books, 1989, pp. 9–10.

15 *Gesammelte Schriften*, Vol. 4, part 1, p. 304. 'Das bucklichte Männlein' was printed in the *Frankfurter Zeitung* on 12 August 1933 and appears in *Berliner Kindheit um neunzehn-hundert*, op. cit., pp. 302–4.

16 Walter Benjamin, 'The Storyteller', in *Illuminations*, ed. Hannah Arendt, London: Fontana, 1992, p. 98.

17 Walter Benjamin, 'Excavation and Memory', in *Selected Writings*, Vol. 2, 1927–1934, trans. Rodney Livingstone *et al.*, ed. Michael W. Jennings *et al.*, Cambridge, MA: The Belknap Press of Harvard University Press, 1999, p. 576.

18 This phrase appears in the file of notes labelled 'N' in *Gesammelte Schrfiten*, Vol.1, p. 579; translated in Gary Smith (ed.), *Benjamin: Philosophy, Aesthetics, History*, Chicago: University of Chicago Press, 1989, p. 52.

19 'Erwiderung an Oscar A.H. Schmitz', *Gesammelte Schriften*, Vol. 2, part 2, p. 752.

20 'Kleine Geschichte der Photographie', *Gesammelte Schriften*, Vol. 2, part 1, p. 371; trans. 'A Small History of Photography' in *One-Way Street and Other Writings*, London: New Left Books, 1979, p. 243. Benjamin uses the term *'verwandt'*, 'allied', a word contained in the title of a novel by Goethe, *Die Wahlverwandtschaften* or *Elective Affinities*, on which Benjamin had written a piece of criticism, completed in 1922.

21 'Das Kunstwerk im Zeitalter seiner technischen Reproduzierbarkeit', *Gesammelte Schriften*, Vol. 1, part 2, pp. 461–2; also in *Gesammelte Schriften*, Vol. 7, part 1, pp. 376–7.

22 Walter Benjamin, *Selected Writings*, Vol. 1, Cambridge, MA: The Belknap Press of Harvard University Press, 1997, p. 303.

23 'Wahrenmung und Leib', *Gesammelte Schriften*, Vol. 6, p. 67.

24 See 'Das Kunstwerk …', *Gesammelte Schriften*, Vol. 7, part 1, p. 368. See also notes for the second version of 'Das Kunstwerk …', *Gesammelte Schriften*, Vol. 7, part 2, p. 666.

25 'Zur Aesthetik', *Gesammelte Schriften*, Vol. 6, p. 127.

26 'Notes' for the essays on mimesis, *Gesammelte Schriften*, Vol. 7, part 2, p. 792.

27 'Notes' for the essays on mimesis, op. cit., pp. 794–5.

28 'Kleine Geschichte der Photographie', op. cit., p. 385 or 'A Small History of Photography', op. cit., p. 256.

29 Walter Benjamin: *Reflections*, New York: Schocken Books, 1986, p. 252 (translation modified).

30 'Das Kunstwerk …', op. cit., in *Gesammelte Schriften*, Vol. 1, part 2, p. 506; 'The Work of Art in the Age of Mechanical Production', in *Illuminations*, op. cit., p. 234.

31 Steven Rose, *The Making of Memory: From Molecules to Mind*, London: Bantam Books, 1993.

32 Freud, *Selected Works*, Vol. 11, op. cit., p. 430.

10

GIVEN MEMORY

On mnemonic coercion, reproduction, and invention

Richard Terdiman

How can you go to Europe, it's the place of death.
(My great-uncle to me before my first trip to Europe, 1961)

In postmodernity, we'll have *non*-identity cards.
(Graffito on a wall in Cieszyn, Poland, 1999)

For Tadeusz, Ewa, and Jakub Sławek

A conference on memory metadiscourses on its own topic.[1] Memory is so constitutive, so indispensable to our intellectual and practical activity to begin with that every cognitive or discursive act or fact is already tangled up in the mnemonic realm. And this is all the more true when memory is itself the matter we reflect upon. Then the imbrication of our cognitive modality and our analytical object becomes truly thorny. The problem becomes something like trying to see vision. This chapter seeks to make explicit memory's implication of its medium in its referent.

Memory contravenes the logic that sober argument strives for. Memory's fluky links and stochastic jump-cuts resist "proper," orderly reasoning. The undeducible associations memory throws up seem less ratiocination than random walk. So, along with the usual scholastic elucubrations that academics find it hard to let go of, my chapter interweaves a somewhat oddball reminiscence and rehearsal of its own genesis: something like recollecting my own remembering of a talk on memory. Since from the mnemonic perspective the present is never sutured or complete, necessarily I begin before the beginning.

Thirty-two hours after I left San Francisco a few days prior to the "Frontiers of Memory" conference, I found myself, via an overnight train from London and a rented car, in Scotland – in the Hebrides, on the Isle of Skye, a place where I'd never been but always dreamed about. Ordinarily, traveling non-stop from San Francisco to London, you fly over Skye at 37,000 feet. I wanted to be there on the ground. But it's a long journey up from London to the Hebrides. Why go – particularly when time is short and one's motivation is entirely imaginary?

The reason is that, like the haunting phrase whose occupation of his brain Mallarmé narrated in "The Demon of Analogy," years ago my memory somehow fixed desire on Skye. I kept recalling the song – "Over the sea to Skye" – that for centuries, since Bonnie Prince Charlie escaped there after the Scottish defeat at Culloden in April 1746, have conjured up the island. I was following Dr Johnson on his voyage to the Hebrides in 1773, when he traversed a Skye that, in his depiction, seems as exotic as Nepal does today.[2] I was remembering Virginia Woolf's *To the Lighthouse*, set on the island.[3] We don't choose these associations, we seem chosen by them. But as a result of their elections, seductively, ineluctably, memory manages us. A lot of what we do answers the demands of the past.

Reaching a bit further back into that mysterious territory of recollection and its hold upon us, I recall that in June 1999, three months prior to my quixotic journey up to Skye, I was in Cieszyn, a small city in southern Poland on the Czech border. The idea for my paper for the London "Frontiers of Memory" conference first arose there. As with Skye, so with Poland: why *that place*? With my personal history and professional profile, one might have thought Poland an improbable destination. Unlike many Jews of my generation, I have no ancestral connection there. What draws me are friends. My Polish friends have a lot to do with who I have become and what I've done over the past decade and a half, with the way things take place for me even when I'm far away doing or thinking about nothing connected with Central Europe.

Friendship – the personal and the discursive connection active here – is a conduct of memory. Like all mnemonically mediated experiences, in an uncanny instantiation of action at a distance, the ties by which friendship calls and binds us assert themselves unbidden, in the "wrong" place, uncontrolled and unconstrained by proprieties of logic and canons of pertinence. As with love, these derogations of conventional appropriateness in no way diminish friendship's force or its demand upon us.

In Cieszyn the impulse for this paper arose in a minor experience of absurdity, or at least of the kind of loopy incongruity that *compels* somatic reaction, corporeal outlet – a disbelieving shake of the head, an astonished and rueful shrug of the shoulders, a bemused smile. My paper mimes and unfolds such a gesture. But memory constantly determines such quirky spasms.

So I wrote this essay under the inspiration or the compulsion of some odd memory associations. People tend to think that the essence of memory is *conservation*. But what can be seen if we look at memory from the opposite direction? Then memory becomes the archetypal technology and register of displacement, mutation, transformation. Memory is the medium for our experience of *difference*. In that sense memory – the paragon of conservation – simultaneously and constitutively undermines this mode of its own functioning. Through its blasé embrace of the most unpredictable relations, through its tolerance for the most discrepant non-sequiturs, memory is the paradigm for *originality* – perhaps the originary practice of such originality in our experience. Without doubt, memory rules the complex of functions and modalities in culture that ensure the reproduction of the *same*. But memory also is the agent of the same's *subversion*.

Memory normalizes the inappropriate and the alien in ways that look like common understandings of creativity. If inventions don't come from *nowhere*, at least, as with the experience of Proust's *madeleine*, they seem to arise in no place we could ever have guessed. Memory acts like the aerolith, the stone that falls unaccountably from the sky. When we are stuck in the box of the here and now, thinking "outside the box" is something memory models for us. In that sense, memory is our template for utopia – it is the source of our imagination of something *else*. "Any where out of the world," as Baudelaire resonantly put it.[4] From whatever locus we are in, memory maps the supersession, the mutation of our place into some other, any other. Memory works because it is the model of the improper, because it *has no place*.

The incident at the origin of my paper demonstrates the eccentricity that many say characterizes what we call "postmodernity" in general. Let me use it to exemplify the absurdity of unrestrainable association that memory generates with the most insouciant disregard for order. That's what I'm remembering now in recalling how this paper germinated three months before the London memory conference. Thus in the summer of 1999, as the fabricated commemorations of the pseudo-millennium frothed themselves up and lurched ever closer, I was in Cieszyn, in the park surrounding the ruins of the eleventh-century castle there, thinking about … about what? What would you think about if you were in southern Poland on a fine June day, on the hill above a slightly tattered former Hapsburg city slowly disengaging itself from socialist drabness? The *memory* point is, you might think about *anything* – just as in "Le Cygne" in 1859, in the vertiginously modernizing heart of nineteenth-century Paris, Baudelaire unaccountably recalled and apostrophized the antique Trojan princess Andromache in an exemplary instantiation of memory's elemental absurdity.[5]

Incongruity is the *name* of the mnemonic. On that day in Cieszyn, what I found myself thinking about were the eerie postmodern disorientations of Los Angeles. The origin of this flight of fancy was not mysterious. Sitting in the castle park I was reading *City of Quartz*, Mike Davis's brilliant book about L.A. I had found it in my friend Tadeusz Sławek's library in Cieszyn. But the choice of this book *there*, from among all the ones on Tadeusz's shelves, exemplifies something like the odd elections that animate memory itself. Why fall upon *that* volume? As something like materialized memory, and functioning in its image, libraries are a regular locus not only of *recovery* but also of *invention*: not just recollection-as-reproduction (retrieving the information you went to find), but also unanticipated and unpredictable discovery.

The logic of *rhetoric* (association, metaphor, metonymy) and the logic of *logic* (propositional deduction and implication) are our two indispensable – and polar – modalities for connection and sense-making. It is memory that models and motivates the first of these modalities. We truncate our faculties if we forget or under-value it.

But (as narratives always say in a paradigm instantiation of the mnemonic experience) back to Cieszyn. Mike Davis's book chronicles the production of Los Angeles as a city without a past, without depth, in effect *without memory*. His L.A is a fabulous construction – part designed, part the consequence of oriented chance – that marginalizes cognizable time and sustainable connection. Los Angeles is the postmodern city before anyone thought to say so. But what a shock montage back viewed from southern Poland! It would be hard to imagine two places more different from each other than Cieszyn where I was thinking about all this, and L.A, where my thoughts took me. In effect I was recalling the city without history from something like the heart of history itself.[6]

Cieszyn is a traditional Central European town, centered around its market square and its baroque town hall. Its winding streets and clustered buildings would remind you of dozens of small European cities, growing slowly over many centuries, incorporating in their development the older elements of their assemblage, altering them hesitantly. Yet, given its location on the southern edge of one of Europe's traditional battlefields, sometimes Cieszyn has experienced violent kinds of alteration. The montage made this history, this penetration by memory, inescapable. It made incongruity, memory's name, immediate. It reminded me of my great uncle's understandable (if repellent) identification of Europe with annihilation that appears as an epigraph to this chapter.

In 1920 Cieszyn was dissevered by politics. In the partition that settled the post-World War I borders of Poland and created Czechoslovakia, Cieszyn was parceled out between the two countries, sliced in two along the Olza, the stream that flows through the middle of what had been one town. The partitioning authorities and the divergent orthographies of the two pertinent tongues gave the now-disconnected pieces of the former city separate names: *Cieszyn* on one side, *Těšín* on the other. Today the River Olza seems too modest to define an international frontier, and the split in the heart of the town seems utterly peculiar. Borders induce thought about the odd couple formed by *difference* and *connection*.[7] Cieszyn radicalizes such reflections.

What could better symbolize dissociation, what could more forcefully instantiate and symbolize the protean links that memory determines between entities despite disjunction, than such an arbitrary split? So looking down from the Cieszyn castle toward the river and across it toward the part of the city that is now another country, I was in a multiple displacement. I was thinking of the history that had created, or de-created this place. I was thinking about Los Angeles, another de-created city. A hundred metres from Poland to the Czech Republic. Twelve thousand kilometers from Cieszyn to California. Is one further from us than the other? In such situations, the distances and differences, material and metaphorical, swirl about us and colonize consciousness. All the marks of culture – those we experience immediately; those mediated by recollection – melt into each other. Everything swims dizzily: geography, sociology, history, politics, psychology, and personal memory.

Then in this mnemonic re-enactment, the question becomes, What place is this? *Where are we?* On one level, the answer is easy. Cieszyn is a charming town of 40,000 whose streets, buildings, and squares are busily rediscovering the charm of their past in the Austro-Hungarian Empire. The city was founded in 810. It has been inhabited for more than a millennium. Simultaneously on another level there, the sorts of wacky – or sinister – incongruities I've sought to register here overwhelm us. Austro-Hungarian Cieszyn is entering the Internet epoch. Today computer stores are tucked away beneath the eighteenth-century arcades that surround the Rynek, the central market square. Internet cafés won't be far behind.

Then communication will take on the same effortlessness with which memory establishes its unpredictable and wanton links. In 1985, when I first traveled to Poland, a letter posted from the USA to a Polish friend on New Year's Day might get a response by April Fool's day. Today my email messages to Poland sometimes get answered before I log out. Time used to signify distance. Now this meaning has been disrupted. We don't know in our bones any more what instantaneity represents.

Around the corner from Cieszyn's main square, in the eighteenth century and through the period of the French Revolution, a Jesuit priest, Father Leopold Johann Szersznik, assembled in his library the works of the Enlightenment *philosophes*. Szersznik's Enlightenment collection is one of the most extensive outside of France. Whence an eerie connection between this unexpected outpost of classical Gallic rationalism, and the archetypal place of modern irrationality: Auschwitz is only an hour's drive from Cieszyn.[8]

What could capture this palimpsestic montage of periods, styles, cultures, histories, and politics – an assemblage even more baroque than the Mitteleuropa baroque in Cieszyn? The tropes of unaccountable *difference*: irony, metalepsis, catachresis. Our accustomed reflex would be *analysis*: sorting out the signifiers, the signifieds, the referents, and elucidating their interactions. Most of the time such rationalization makes sense. But on the ground in Central Europe, the perverse density and complexity of association itself becomes the phenomenon to be seized. Rationalized, the essence disappears. This is because the heart of the experience is an unaccountable relation, a history – a memory – of difficulty, loss, and pain. Fredric Jameson put it resonantly: "History is what hurts...."[9]

In Cieszyn, history reproduces and foregrounds this painful parachronic structure. Before the re-establishment of Poland in 1920, when Cieszyn was German, its name was *Teschen*. In June 1999 in Cieszyn's Cultural Center on the square, there was an exhibition that coupled images of the Polish *fin de siècle* a hundred years ago – reproduced from postcards mailed back to their family at home by Germans vacationing in Lower Silesia – with photographs of the same places in Cieszyn now. It's amazing how little has changed. And it's staggering how much. It seems as far from Teschen to Cieszyn as from Paris to Andromache's Troy. Memory fuses such links as if the distances could simply be annulled. Yet what's happened in the interval can be read in the very fact that

190

such museology can never elide the consequentiality of what cannot appear, the history of what in this place has brought this *then* to *now*.

I first went to Cieszyn in March 1985, driving from Paris with my friends the Sławeks. In those dismal days after Jaruzelski's December 1981 crackdown on Solidarność, crossing into Poland from fraternal Czechoslovakia was an irksome adventure. *Our* adventure in 1985 included a full body cavity search, from which even my friends' then-eight-year-old son Kuba was not exempted. When Tadeusz asked the border guards why they'd singled us out, they responded, hadn't he been active in Solidarność? Tadeusz acknowledged that he had. My pants cinched back up, I observed this dialogue, occurring in a language I didn't understand. Almost anywhere in the world the guard's shrug in response would have communicated *What did you expect?* What do you expect, you were in Solidarność, we crushed you, now we get to humiliate you if we feel like it. The point is not that you might have secreted clandestine tracts up there. The point is, *we can do what we want.*

This was in 1985. I mention the date because that sort of attitude, assuming authority and domination, seeks to assassinate memory. It tries to dissolve temporality, it projects timelessness, inexorability, inevitability.[10] But in Poland the seemingly sovereign arrogance of the Jaruzelski martial law regime couldn't and – to the surprise of almost everyone – didn't last forever. Now it's well into the process of "becoming just a memory." In 1989 following the Round Table, Poland became the first of the Socialist Bloc countries to begin the leap into parliamentary democracy and nascent capitalism. Such is the casual absurdity of contemporary history.

Memory is *always* absurd in this way. Today my Solidarność dissident friend Tadeusz Sławek, so badly treated by the border guards in 1985, is Rector of the University of Silesia in Katowice. In a way, nothing's changed: he has not cut his hair, still down to his shoulders as it was in 1985. In 1997, at his instigation, the University of Silesia awarded Derrida a doctorate *honoris causa*. Derrida came to Katowice and responded with a moving oration – about the difficulty and necessity of orations, about generosity, ceremoniality, and hospitality, about uncanny and inscrutable relations across heterotopia, between diverse systems, periods or parts of the world – and, perhaps more consequential than any of his other themes, about the painful specificity of Poland's historical, political, social, and cultural experience in the lifetimes of many of those who, having lived through the war and through post-war Communism, were still there to attend the ceremony at which Derrida spoke.[11] Jacques Derrida in Poland: connections that we would never have thought of happened anyway. The point is, they happen all the time.

Cieszyn is perched on top of archaeological, historical, geopolitical depths that the most interesting contemporary understandings of Los Angeles (or of the postmodern) would seem to render inconceivable. Yet memory doesn't require us to feel astonishment at the disparity. It accustoms us to the incongruous, it naturalizes the paralogistic. Today in Cieszyn the border guards on the bridges over the Olza don't appear to remember 1985 and their awkward intimacy with my friends and me. Today they couldn't be more blasé. In 1985 it took us five hours to cross from Czechoslovakia to Poland. Today you can walk over the Olza bridges to the Czech Republic and back again in 20 minutes. Difference is being banalized.

When I was in Cieszyn in 1985 and again in 1987, before the government change, political discussions with my friends there turned in an endless regress. Someone would hope that Jaruzelski would allow some relaxation after the crack-down so that Poland could return to something closer to 1981. Automatically someone else would respond that if the liberalization got out of hand, well, the Soviets didn't have to invade Poland, they were already there. A perfect feedback system, self-correcting for any excess in optimism, for any naive fantasies of neo-Enlightenment progress. No leaps, just logic. But what happened was a leap: more like memory than like logic. No one deduced the revolutions of 1989 and 1990.

Isn't the by-word of the past decades that such eccentricity has increasingly been normalizing itself? The blasé incongruities that characterize the memory realm seem to propagate. Jaruzelski is still there with his inscrutable sunglasses. But suddenly he is being scruted himself. The new government indicted him for crimes from the 1970s when he was serving as Minister of War. So Jaruzelski also functions as a memory palimpsest. Then my *dis*-locations or *re*-locations or *bi*-locations or *meta*-locations, like the ones from San Francisco to Cieszyn to Skye to London, become nothing more than a figure, an entirely routinized exemplification, of the shape of experience that has been and is still being constructed in postmodernity, of how we live now.

What experience is that? It feels like the ungovernable lability of memory. Our cognition and evaluation of difference has an archaic template in the functioning of recollection. The everyday experience with which our mnemonic faculty familiarizes us allows us, without the sort of psychic dissociation that would render us non-functional, to find ourselves instantaneously somewhere else. Less and less does such incongruity surprise. Materially, geographically, electronically we are realizing in postmodernity the seemingly effortless and atemporal leaps that memory has been accomplishing for all of history. Practical existence, everyday life, appear to be catching up with our psyche. Life – in the First World at least – increasingly seems to evade constraint and outflank limitation. In general it might feel as if we were living postmodernism as an incessantly disappearing homeland.

The most evident analogue for our hyperbolic ability to flourish in dissociation might be the bewildered non-location we experience on the Web. In this utopia you can be anywhere at 56 K; but *where are you?* Presumably, in a generation or less, such experiences of junction-in-disjunction will be so routine as not to produce the slightest vertigo. Younger people will never have known *not knowing* the world's near-simultaneity and its electronic ubiquity. But for me this dazed non-situation still feels spooky, just as it felt spooky to sit under the trees in the park in Cieszyn and remember L.A, and to recall Poland before the government change, even to remember a future moment in London where I was going to be going with this attempt to theorize the constitutive incongruity of memory.

Now I want to ask how we might understand this perception that the associative dissociations of memory converge with the disseminations of postmodernity. Does that make postmodernism *true*? We talk about conjuncture determining experience. Does that mean that a new logic has taken over perception and experience, or that we have no freedom of action within such a structure? Is postmodernity more than a periodized modality of contemporary life? Is it the end of history? Is it our *sentence*?

That can't be so – because we are developmental beings, because memory with its unending and uncompassable associations is the modality of culture itself.[12] No time – particularly the present – is ever simple or sutured. Nothing comes from nowhere, the slate is never "previously" clean. Wherever we look, culture has already recorded its inscription and imposed its servitudes. Even the chanciest leaps, the most apparently incomprehensible hiccups of history, occur upon the basis of a substrate laid down and retained somewhere in a memory register. Every cultural element that enters circulation and consciousness pushes against contents already present in the field. So the contention never stops, there never is just *one* way of conceiving or experiencing the world. A dialectic, a complex set of determinations and constraints, marks the way that we can theorize the generation of modes of existence themselves. And memory is essential for recovering the parts of the picture that doxa seeks to force outside the frame, to cause us to forget.

All discourses, all experiences, thus arise *situated*. The conservative register of memory – our tenacious internalization of facts, practices, learned behaviors, consecrated modalities for doing and thinking *anything* – is so constitutive a faculty that, even given its domination over us, still we struggle to augment and preserve it. We are born into memory, bound to it, and we fight fiercely to hold on to it. Entropy – the loss of patterned conduct, of pre-scripted thought – haunts us, and we resist the dispossession of the past that, even as it complicates our present, makes the present possible. So the present is never absolute. There is always another side, there is always more in memory.

Yet as people have been saying for a long time – certainly since the nineteenth century when Marx and Nietzsche framed the issue as a diagnostic anxiety[13] – memory's conservative function is always contradicted or counterbalanced by a more or less deliberate stochastic force working *against* the preservation of constituted practice and doxa, undermining their conservative vocation to make the present only a timeless reproduction of the past. In this, the limitless and eccentric associations of memory serve as a paradigm for the production of the new.

In the memory world anything can connect with anything. But some associations are more important than the randomized average. In the light of my discussion of memory's ambiguous or "bipolar" vocation – both to retain and to subvert, to remain focused on the facts and simultaneously to spin off into fantasy – I want to conclude with some thoughts about how we might make sense of the "theoretical" enterprise itself. For however surprising it might seem, I think the connection between memory and theory is a strong one. I want to claim there is an isomorphism between memory's oscillation between different and seemingly irreconcilable "interpretations" of the world it references on the one hand, and on the other theory's seemingly unconstrainable variability in connection with its object.

Just as no referent commands our recollection of it, just as we can recall *anything* under the stimulus of any other, in the same way no conceptual object self-interprets nor determines the theory that will cognize it. You can read *Hamlet* in multiple ways, through multiple theoretical lenses. *Hamlet* won't protest. But this raises a puzzle. How can the world be so wanton, so porous to recollection or interpretation? How can we understand or maneuver in a universe so underdetermined as to permit, even to invite, such disorderliness?

This unsettled and unsettling configuration of the worlds of recollection and comprehension seems to come into focus in the aporetic antifoundationalism of the postmodern period. What might we make of the apparent congruence between what I termed the stochastic functioning of recollection on the one hand, and the seemingly limitless links and disseminations that characterize "postmodernism" on the other? Are these the same instabilities and the same uncertainties?

Seeing these characteristics of memory and theory in this way depends upon an evolution in the history of understanding itself. One of the conditions of its possibility has been the rise, since the Enlightenment, of a broad notion of social constructionism – the idea that social and cultural things are not positively (or positivistically) just *there*, but that they are always devised and determined in relation to some interpretive or cognitive need. This view has had profound and progressive influence in understanding the formation of complex social entities, and in destabilizing the self-evidence of hegemonic ideologies. It has liberated thinking about the constraints and opportunities of the social world, and consequently has empowered action to remake this world. Indeed, social constructionism was *itself constructed* to precisely this end.

But in our own day this notion of the constructed nature of our reality has mutated into a different one, a radical relativism that, in the guise of further liberation, really stops any concerted social action in its tracks. Social constructionism thought that things were made in response to need and desire. This making was never conceived as uncomplicated, effortless or randomized. Some contemporary constructions of social constructionism, on the other hand, elide these constraints. They project an immediate, unrestrained, and painlessly voluntaristic reformulation of the world, a kind of "Ruby Tuesday" evasion of any material bond or social constraint. They imagine fostering liberation. But what they produce is passivity in the face of muddle. The question is, are memory and theory like *that*?

The answer may lie in looking closer at social constructionism. What ought to be remembered in the supposedly social-constructionist doxa of postmodernism that I alluded to just above is the construction of social constructionism itself: the liberation of human possibility that lay at its origin and defined its objective. The social construction of any element of reality (and of any theoretical paradigm in particular) is not simply random or voluntaristic, it is *responsive* and stringently *adaptive. It is tightly bound to concrete situations.* And so, despite its seeming arbitrariness, is memory. So to understand such constructions, we need ourselves to construct the relationship between the situation they sought to confront and the human creativity that answered this. This makes the variance of recollection or the clash of theories more a matter of differential or differently focused understandings – akin to what the physicist Niels Bohr termed "complementarity" – than of theological conflict, randomness, or simple caprice.[14]

What do our theories theorize *about?* and how can a notion like "complementarity" help us make this work more productive? To begin with, we think about (just as we remember) what *troubles* us: no problem, no cogitation. By definition, "trouble" is something we haven't yet resolved. This means that no stable way of framing or understanding it yet exists. Whence a multiplicity of – apparently irreconcilable – lines of attack and proffers for comprehension: *different* theories. These are the elements of complementarity. They are imagination's diverse responses to difficulty. So in the perspective of a task to be performed, of a problem to be addressed, contention in the theory realm is better conceived as *hunt* than as *race*: as people chasing a common objective, rather than battling the other guy. This could help us frame a more propitious form for reflection on the theoretical wrangles that regularly characterize cultural conjunctures. It is the basis for an *ethics of theory.*

If we conceive our theoretical models as joined in a hunt, as seeking, however diversely, to resolve the uncertainties that trouble us, then the conditions of possibility both for understanding and for assessing them are fostered. Our activity in building and using models always involves choices that define what we can see and say. As I argued earlier, there is no self-interpreting text; there is no element of the world that chooses its theory for us, or tells us unambiguously how to apprehend or understand it. If so, then the chaotic theoretical relativism and subjectivism that I discussed might appear to loom, and to doom any attempt to adjudicate between competing and often discrepant models. It might seem that we could think *anything at all.* But in the face of this multiplicity in the theoretical field, are we obliged to accept a kind of Tower of Babel jumble, in which (if I can badly mix a metaphor) a thousand theories bloom, but none does really well?

But our models are determined, even if this determination is not simple or single. In this they resemble recollection: multiple, unpredictable, but always eventually comprehensible. Associations are myriad, but they are not haphazard. While we cannot *fore*-see what may arise in recollection, we can always *after*-see what memory comes up with. And we can figure out why. Theory parallels this

Owl of Minerva genesis in a necessary logic of *Nachträglichkeit*: meaning presides over the production of any mental content, but on the other hand meaning is not necessarily readable on the surface of the experience, or simultaneously with it.[15]

So we *choose* our meanings, they emerge neither out of some revealed truth of the world nor as the result of random and incomprehensible arbitrariness. It is important to be aware both of the contingency and of the opportunity-costs of these choices – particularly of the ones that seem self-evident at any moment. I *do* construct my understandings and my meanings. So does the other guy. But that doesn't imply that everything is simply up for grabs, that anyone's meaning carries the same legitimation as anyone else's. The question is, is there a principled basis for reformulating the disengaged relativism that today many radicalized social-constructivist or post-structuralist positions entail? In the memory world, this would be like restoring a calculus of *pertinence*. Trying to recollect your phone number, you might instead come up with a pink elephant. You might even be able to reconstruct why that content unexpectedly arose in consciousness. But likely you will keep working at remembering until you find your phone number. Some analogous hierarchization of purposiveness seems necessary in the world of theory. Recollection appears end-directed, though we have seen – or at least I have argued – that such a pragmatic objective is accompanied or even subverted by a much less evidently teleological function, the uncompassable creativity for which associative memory is our archetypal model. Theory has a parallel doubleness built in. But that doesn't mean it can or should exist without any constraint at all.

So I would argue for a powerful skepticism about the radically relativist position taken today by many in postmodernism or under its influence. This skepticism seems justified on the basis of two related questions. First, we need to think again about the determinations, the pressure that any theory's *referent* puts on the formulation by which it proposes to make sense. This is like recalling that it was your phone number you were trying to remember. The world answers back to theory as it does to recollection. Second, we need to ask whether there is any principled basis for invoking ethical, social, and political considerations to help us navigate in theory's seemingly unregulated market, so that choices can be made to reduce the seeming randomness of model building and selection.

The theorists of theoretical relativism rightly maintain that there is no objective place from which hierarchies of models can be neutrally ordered, best to worst. But most arguments about whether *her* theory is better than *his* are badly formed. We need to find the grounds of *commensurability* that could make a comparative judgment – of range, of efficiency, of effectiveness, maybe even of beauty – possible. This means paying much greater attention to specifying the means and objectives of models than has often been the case in the theory wars.[16] We need to restore a strong notion of *agency* to the making of our paradigms. Models *do* imply choices. A theory *is* always constructed. But it would be a mistake to treat these effects of volition and creation as if they were no more than the random and incomprehensible result of caprice – no more (to return to my memory analogy) than it would make sense to treat the breathtaking leaps of mnemonic association as if they were *simply* random or incomprehensible.

A randomizing Saussurian model won't do the work we need done in the human sciences. The arbitrary can sustain understanding neither of theory nor of memory. In the cultural realm, connections are motivated, not motiveless as in Saussure's account of the signifier's relation to its signified. There may be no reason English names it *cow* and French calls it *vache*. But this is a *disastrous* analogy for the way models of social or cultural understanding arise and function. To say that no referent can unambiguously determine the theory that accounts for it is far different from saying that every theory has equal status in the marketplace or before the law of paradigmatic existence. As the product of theoretical labor that functions in the way all labor does, a model is constructed within a web of intentions and determinations, just as memory is deployed, among other tasks, for remembering phone numbers. If we allow those intentions and determinations to remain unspecified or mystified, the more fools we.

The choices that form a theory, then, are motivated and differential. And they can be elucidated. We need to insist that the oriented choosing that constructs the model be brought as fully to light as can be achieved, and that the consequences of this complex of choices be specified. Your right to construct your theory shall not be abridged – no more than your right to remember anything that comes to mind. But none of us has a right to heedless indiscrimination in our choosing. And once choices are made and models are constructed, we need to ask what their range and strength might be, what their areas of blindness or underdevelopment are. This is the consecrated and still essential role of critical thinking; the old Hegelian notion of self-reflexivity remains a good idea. And if for social or ethical reasons we believe it is imperative to focus upon the things that a given theory blurs, then we might find a principled basis for critiquing any model that veils them.[17]

Because the problems to which it responds are emergent and unresolved, theory arises in an effort to displace established modes of thought and disciplinary practice, to destabilize self-evidence, to lift the weight with which the past presses down on practice and on thinking. For *ex hypothesi* the past has not solved the present problem. On the other hand, this activity of renewal necessarily references the very modes it seeks to supplant. Their weight is always there; *then* still bears upon *now*. We can see how the duplex, "bipolar" paradigm of memory – indissolubly linking coercion and creativity – models for this constituting ambivalence.

How far can the originarily dissident and disruptive vocation of what we call "postmodernity" propagate before it simply becomes uncritical and conservative doxa? I'd like to suggest that the resources and the structure of memory can help us answer this question. There are cultural and human regularities that overarch individual and specific situations – or else theory wouldn't be possible at all. But theories never get entirely free of the dialectic between specification and generalization.

Typically they want to transcend their originary situation toward a horizon of universality. No discourse, theoretical discourse particularly, can constrain our interpretation of it so as to preclude or foreclose finding meanings that will answer the different demands of diverse situations. Post-structuralism, as is notorious, was subtly transformed when it was imported from France into the English-speaking countries, so that finally (to take a pertinent case) Derrida found himself saying what many powerful thinkers have said before him, that he didn't entirely recognize himself in what others were doing in his name.

Like all theories, deconstruction was a message in a bottle. It floated off, generously but unpredictably. So to return to one of the memory loci I've been evoking in this talk, during the Communist era in Central Europe that ended at the beginning of the 1990s, the fascination in Poland, in the Czech Republic, and in Hungary with deconstruction – exemplified by the honorary doctorate given to Derrida in 1997 by the University of Silesia as I mentioned – obviously can't be understood by assuming that post-structuralism's intervention in the discourses of the Socialist Bloc functioned in the same way as it did in France, Britain, or the USA.

It will be evident that this essay has some of the associative, meandering quality that we identify with the unconstrainable processes of memory. At least *some* of this non-deductive, associative quality has been intentional. We can write the narrative of such associations, but often they're not obvious by inspection. To conclude what I have to say, and since I've already mentioned Virginia Woolf, I want to recall that recollection, and end with a short passage from Woolf's autobiographical memoir, "A Sketch of the Past." At its beginning, she wrote as follows:

> Two days ago – Sunday, 16th April 1939 to be precise – Nessa [Woolf's sister] said that if I did not start writing my memoirs I should soon be too old.... There are several difficulties. In the first place, the enormous number of things I can remember; in the second, the number of different ways in which memoirs can be written. As a great memoir reader, I know many different ways. But if I begin to go through them and to analyse them and their merits and faults, the [time] ... will be gone. So ... I begin....[18]

The memory and the theory mysteries are all strikingly present here. On the one hand, the past (conservational memory) is so overwhelming that its weight can drown us. On the other hand, there are so many different and irreconcilable ways to recall – or to interpret – our recollections (associational memory) that the plethora can stop us dead. We call the different modes of representation between which Virginia Woolf was momentarily poised *theories*. Woolf was claiming for herself the writer's privilege of jumping over methodological quibbling, and plunging into the midst of mnemonic and representational practice.

But whatever the case may have been with Woolf, we have a different sort of responsibility regarding theory and interpretation than she did. I think literary critics and interpreters in the human sciences have to be particularly reflective and judicious concerning these. Thus to my mind, figuring out what Woolf termed the "merits and faults" of the diverse ways we might practice our understanding is as important as unreflectively practicing them.

What do we learn from memory? Of course, that's the problem. We learn everything from it. Memory is *too much*. But in particular and for this reason, memory tells us how complicated things are. An important part of our job is to honor those complications. As we do our theoretical work or write our cultural historiography, we need to remember this daunting – and liberating – mnemonic intricacy. Doing so might help us see beyond the doctrinal polarizations that stress much thinking in postmodernity concerning relativism, or referentiality, or signification. It might even help us remember postmodernity itself as one of the strands of a memory much richer and more complicated than the one contemporaneity itself often projects.

Notes

1 This paper was written for and presented at the "Frontiers of Memory" Conference in London in September 1999. The essay was so closely tied to its occasion, and reflected so explicitly upon it, that altering its subjective, self-referential bearing would subvert its objective. In this printed version I have clarified points in the argument, and added appropriate documentation. But the essay's situational, even eccentric character, and its geographical and chronological allusions centering upon the place and moment of the conference, remain.

2 See Samuel Johnson, *A Journey to the Western Islands of Scotland* (orig. publ. 1775), ed. Peter Levi, London: Penguin, 1984.

3 *To the Lighthouse* is a book about memory if ever one existed. Many scholars believe the novel's setting in Skye is a fictive displacement from the house in Cornwall where the Stephen family spent summers during Woolf's childhood. But for me in the thirty years since I first read it, *To the Lighthouse* has always been about Skye. Sometimes memory doesn't want to be bothered by the data.

4 "Le Spleen de Paris," XLVIII, in Charles Baudelaire, *Oeuvres complètes*, ed. Y.-G. Le Dantec and Claude Pichois, Paris: Gallimard-Pléiade, 1961, pp. 303–4.

5 I described this in Terdiman, *Present Past: Modernity and the Memory Crisis*, Ithaca, NY: Cornell University Press, 1993, ch. 4.

6 Here I conceive Poland's catastrophic engagement with and implication by "history" as exemplary on the grounds not only of the epochal consequentiality of what happened to and in Poland in the twentieth century, but of history's own constitutive implication in what is lost, destroyed and dead. Michel de Certeau made this latter point movingly in *The Writing of History*, trans. Tom Conley, New York: Columbia University Press, 1988, ch. 1. Certeau speaks of history opening for the past what he terms "scriptural [or textual] tombs" (p. 2). Jacques Derrida, in his speech at the University of Silesia to which I will return below, sought to specify Poland's exemplarity in relation to history and catastrophe; see Jacques Derrida, "Discours," in *Jacques Derrida: Doctor Honoris Causa Universitatis Silesiensis*, ed. Tadeusz Rachwał, Katowice, Poland: Wydawnictwo Uniwersytetu Slaskiego, 1997, p. 116.

7 See Terdiman, "The Marginality of Michel de Certeau," *South Atlantic Quarterly (SAQ)*, 100(2), 2001 (special issue on Michel de Certeau, ed. Ian Buchanan), pp. 397–419.

8 On Father Szersznik, see Janusz Spyra, "Leopold Johann Scherschnik (1747–1814)," *Oberschlesisches Jahrbuch*, Vol. 7, Berlin: Gebr. Mann Verlag, 1991, pp. 91–110.

9 Fredric Jameson, *Political Unconscious: Narrative as a Socially Symbolic Act*, Ithaca, NY: Cornell University Press, 1981, p. 102. The passage runs:

> History is therefore the experience of Necessity, and it is this alone which can forestall its thematization or reification as a mere object of representation or as one master code among many others. Necessity is not in that sense a type of content, but rather the inexorable *form* of events.... Conceived in this sense, History is what hurts, it is what refuses desire and sets inexorable limits to individual as well as collective praxis....

10 The idea of such purging of the mnemonic has been widely discussed since Pierre Vidal-Naquet published his *Assassins of Memory: Essays on the Denial of the Holocaust*, trans. Jeffrey Mehlman, New York: Columbia University Press, 1992.

11 See Jacques Derrida, "Discours," op. cit., pp. 110–24.

12 On this point, see Terdiman, *Present Past*, op. cit., p. 3 and n. 1.

13 Karl Marx, *The Eighteenth Brumaire of Louis Bonaparte*, Moscow: Progress Publishers, 1954; and Friedrich Nietzsche, "On the Uses and Disadvantages of History for Life" (1874), in *Untimely Meditations*, trans. R.J. Hollingdale, Cambridge: Cambridge University Press, 1983, pp. 59–123.

14 The notion of "complementarity" has recently been foregrounded for non-physicists by Michael Frayn's *Copenhagen*, London: Methuen, 1998, a semi-fictionalized dramatic account of Bohr's encounter with Heisenberg in 1941. Roughly speaking, "complementarity" was Bohr's theoretical response to Heisenberg's celebrated concept of "uncertainty" (perhaps better translated as "indeterminacy"). Non-physicists like me need to be aware and to acknowledge that we are using these terms in ways that physicists would likely find to be highly metaphorized, if not simply wrong. If it's any comfort, Frayn, as he acknowledges in his "Postscript" (see esp. p. 99), was himself in the same situation. Frayn specifically associates Heisenbergian "uncertainty" with human memory (p. 124). And in his last years, Bohr sought to point out ways in which the idea of complementarity could throw light on many aspects of human life and thought beyond physics.

15 The Owl of Minerva is Hegel's famous symbol for understanding's *post festum* functioning, its after-the-fact temporality; see *Philosophy of Right* (1821), Preface. *Nachträglichkeit* ("deferred action") is Freud's term for an interpretation that retroactively modifies or replaces another that is more simultaneous with a given experience; see J. Laplanche and J.-B. Pontalis, *The Language of Psycho-Analysis*, trans. Donald Nicholson-Smith, New York: W.W. Norton, 1973, s.v. "Deferred Action."

16 The multiple methodological paradigms in the human sciences vie with each other for theoretical predominance in a familiar structure of contention. One way to increase understanding of this configuration of conflict is to assess what each model has to say about fundamental categories of cognition and representation of the world. What is new when such models are brought to a comprehension of the cardinal modalities of human thought and activity – like "time" and "memory" for example? How well is comprehension furthered when such models are deployed? I cannot discuss this question further here. But with regard to memory it is a constant preoccupation in my book *Present Past*, op. cit. And I hope to produce a parallel consideration of models of temporality in a book to be called *Taking Time*, now in progress.

17 From a quite different perspective, the philosopher Alan Garfinkel comes to convergent conclusions in *Forms of Explanation: Rethinking the Questions in Social Theory*, New Haven, CT: Yale University Press, 1981; see esp. chs 5 and 6. Garfinkel argues that in

our discourse about the social world there is always what he terms an "ethics of explanation": "Choosing one explanatory frame over another has value presuppositions and value consequences" (p. 156). Despite the liberations of textuality, these presuppositions and consequences are what we are *not* free *not* to bring to light and expose to critique.

18 From "A Sketch of the Past," in *The Anatomy of Memory: An Anthology*, ed. James McConkey, Oxford: Oxford University Press, 1996, pp. 316–28 at 316.

11

MEMORY IN A MAUSSIAN UNIVERSE

Michael Lambek

This chapter throws into play a number of oppositions: memory and history; Western modernity and an alternative I refer to as Maussian (after the great French anthropologist Marcel Mauss); personage and individual; social person and psychological self.[1] These oppositions are unstable – they shift with time and perspective and they are not precise equivalents. They are also somewhat exaggerated and function as ideal types and heuristic devices to enhance the exploration of a cultural world rather different from one in which events like conferences entitled 'Frontiers of Memory' take place. It is the argument of the essay that the pairs are interdependent; specifically, here, that conceptualizations of memory and history are dependent on conceptualizations of social persons. In a Maussian universe – one in which social persons are understood as personages rather than exclusively as individuals – a distinction between 'memory' and 'history' is by no means obvious.[2]

The (triumphal) history or historical consciousness said to be uniquely characteristic of Western societies has often been associated with literacy. In such arguments, whatever the attention given to the poetics of oratory or the training in memory, the oral ('pre-literate') society is inevitably characterized by an absence or lack. Implicitly the question is, what kind or degree of history is possible in the absence of writing? The argument presented here disregards the oral/literate divide or debate and rejects the separation of history from memory as discrete modes of knowing and transmitting the past that it seems to presuppose. Instead, I locate what, for want of a better word, I will call historicity, within social reproduction broadly defined, and specifically with respect to the reproduction of social persons. I locate a specific medium of historicity (consciousness and practice) significant among Sakalava of north-west Madagascar. I emphasize the positive attributes of this medium, and contrast it to a problematic development in the discursive constitution of Western relationships to the past.

Sakalava spirit possession

In north-west Madagascar royal ancestors provide a source of blessing for the living. Members of the royal clan are individually distinguished within a genealogy that extends over several centuries. Around 1700 they established the Sakalava kingdom of Boina that remained very powerful for over a century until it was partially eclipsed by the expanding Merina kingdom and eventually appropriated by France (from 1895 until 1960). Under French rule, descendants of the once powerful monarchs were given minor administrative positions; in the postcolonial period their individual fortunes have waxed or waned according to whether and how they have been situated in the new economy and political order, but living royals remain prospective ancestors.[3]

The main point is that the social presence of individual members of the royal clan does not disappear at death; upon burial, their spiritual remains are transformed into *tromba* spirits who possess the living. Former rulers establish relations with spirit mediums who come to be recognized as legitimate vehicles for particular royal ancestors. During states of dissociation (trance) the spirits rise in them and speak, dress, consume, and generally comport themselves as they were at the times of their deaths, producing portraits that while traditional, typical and ostensibly direct, also require some contribution of energy and imagination on the part of the mediums in the present. Becoming a spirit medium changes a person's life. It entails both a rewriting of the script of their own personal history such that earlier life events can be interpreted as previously unrecognized signs of the spirit's presence, and numerous adjustments in daily practice, notably in striving to maintain a state of purity through the observance of many taboos. Both in their punctuated trance performances as spirits and in their continuous daily practice, spirit mediums conserve, and enliven older ways of living, of constructing and channeling a flow of power, and of looking at the world. They bring to the present powerful voices from the past, more exactly, from the specific periods of the past to which each of the spirits who possess them belongs. These voices, habits, and outlooks are not blurred or synthesized with one another but remain distinctive.

Each spirit presents itself in character, a character that is reproduced from generation to generation of mediums and which, in many instances, is reinforced discretely by narratives about the ancestor. The characters are not reproduced as isolated individuals but in the relationships they established with one another, as spouses and lovers, parents and children, siblings and rivals. Their identities are also grounded, quite literally, in the physical presence of their bones, artifacts, tombs, and tomb custodians. In effect, then, Sakalava have a system comprised of three media or registers for reproducing the past: performances and practices of the spirit mediums; narratives about past monarchs; and the physical remains (bones, artifacts, architecture), and their curators.

Although these registers are closely related, I will attend here only to the spirit mediums. What I hope to evoke is their exemplary nature. Within Madagascar they are exemplary for shouldering the burdens of history, bearing the historical consciousness and the historical conscience of their communities, and doing so with wit, verve, provocation, eloquence, and elegance, seriously, but not without a tinge of irony. They do not provide mere static representations of the past but give it voice and agency. Insofar as spirits continue to speak in and to the present, such novel acts and their consequences can in turn become incorporated into the record. Their practice is exemplary for non-Malagasy, I suggest in traditional anthropological fashion, not to be imitated, but for putting into perspective the commemorative and historical representations and practices of our own cultural milieux.

While a given spirit medium may have anywhere from two to a dozen spirits, only one is expected to arrive on any given occasion. Coordination among mediums enables the presentation of tableaux in which royal ancestors from various generations assemble. Those who observe these tableaux are not passive spectators but supplicants and addressees – whether amused or fearful, they are engaged by the spirits and engage them, request advice, receive blessings, and assist the spirits in their sometimes tortured or flamboyant entrances into and exits from the bodies of the mediums.

In presenting ancestors as sentient speaking beings, mediums are linked vehicles for a collective past. Yet as each spirit has made its way into the body and life of a particular host, often by a trail of sickness or misfortune, the lives of medium and spirit, hence the individual and collective, are intertwined. For example, most senior spirits are described as *mashiaka*, irascible and punitive. This recalls the power of the monarchs when they were alive, and, more saliently, the way they punish their mediums. Both dimensions are relevant; narratives that recount their violent acts in the past reinforce their aura in the present, while the travails of the mediums afford an embodied rehearsal of the inclinations of the historical figures and a convincing exhibition of the nature of ancestral kingship and of power more generally. (Today no living monarchs would dare to act towards their subjects with the intransigence and violent impatience displayed by their ancestors.)

In a significant essay, Marcel Mauss referred to the participants of certain societies as *personnages*.[4] By this he meant that they held social roles, as though cast in a continuous theatrical performance. The sociological use of 'role' is a much weaker version of this concept because the personage refers to an integrated totality, not a specific function. Moreover, the personage is constituted with reference to the cosmological order of which it is a part, in contrast to the modern individual who is seen as unique, distinct from, and possibly in some opposition to the world. Significantly, the personage is understood as a position that perdures irrespective of the person who fills it. The personage represents a kind of fusion of the person with the office. Elements of such a system are visible in the British monarchy or American presidency where incumbents are in some sense identified with their predecessors. But in the Maussian universe everyone ('all free men')[5] might hold such positions, that is, live their lives as manifestations of them. The personage is intrinsically relational and perduring.

Mauss did not concern himself much with the relationship between personage and the psychological individual or self within given societies, preferring to examine the historical development of the latter concept from the former.

Yet, without succumbing to an extreme form of dualism, it is inescapable, as Mauss himself put it, 'that there has never existed a human being who has not been aware, not only of his body, but also at the same time of his individuality, both spiritual and physical.'[6] For contemporary Sakalava spirit mediums the relationship between personage and other dimensions of social and psychological identity is palpable. As self-aware individuals they live in lively tension as or with their personages rather than being entirely subsumed by them.[7] However, rather than seeing the self and personage as radically different in origin or in some sense opposed, I understand the difference to be produced, worked out, and eventually transcended by means of ethical practice, a practice that entails precisely the mix of 'memory' and 'history' at issue here.

In the course of their daily lives, mediums act as both their personages and themselves, thus as both exemplary monarchs and as the exemplary subjects who bear them. Spirit and host are understood by Sakalava as discrete persons, yet inevitably each helps to render meaningful, vivid, and apt the experience and practice of the other. Spirit mediums can be understood to engage in a three-fold task – performing as their characters, the spirits; building their careers, as mediums; and living their lives, as themselves, a project that must ultimately integrate the others.[8] These are not actually discrete tasks but intricately intertwined as the emergent products of ongoing practical judgment (phronesis).

In its ambiguity as to whether it is mediums who possess spirits or vice versa, spirit possession destabilizes the notion hegemonic in the West of autonomous possessive individuals, discrete subjects who carry even their memories as 'things.' To be possessed is to be more than oneself, to be embedded in relations with others, rather than to own property. Possession instantiates intersubjective relationships, both between individual hosts and spirits, and among the various perduring personages. The very relationship of present to past is constituted as one between subjects rather than of subject to object. Thus Sakalava maintain the relevance of certain past actions and relations within the present. These relationships are the substance of a historicity which is situated between parties rather than separately enclosed within them. Insofar as it is relational rather than possessive (not *my* memory/history, but *our* mutual commitment), there is no clear divide between past and present or collective and individual. Through recurrent appearances, remarks, acts, and observance of taboos, spirits and mediums remember and enliven – keep alive – commitments. These commitments are embodied, not simply objectified; a matter of relational and relative status rather than fixed contract; gift-like rather than commodity-like. Historicity has an insistent moral dimension.[9]

Medium meets medium

Consider the following incident. Madame Doso was a well-known spirit medium in Mahajanga throughout the 1990s. Among the spirits who possessed her were Mbabilahy, recognized as male founder of the dominant (Bemihisatra) royal faction and alive during the first half of the eighteenth century, and Ndramandaming, a male descendant of Mbabilahy who lived during the height of the French colonial period in the twentieth century and is remembered as a provincial 'governor' who visited France. Ndramandaming appears as an urbane Christian with the dress and habits of an official in the French colonial regime.[10] In July 1996 Mme Doso reminisced with chagrin about the occasion when a satisfied client and 'male friend' (*rahalahy*) of Ndramandaming had rewarded her with the gift of a television set. Although delighted, she had been able to keep the set only a few days. What had happened?

Mbabilahy did not like the television. One night when Mme Doso was watching a show, he suddenly rose [in her] and tried to smash the screen. He was afraid of the violence displayed on the programme and the weapons he didn't know. The programme she was watching at the time, Mme Doso said, switching from Malagasy into French, was about *la guerre en Indochine*. What particularly frightened Mbabilahy were the guns. He lived long ago, she explained, in the time of brigands (*fahavalo*) and had no experience of Western (*vazaha*) things. So she was forced to give the TV away.

This is a complex statement about a complex act. It typifies the historicity of Sakalava spirit performance in working forward rather than backward. Rather than consisting simply of figures in the present reminiscing about past experience, as Mme Doso herself might do, figures from the past, like Mbabilahy, express an immediate experience of disorientation with respect to the present. In a sense this spirit from two centuries ago could represent all living adults for whom television has been a new and initially disconcerting experience, but he also bears the cumulative apprehension of the entire transformation from the pre-colonial to the postcolonial era and the disjunctures in experience produced by time and travel and along lines of class and education.

Change is often legitimated for Sakalava by explaining it to royal ancestors and acquiring their acquiescence and comprehension. So, while spirits are sometimes presented as historically naive, at other moments they become the wise assimilators of novelty into the ongoing tradition. The spirits provide reflexive awareness in counterpoint to the ostensible naiveté of the mediums and other people who would simply accept what comes. Or rather, the obstinacy of the spirits requires people to take a more reflective stance toward the changes taking place in the present, not to let them pass unremarked. The spirits, and the past they come from, demand to be taken into account. In her eagerness to enjoy the TV, Mme Doso had probably forgotten to explain its nature to her spirits and to ask their permission to keep it in the house.

Thus, the past may be said to be kept alive in a number of senses; alive in that it speaks and, when change is addressed, is spoken for; alive in the sense that it continues to provide a series of positions from which to interpret the present (note that Mbabilahy's perspective takes precedence here over the alternate perspective of his descendent, Ndramandaming); and alive in the sense that it is not fixed or stagnant but can acquiesce to change. Ideally, ancestors are addressed and respond; acknowledged, they acknowledge the present. The voices from the past are both responsive and responsible; the past contextualizes and renders the present meaningful, but it does not fix or limit it. The present does not serve as a memorial *to* the past, kept frozen by its sense of fear or homage (as might be the case in neurotic illness or ultra-conservative ideology), but rather changes deliberately, with reference to the past. We might say that action in the present is sanctified by the past.[11] The mutual commitment of present to past, and past to present, is central.

Mbabilahy's actions speak not only to the present, that is to the consumption of television, but also to a period that is past relative to the present but future relative to Mbabilahy's life, namely French colonial aggression. Mbabilahy rejects the activities of French colonialism as upheld by Ndramandaming and as visibly exemplified by the Vietnam war.[12] Modern violence is not opposed to a romanticized pre-colonial past. After all, the spirit responds to the display of colonial violence with his own threat. Mbabilahy, like most senior spirits, is described as cruel or violent (*mashiaka*). And the medium depicts the era in which Mbabilahy lived as a time of brigands, implying a condition of insecurity rather than of order, a state, in effect, of violence of its own. The medium brings to bear a colonial or modern view of the past as anarchic, in some discrepancy to the way she generally defers to Mbabilahy and his pronouncements. Thus the past is neither homogenized nor idealized. It is seen from multiple perspectives and multiply voiced.

Insofar as the spirit's reaction to the powerful weaponry is one of fear, the display may be said to ruefully acknowledge the facts of history, the eventual subordination of the Sakalava to France after Mbabilahy's time (and, we might add, the success of television). Mbabilahy's response to the danger is one of disquiet – he does not recognize the guns – yet it occurs long after the fact. Hence the location of this appraisal is both prospective and retrospective. This is only curious if we think in terms of the linearity of history, not if we think in terms of the temporal fluidity and thickness of memory. In memory, the prospective and retrospective speak continuously to each other, anticipation conceived in terms of recollection and vice versa.[13]

This vignette demonstrates the artificiality of separating the public from the private or the subjective from the objective. Although Mbabilahy is a public figure, a personage, the act of threatening the television in response to disturbing scenes took place in the house of a single medium and was not widely known. (Insofar as it was known, it served to further legitimate the medium's possession, thicken peoples' understanding of Mbabilahy, and widen reflection on time, history, and change.) It was a novel act, a creative response on the part of the personage, in character so far as Mme Doso understands that character, but not part of a collective ritual script. That it happened at all and how widely she disseminated the story were aspects of her disposition and situated judgment.

Mme Doso's performance undoubtedly drew on her own experience. Unlike Mbabilahy, she had a cosmopolitan outlook. She was a moderately well-off widow, probably in her late sixties at the time, who for many years had been married to a man from the Comoros whose profession was none other than soldier in the French army. With him she moved between military bases throughout Madagascar and in La Réunion; along the way she must have heard a good deal about French and American military exploits in Vietnam. However, that the fear of guns lies deep is suggested by the fact that yet another of her spirits is someone whose character is epitomized by his death from gunshot wounds (inflicted by Merina soldiers at a time when they were bent on conquering the Sakalava). All spirits must avoid the things associated with their deaths and the main impact of this spirit upon Mme Doso's life is that she has to withdraw at the climax of the annual festivities at the major shrine in Mahajanga in anticipation of the rifle that is let off.

Mme Doso herself does not shun television. She relinquished her set with considerable regret. In 1998 I often found her gazing avidly at the television owned by one of her tenants. In the intervals between her strenuous activities as a medium, housekeeping, and making pickles and cakes to sell for a bit of cash, she watched news, sports events, and French films. She has explained to me that after negotiating with Mbabilahy she can watch TV as long as the programme is not about war. In a way, she speaks to my own ambivalence about seeing the portrayal of suffering on the nightly news. It is as though, to quote a Malagasy colleague, the spirit functions as a kind of microchip censoring device.[14]

Spirit mediums like Mme Doso provide marked acts of witness, responding to external events, like the reception of television or military violence by drawing not only on their own earlier life experiences, but on those of the historical personages whose trustees they are. Such acts of witness and recollection have both personal and public relevance. The conjunction of present lives and past ones challenges any simple distinction between 'memory' and 'history' as discrete forms of giving voice to the past. Insofar as we understand by 'memory' the practical subjectification of the past and by 'history' its discursive and disciplinary objectification, so it becomes difficult to classify Sakalava practice. Spirits speak out as the conscience of history; subjectively located, this history may also be described as memory. Both terms, 'history' and 'memory,' can serve useful rhetorical functions, but it appears that any reified distinction between them is socially produced; in a Maussian universe like that of Sakalava spirit possession, history and memory are not discrete and fully distinguished.[15]

However, Sakalava experience is certainly not monistic. In the face of current theoretical interest in embodied mimesis, I emphasize that the spirit's passionate response to the televised images is in counterpoint to the medium's dispassionate retelling of the event.[16] This shift to a more distanciated, even objective perspective is critical to what is at issue here and typical of possession's ability to produce a recontextualization of its acts. There is in possession what Ricoeur has referred to as a 'dialectic of distanciation and appropriation' with respect to the reception of texts or what Loewald refers to as transitions between representational and enactive remembering.[17] Here is where the germ of a split between the subjective and the objective is to be found, in which a perspective we can call 'history' is forged in relation to a perspective we can call 'memory.' The inherent communicational triad of possession events – the fact that host, spirit, and interlocutors speak *to* each other and with discrete voices – as well as the necessity of redundancy – that mediums must be told what their spirits said and did when they were in trance – provide the means for increasingly detached and reflexive responses, much as in the successive retelling and inscription of a dream narrative. Moreover, in many instances it is the spirit who responds dispassionately to the passionate or incoherent utterances of host or clients.[18] In this process events become increasingly abstracted by means of regnant cultural models, shifting into the discursive realm of linguistic representation and becoming available for new kinds of entextualization.[19]

I venture that through the cultivation of this dialogic or polylogic space in which both enacted and representational memory are validated, spirit possession provides the means for a kind of working through of history roughly analogous to what psychoanalysis is said to offer individual experience. Mediums, qua personages, draw on the collective past to articulate their situations, but likewise their practice serves as a model for collective historicity and assimilation of change. In its emergent reflexivity mediumship is both a personal and a collective practice through which, and in a manner somewhat akin to psychoanalysis:

> Being a person is now understood to be a much more complex business, a dialectic between the 'I' that does things, assigns meanings, makes, honors, and betrays commitments and loyalties, and the 'I' that *knows* some of the things done, meanings assigned, commitments undertaken, honored, and betrayed.[20]

A final point to make about Mme Doso's story is that from Mbabilahy's perspective there is no difference between the scene portrayed on television and reality. There is some humor in the fact that he appears to mistake the one for the other. But this, in turn, produces a reflection on the ontology of possession itself, its own relation, so to speak, to reality, and ultimately on the relationship between television and spirit possession as alternate, and possibly competing media, for transmitting and juxtaposing images and for provoking reflection on temporal passage.

The risk of romanticized objects

Western media do offer some points of comparison with spirit mediums. Perhaps the modern novel, with its exuberant and multiple voices, comes closest to the dialogic play with temporality made possible by spirit possession.[21] And perhaps it is novelists who capture this best in words. Thus in *Moon Tiger*, Penelope Lively has her protagonist – an iconoclastic historian – say:

> The collective past ... is public property, but it is also deeply private. We all look differently at it. My Victorians are not your Victorians. My seventeenth century is not yours. The voice of John Aubrey, of Darwin, of whoever you like, speaks in one tone to me, in another to you. The signals of my own past come from the received past. The lives of others slot into my own life....[22]

But the dominant discursive regimes and representations of person and memory suggest differences. Instead of the dense dialectical play of emergent subject and object and the creative tension between personage and individual, there has developed a polarization of objectifications and subjectifications. The personage is replaced by an overly objectified individual, constituted through the effects of governmentality, bio-politics and, as Hacking would have it, memoro-politics, and an overly subjectified individual whose qualitative uniqueness and autonomy are celebrated in liberal humanism.[23] Conceptualizations of memory are divided between the sciences of memory – cognitive psychology, neurology, and the various forensic experts trotted out as consultants and witnesses – on the one side, and literary reminiscence, psychoanalytic insights and their popularization, on the other. On the one side memory is conceived as a natural object or process available to the gaze of experts; on the other, memory is the means and substance of unique, private, deep, ambiguous, unpredictable, yet essential subjective experience. The subjective memories of individuals are in turn distinguished from the objective accounts of professional historians. If historians further demonstrate a strong preference for written records as grist for their own textual production, one may suppose this is not because they believe texts are inherently less distorted by interest and sentiment than memory but because they are fixed and do not change their minds.

I suggest that the objectification and the subjectification of memory have become excessive in Western discourse, both in much disciplinary work and in popular culture. What we risk thereby is the constitution of memory as a romanticized object. This is the term Hannah Arendt used to describe the way personality becomes naturalized in racism. Jews and Jewish culture are replaced by 'Jewishness,' which, as Richard Handler puts it, 'like personality, was taken to be innate, an inner quality characteristic of both Jewish individuals and the Jewish people.' [24]

The romantic objectification of memory proceeds as a vehicle for, and an expression of, the extreme individualism characteristic of modernity, and also, in part for those who wish to counter this, as the expression or vehicle of a collective, popular, national, or subaltern truth. In either case, memory becomes the locus and ground for some posited essential identity, 'bestow[ing] a high sense upon the common, a mysterious appearance upon the ordinary, the dignity of the unknown upon the well-known.'[25] Attempts to apprehend this 'real me' or 'who we really are' are of course inevitably compromised.[26]

To say that memory becomes a romanticized object is also to imply a change in the sensibility of memory and the meaning of remembering. It has become

important to remember – to remember to remember. Self-conscious remembering permeates life. We must remember to take photos on a family vacation –
and subsequently remember to look at them and to be cognizant of the fact that
we *are* remembering. Memories are acquired and consumed, like souvenirs, but
to be without memory is to be that much less a self.

Anthropology, like other fields, has recently turned its attention to memory
and it has done so for good reason. 'Memory' serves well to highlight the intrinsically temporal, historical nature of self and of culture, and to reveal the
contested, polyvalent nature of social life in which acknowledgment and conceal-
ment of the exercise of power are central. Many anthropologists and historians
appreciate that memory is the history that cannot be written, that eludes codifica-
tion, that remains stubbornly discreet and that refuses consistency and fixity.[27]
Gold and Gujar point out that it is precisely the interest 'to privilege discord over
monolithic essentializations' that favors memory over documentary history. This is
an approach that 'distrusts records … privileges stories.' They cite LeGoff's
description of 'a coursing collective memory … overflowing history.'[28]

While these scholars are not inattentive to the violence of inscription, there
remains, even in the best work, a curious tension between looking to memory for
a new source of authority, the authority of the subaltern, and looking to memory
in order to defer and displace the very idea of certainty and authority. The resolution to this is by no means obvious; as many have begun to ask about
postmodernism more generally, why do we question the existence of authority
just at the moment when our authority is being eclipsed by that of others?
Whatever the case, the risk is that we assume that somewhere there exists pure
and unsullied memory, memory which accurately reproduces the experience of
its subjects and that is their unique possession, that holds or moulds their
essence, that is itself an essence.

In making 'memory' the object of study, we run the risk of naturalizing the very
phenomenon whose heightened presence or salience is in need of investigation.
The history of social science is full of examples of analyses of nationalism or
ethnicity that contribute to the constitution of those objects whose existence they
ought to bring into question. Psychology and psychiatry provide equally
compelling examples, not least in the realm of ostensible memory-induced
illnesses. Foucault has generalized this process in his concept of discourse, though
in the case of memory (as of nationalism in Handler's analysis), the issue is less that
scholars produce the phenomena of which they speak than that they share and
reinforce the broader public discourse. So the question is, how can we understand
memory without enlarging its discourse? How do we acknowledge the salience of
memory without contributing to either its objectification or romanticization? (If
the traditional problem for anthropologists has been how to get inside the language
of their subjects, the contemporary dilemma is how to step outside it.)

A key to stepping outside and illuminating a comparative account is to
discover the cultural logic underlying the cycle of ideological production.[29] It
may be found in Handler's insight that romantic objectification is the outcome of

a logic of possessive individualism, 'the modern fascination with … irreducible individualized units, bounded, homogeneous, and continuous.'[30] As a property of such units memory takes on the same qualities of boundedness, homogeneity, and continuity – and indeed serves to reproduce them. An alternative to seeing memory as either private or as public, where the public is but a vision of the individuated private writ large, and an alternative to seeing memory as either objective or as subjective, where the subjective is but a vision of the objective romanticized – is to see memory as practical and relational.[31]

The search for alternatives to possessive individualism returns us to the Maussian world of personages. At first sight this may look like a familiar and equally romantic project: the West versus the Rest. I would qualify this predictable opposition in three ways: first, there is not simply a single 'other' to the logic of possessive individualism – South Asian hierarchy, East African segmentary relativism, Melanesian dividualism, and Amerindian perspectivism come to mind.[32] Second, the presence of alternate models need not be mutually exclusive; they may be found side by side in many, if not all social settings, perhaps one dominant and explicitly articulated and the others relatively mute, or their incommensurability unmarked.[33]

The final way to overcome the opposition is to realize what we share. Sakalava mediums remind us that memory is history located in relatively subjective space; history is memory located in relatively objectified space. History is memory inscribed, codified, authorized; memory is history embodied, imagined, enacted, enlivened. Memory provides an agile, existential, indeterminate practice that draws on and supports history even as it offsets the weight of history's powerful claims. Yet many events and perspectives are occluded or excluded in both modes.

Conclusion

In Madagascar, numerous spirit mediums become the exemplary personages of the Sakalava world; by means of a complex division of labor they reproduce the characters of the royal clan from generation to generation and add new ones as members of younger generations of royalty die. Sakalava historicity is mediated through the minds and bodies, the practical consciousness and dispositions of the spirit mediums, and articulated by means of the characters of the historical personages and their relationships. In bearing Sakalava historicity – in carrying its weight, in passing it on – the mediums also have to bear – to suffer – it. They bear it and make it available for others, with dignity, agility, and imagination, circumspectly and dialogically, from the situated position of a subject to situated addressees, never from the neutral space of the objectivist gaze: thus never baring – exposing, essentializing – it.

Memory is a field in which the relation of existence to essence is negotiated, both in theory – in the ways in which we talk about memory and the things we use it to signify – and in practice, both collective and personal – in the ways in which we navigate our lives, and keep our balance between 'speaking the present' and 'speaking the past.'[34] Treating memory as romanticized object risks the subsumption of existence by essence. In so doing it risks missing the very thing that I argue is central to memory, namely continuous practical judgment in the living of a moral life, a life judiciously composed of both action and reflection, of retaining and letting go, of initiating and terminating commitments, of speaking the future and speaking the past. As Fingarette put it, 'Guilt is retrospective, but responsibility is prospective…. To accept responsibility is to be responsible for what shall be done.'[35]

Memory is at once representation and practice, making and doing, in Aristotelian language, poiesis and phronesis. These conjoin differently in different cultural contexts and historical moments, producing distinctive 'imagined continuities' and asking different things of us, but perhaps always to seek a golden mean of responsible memorial practice. Regardless of the presence of specific cultural registers like spirit possession, I suggest that the way to mediate the extremes of objectification and subjectification is through attention to practice. I defer to Hans Loewald for the last word:

> The microdynamics of memory is the microcosmic side of historicity, i.e., of the fact that the individual not only *has* a history that an observer may unravel and describe, but that he *is* history and makes his history by virtue of his memorial activity in which past-present-future are created as mutually interacting modes of time.[36]

Notes

1 Earlier drafts of this paper were presented at the symposium 'Possessed by the Past: Psychoanalysis, Psychiatry, Sakalava,' University of Toronto, 16 April 1999, and at the conference on 'Alternative Forms of Memorialization: Memory and the Art of Recovery,' University of Virginia, 23 April 1999, as well as at the 'Frontiers of Memory' conference, Institute of Education, London, 17–19 September 1999. For advice and encouragement I wish to thank Paul Antze, Chris Colvin, Ann Gold, Kate Hodgkin, Antonia Mills, Susannah Radstone, Jacqueline Solway, Emmanuel Tehindrazanarivelo, and the various interlocutors on the previous occasions. Susannah Radstone has been particularly helpful. I am indebted to the Social Sciences and Humanities Research Council of Canada for supporting the research on which it is based, and of course to Mme Doso for her patience, wit, and creativity.
2 To qualify, no society operates with a single, fully consistent mode of understanding the past.
3 Jean-François Baré, *Sable Rouge: Une monarchie du nord-ouest malgache dans l'histoire*, Paris: L'Harmattan, 1980; Gillian Feeley-Harnik, *A Green Estate: Restoring Independence in Madagascar*, Washington: Smithsonian Institution Press, 1991; Michael Lambek, 'The Sakalava Poiesis of History: Realizing the Past through Spirit Possession in Madagascar,' *American Ethnologist* 25(2), 1998, pp. 106–27, and 'The Value of Coins in a Sakalava Polity: Money, Death, and Historicity in Mahajanga, Madagascar,' *Comparative Studies in Society and History* 43(4), 2001, autumn. A more comprehensive account of the material described here, is *The Weight of the Past: Living with History in Mahajanga, Madagascar*, New York: Palgrave Macmillan, 2002.

4 Marcel Mauss, 'A Category of the Human Mind: The Notion of Person; The Notion of Self,' trans. W.D. Halls, in *The Category of the Person*, ed. M. Carrithers, S. Collins, and S. Lukes. Cambridge: Cambridge University Press, 1985 [1938], pp. 1–25.

5 Ibid., p. 7; cf. Marie Mauzé, 'The Concept of the Person and Reincarnation among the Kwakiutl Indians,' *Amerindian Rebirth*, ed. A. Mills and R. Slobodin, Toronto: University of Toronto Press, 1994, pp. 177–91. Among Sakalava both mediums and tomb custodians identify with specific personages, though I address only the former here. Mediumship is in principle open to everyone; according to Sakalava it is the spirits who select their hosts.

6 Mauss, op. cit., p. 3; cf. Michael Lambek, 'Body and Mind in Mind, Body and Mind in Body: Some Anthropological Interventions in a Long Conversation,' in *Bodies and Persons: Comparative Perspectives from Africa and Melanesia*, ed. M. Lambek and A. Strathern, Cambridge: Cambridge University Press, 1998, pp. 103–23.

7 The situation may be compared to the analysis of the 'I' and the 'me' developed by G.H. Mead, *Mind, Self, and Society*, ed. Charles Morris, Chicago: University of Chicago Press 1962 [1934].

8 For comparison with Western actors and actresses, Michael Lambek, 'Graceful Exits: Spirit Possession as Personal Performance in Mayotte,' *Culture* 8(1), 1988, pp. 59–69. 'Character,' 'actors,' and 'drama' are all words used by Mauss. Among the Kwakiutl, 'the drama is more than an aesthetic performance. It is religious, and at the same time it is cosmic, mythological, social and personal' (op. cit., pp. 7–8).

9 Michael Lambek, 'The Past Imperfect: Remembering as Moral Practice,' in *Tense Past: Cultural Essays in Trauma and Memory*, ed. P. Antze and M. Lambek, New York, Routledge, 1996, pp. 235–54.

10 Mbabilahy is short for Mbabilahimanjaka, itself the popular name for Ndrananilitsiarivo, a grandson of Ndramandisoarivo. For further depiction of Ndramandaming, see Lambek, 'Sakalava Poiesis,' op. cit.

11 On sanctification, Roy A. Rappaport, *Ritual and Religion in the Making of Humanity*, Cambridge: Cambridge University Press, 1999.

12 The war might also serve as a displacement of the violent quelling by the French of the Malagasy revolt of 1947, but this is not explicit and not, I think, terribly significant here.

13 Edward Casey, *Remembering: A Phenomenological Study*, Bloomington: Indiana University Press, 1987; Hans Loewald, *Papers on Psychoanalysis*, New Haven, CT: Yale University Press, 1980; Brad Weiss, 'Dressing at Death: Clothing, Time, and Memory in Buhaya, Tanzania,' in *Clothing and Difference: Embodied Identities in Colonial and Post-colonial Africa*, ed. H. Hendrickson, Durham, NC: Duke University Press, 1996, pp. 133–55.

14 E. Tehindrazanarivelo, personal communication.

15 Spirit possession is of course only one modality of Sakalava historicity.

16 Lambek, 'Body and Mind,' op. cit; Michael Lambek, 'The Anthropology of Religion and the Quarrel between Poetry and Philosophy,' *Current Anthropology* 41(3), 2000, pp. 309–20.

17 Paul Ricoeur, *Interpretation Theory*, Fort Worth, TX: Texas Christian University Press, 1976, pp. 43–4; Loewald, op. cit., pp. 164–5.

18 Michael Lambek, 'Spirits and Spouses: Possession as a System of Communication among the Malagasy Speakers of Mayotte,' *American Ethnologist* 7(2) 1980, pp. 318–31 and *Knowledge and Practice in Mayotte: Local Discourses of Islam, Sorcery, and Spirit Possession*. Toronto: University of Toronto Press, 1993.

19 Compare Janice Boddy, *Wombs and Alien Spirits*, Madison: University of Wisconsin Press, 1989 and Niko Besnier 'Heteroglossic Discourses on Nukulaelae Spirits,' in *Spirits in Culture, History, and Mind*, ed. Jeannette Mageo and Alan Howard, New York: Routledge, 1996, pp. 75–97.

20 Stephen A. Mitchell, *Relational Concepts in Psychoanalysis*, Cambridge, MA: Harvard University Press, 1988, p. 265.
21 See especially Mikhail Bakhtin, *The Dialogic Imagination*, ed. Michael Holquist, trans. C. Emerson and M. Holquist, Austin: University of Texas Press, 1981. But literature, and even theatre, lack the embodied qualities, the awesomeness of the mediums' transformations between pain, power, and pleasure, their negotiation between asceticism and excess, the combination of strangeness and everydayness, and the insistent interpellation of the present by the past.
22 Penelope Lively, *Moon Tiger*, London: Penguin, 1987, p. 2.
23 The difference is not one of psychic structure, rationality, or inner subjectivity, but of social structure, discursive formations, and dominant cultural ideologies. On memoro-politics, Ian Hacking, 'Memory Sciences, Memory Politics,' in Antze and Lambek, op. cit., pp. 67–87.
24 Hannah Arendt, *The Origins of Totalitarianism*, 2nd edn, New York: Meridian, 1958, p. 169, as cited in Richard Handler, *Nationalism and the Politics of Culture in Quebec*, Madison: University of Wisconsin Press, 1988, p. 190.
25 Novalis, 'Neue Fragmentensammlung,' in *Schriften*, Leipzig, Tome II, 1929 [1798], p. 335, as cited by Arendt, op. cit., pp. 167–8.
26 Handler, op. cit.
27 Antze and Lambek, op. cit.; Jonathan Boyarin (ed.) *Remapping Memory*, Minneapolis: University of Minnesota Press, 1994; Jean Comaroff, *Body of Power, Spirit of Resistance*, Chicago: University of Chicago Press, 1985; Ann Gold and Bhoju Ram Gujar, *In the Time of Trees and Sorrows: Nature, Power, and Memory in Rajasthan*, Durham, NC: Duke University Press, 2002; Gerald Sider and Gavin Smith (eds) *Between History and Histories: The Making of Silences and Commemorations*, Toronto: University of Toronto Press, 1998; Richard Werbner (ed.) *Memory and the Postcolony*, London: Zed Books, 1998.
28 Gold and Gujar, op. cit.; Jacques LeGoff, *History and Memory*, trans. S. Randall and E. Claman, New York: Columbia University Press, 1992, pp. 97–8.
29 Another avenue is that of historians of science who, following Foucault, seek the points of emergence or transformation of discursive formations. See Ian Hacking, *Rewriting the Soul*, Princeton: Princeton University Press, 1995 and op. cit.; Allan Young, *The Harmony of Illusions: An Ethnography of Post-Traumatic Stress Syndrome*, Princeton: Princeton University Press, 1995 and 'Bodily Memory and Traumatic Memory,' in Antze and Lambek, op. cit., pp. 67–87.
30 Handler, op. cit., p. 189.
31 Parallel arguments may be made by means of the psychoanalytical literature; indeed my thinking has been inspired by the relational arguments that have been replacing those based on the drive model. Mitchell, op. cit., provides a useful survey of the lively and diverse developments within relational psychoanalysis.
32 Respectively, Louis Dumont, *Homo Hierarchicus*, trans., Mark Sainsbury, Chicago: University of Chicago Press, 1970 [1966]; E.E. Evans-Pritchard, *The Nuer*, Oxford: Oxford University Press, 1940; Marilyn Strathern, *The Gender of the Gift*, Berkeley: University of California Press, 1988; and Eduardo Viveiros de Castro, 'Cosmological Deixis and Amerindian Perspectivism,' *Journal of the Royal Anthropological Institute* 4, 1998, pp. 469–88. On alternate forms of historicity see also Maurice Bloch, 'Internal and External Memory: Different Ways of Being in History,' in Antze and Lambek, op. cit., pp. 215–33. To be sure, most of these models are foreshadowed in Mauss and have been contested elsewhere.
33 Lambek, *Knowledge and Practice in Mayotte*, op. cit.
34 Alton Becker, 'Text-building, Epistemology, and Aesthetics in Javanese Shadow Theatre,' in *The Imagination of Reality*, ed. A.L. Becker and A. Yengoyan, Norwood, NJ: Ablex, 1979, pp. 211–43 and Maurice Bloch, 'Symbols, Song, Dance and

Features of Articulation,' *Archives Européenes de Sociologie* 15, 1974, pp. 55–81, reprinted in Bloch, *Ritual, History and Power*, London: Athlone, 1989.

35 Herbert Fingarette, *The Self in Transformation: Psychoanalysis, Philosophy, and the Life of the Spirit*, New York: Basic Books, 1963, p. 165.

36 Loewald, op. cit., p. 146.

INDEX